Language and Human Relations

The way in which people address one another is crucial to expressing social relationships and is closely linked with cultural values. In English we call some people by their first names and others 'Mr' or 'Ms', followed by their surname. In some other languages there are different ways of saying 'you' depending on the degree of social distance. Exploring practices in the family, school, university, workplace and in letters, this book reveals patterns in the varied ways people choose to address one another, from pronouns to first names, from honorifics to titles and last names. Examples are taken from contemporary English, French, German and Swedish, using rich data from focus group research, interviews, chat groups and participant observation.

MICHAEL CLYNE is an Honorary Professorial Fellow in the School of Languages and Linguistics at the University of Melbourne.

CATRIN NORRBY is an Associate Professor and Reader in Swedish in the School of Languages and Linguistics at the University of Melbourne.

JANE WARREN is an Honorary Fellow in the School of Languages and Linguistics at the University of Melbourne.

Language and Human Relations

Styles of Address in Contemporary Language

Michael Clyne
Catrin Norrby
Jane Warren
University of Melbourne

CAMBRIDGE
UNIVERSITY PRESS

CAMBRIDGE UNIVERSITY PRESS
Cambridge, New York, Melbourne, Madrid, Cape Town, Singapore, São Paulo, Delhi

Cambridge University Press
The Edinburgh Building, Cambridge CB2 8RU, UK

Published in the United States of America by Cambridge University Press, New York

www.cambridge.org
Information on this title: www.cambridge.org/9780521870627

First published 2009

Printed in the United Kingdom at the University Press, Cambridge

A catalogue record for this publication is available from the British Library

Library of Congress Cataloguing in Publication data
Clyne, Michael G., 1939–
Language and human relations : styles of address in contemporary language /
Michael Clyne, Catrin Norrby, Jane Warren.
    p.   cm.
ISBN 978-0-521-87062-7
1. Forms of address.   2. Politeness (Linguistics)   3. Grammar, Comparative
and general–Honorific.   4. Grammar, Comparative and general–Pronoun.
I. Norrby, Catrin.   II. Warren, Jane, 1958–   III. Title.
P40.5.F67C59   2009
306.44–dc22
2008049143

ISBN 978-0-521-87062-7 hardback

Table of contents

Tables and figure

Figure

Abbreviations and transcription conventions

FN	first name
LN	last name
hon	honorific
PO	participant observation
FG	focus group
Q	questionnaire
…	a hesitation of three seconds or more
[…]	ellipsis
<What do you say?>	Question by moderator during an informant's turn at talk is given in angel brackets

Acknowledgements

In a project of wide dimensions such as this one it is impossible to thank all those who deserve thanks, so we will have to do so collectively. We are indebted to our many participants and others who have shared their perceptions and expectations of address. Without them this book could never have been written.

While the book has three authors, it is actually a combined effort of a much larger group of people. Our colleague, Heinz-Leo Kretzenbacher, was the fourth chief investigator on the project, providing ideas and valuable insights, but had to withdraw during the writing of the book for personal reasons. The data collection 'on the ground' through focus groups and/or interviews was carried out by Emmanuelle Guérin, Jo-anne Hughson and Christophe Mafart (in Paris), Elīzabeth Ober (Toulouse), Kristin Gogolok (Leipzig), Daniel Kraft and Sandra Lachmann (Mannheim), Maria Weissenböck (Vienna), Jenny Nilsson (Gothenburg), Heidi Nyblom (Vaasa), Russell Aldersson (London), Adam Brandt (Newcastle upon Tyne) and Muiris Ó Laoire (Tralee). Jo-anne Hughson and Doris Schüpbach were of invaluable assistance not only for the transcription and analysis of data but in innumerable ways throughout the project. Leo Conroy, Jenny Nilsson, Heidi Nyblom and Maria Lindaräng helped prepare the data for analysis. Felicity Grey provided statistical assistance. Sandra Kipp generously made available her considerable writing talents by reading the manuscript and providing advice on how to improve it in content and form. We acknowledge gratefully the input from an anonymous reviewer. The Institut für deutsche Sprache (Mannheim), the Institute for Applied Linguistics and Translation Studies (University of Leipzig), the Department of Applied Linguistics (University of Vienna), the Department of Swedish Language at University of Gothenburg, and the Department of Nordic Languages at Vaasa University all provided facilities for the project.

The project was financed by the Australian Research Council. The grant was supplemented by funding from the School of Languages and Linguistics, University of Melbourne, and the Alexander von Humboldt Foundation.

It is our hope that all who have made this possible will on reading it feel that their efforts and generosity have been worthwhile.

Our thanks are also due to Andrew Winnard and his colleagues at Cambridge University Press for their kindness and support in every stage of the production of this monograph.

MC, CN, JW

1   Introduction

The way we address one another – the use of second-person pronouns such as English 'you', first names, last names and titles – is crucial in marking social relations and is critical to human relationships. As Joseph (1989) points out, address usage encodes the relationship and attitudes of interlocutors perhaps to a greater extent than other aspects of language and is thus more open to cultural variation. It reflects cultural values and acts as an indicator of major social and political changes that affect human relationships and social networks. The study of address systems and rules thus not only has significance for linguistics but also informs research into social structures and social change.

1.1   Address across languages

This book, based on empirical data, examines changes in the address systems of three western European languages, French, German and Swedish, and to a more limited extent English. It explores the impact on these systems of sociopolitical changes and events, particularly since the 1960s. The 1960s were an important turning point not only in Europe but also in the Americas and Asia. The spirit of the time was one of social revolt and oppositional politics, which differed from country to country. Reassuringly conservative after the shock of World War II, the national cultures of Europe have been radically challenged since the 1960s, not only by the ideological divides and shifts along with new expressions of solidarity during and after the student uprisings of 1968 in western Europe, but also by the social and cultural effects of ongoing European integration, the end of the Cold War in the late 1980s, globalisation, and the spread of Anglo–American cultural influence (through its single address pronoun *you*).

The effects of these developments have been felt in different ways in the countries and sites we examine here. In France and Germany, they were experienced most immediately in the universities, where students led the way in changing patterns of use of address pronouns. France experienced considerable social change in the post-68 years, but there was a gradual return to more traditional social stratification. France continues to be a stratified society in which early educational choices determine to a greater or lesser extent workplace and life opportunities. At the same time, the broader social context is currently one in which there is a growing tendency towards individualism rather than a focus on collective concerns, as is the case in other western societies. In Germany, the end of the Cold War and the subsequent unification of West and East Germany have created a new set of sociopolitical conditions, as communist and capitalist values have come into contact. Sweden and Finland in the post-war era have been characterised politically by a strong social democrat movement, with an emphasis on egalitarianism. In addition, across Europe – and around the world – new information technologies such as email and the internet are currently having a considerable impact on language usage, particularly among the younger sections of society.

Each of the languages discussed in this book contributes a different set of issues to the way in which people are addressed. The book investigates both pronominal and nominal address in French, German and Swedish – that is, pronouns of address, as well as the use or absence of first names, surnames and titles. English (actually the English and Irish national varieties, for we are focusing on Europe) is used as a point of reference to better understand the changing significance of modes of address in the other three languages.

Each language offers a large variety of linguistic means for the expression of a speaker's personal and social orientation to others through address (Crystal 1993: 7). These means can range from avoidance of direct address to the use of pronouns (such as the French *tu* and *vous*) and verbal forms ('*Viens ici!*' ('Come here!')) using the *tu* form, as opposed to '*Venez ici!*' using the *vous* form, from terms of endearment (*chéri, mon amour*) to honorifics[1] and/or titles plus last names (*Madame Depardieu, Monsieur le professeur Blanc*) and to combinations of all these. Each language has its own inventory of terms of address. For example, while there is pronominal variation in the address systems of French, German and Swedish, English has little or no pronominal address choice, with the pronoun *you* almost universally the sole address pronoun.

Table 1.1 shows basic similarities between the systems of French, German and Swedish, with all three languages making a distinction between singular and plural on the one hand and less formal and more formal on the other.

If we compare the three languages in the table, we find the following:
1) French and Swedish have two pronouns to mark distinctions in the singular only, whereas German has two pronouns in both the singular and the plural.
2) When addressing someone in French or German, the choice of address pronoun has consequences for the verb form. For example, the sentence 'You gave me a fright' can be rendered in French and German in two ways, with two distinct verb forms: *Tu m'as fait peur / Vous m'avez fait peur, Du hast mich*

---

[1] We use the term 'honorifics' to refer to expressions such as the English *Mr, Mrs* and *Ms*, which are combined with a surname, and expressions such as *Sir* and *Madam* used vocatively. The term 'titles' refers to professional titles, such as *Dr* and *Professor*.

Table 1.1 *Address pronoun systems in French, German and Swedish*

	French	German	Swedish
Singular			
less formal (T)	*tu*	*du*	*du*
more formal (V)	*vous*	*Sie*	*du*
			ni
Plural			
less formal (T)	*vous*	*ihr*	*ni*
more formal (V)	*vous*	*Sie*	*ni*

erschreckt / Sie haben mich erschreckt. This even applies in the imperative, where the pronoun is not used, as in French '*Viens ici!*' (T form, named after *tu* in Latin) and '*Venez ici!*' (V form, after *vos* in Latin) ('Come here!') and German '*Komm mal her!*' (T form, singular) and '*Kommt mal her!*' (T form, plural). In Swedish, all verbs have the same ending, regardless of person.

Each of the four languages under investigation has opportunities for combining pronouns with (a) names – first names, last names or both (*Brian, Smith, Brian Smith*); (b) honorifics and/or titles and names (*Ms Moneypenny, Madame Goncourt, Herr Müller, Frau Doktor Meier, Professor Bergkvist*). In addition, in French and German it is possible to combine honorifics and titles (*Monsieur le docteur, Frau Professor*). For each of the languages, a distinction was traditionally made between the honorific used to address a married woman (*Mrs, Madame, Frau, Fru*) and that used to address an unmarried woman (*Miss, Mademoiselle, Fräulein, Fröken*). The fact that women's marital status is linguistically encoded in this way has been hotly debated in recent times and has led to gender-inclusive language planning in several languages (e.g. Pauwels 1998). For example, in English the term *Ms* has been created and promoted as the equivalent to the unique honorific *Mr*, which gives no marital information. In German, the married honorific *Frau* has been generalised to address all women. In French, a shift to *Madame* is under way, but *Mademoiselle* is still in use. For Swedish, marital status is not indicated for either men or women since honorifics have largely been abandoned.

The following sections present an overview of address forms in each of the four languages, a brief description of the research sites and an outline of the book structure.

1.2 English

English provides the opportunity to examine how mainly nominal forms can be used to make similar distinctions to those made by the combination of pronominal and nominal forms in other languages. Address forms in English have been typically used as follows:

 (i) Standard English has only one pronoun of address, *you*. This means that, in contrast to a language such as French or German, an English speaker does not have to make a conscious decision before speaking about which pronoun and corresponding verb form to use.

 (ii) Given the generic nature of *you* in English, it is relatively straightforward to avoid any direct expression of closeness or distance towards one's interlocutor.

 (iii) English has other ways of expressing personal and social orientation to others through address. For example, when English speakers are being very formal, they can use honorifics such as *sir* or *madam*, and when they wish to express informality or intimacy they can use terms of endearment such as *mate* or first names and nicknames.

 (iv) The pronoun *thou* is restricted to some British English dialects (Wales 2003: 175–8) or particular religious communities (Birch 1995).

 (v) Non-standard plural forms such as *youse* in British English and Irish English varieties are a means of introducing a number distinction that is absent in standard English pronominal address.

Recent developments in British English address practices include an increasingly widespread use of first names in work contexts and service encounters, possibly influenced by patterns in American English, and the spread of terms of endearment such as *mate*. These aspects will be investigated in Chapters 3 and 4.

1.3   French

French offers the opportunity to examine how, in a society in which language has long been monitored and regulated, an area such as address nevertheless reflects changing social values and patterns of interaction. In particular, the choice of French allows fruitful and illuminating comparisons with German with which it shares several address practices.

The typical patterns of address usage in French in vogue in the 1960s could be described as follows:

 (i) *Vous* was the default address pronoun and was used in encounters with strangers and with older people.

 (ii) *Tu* was generally used within the nuclear family and with close friends and was the pronoun of solidarity (Brown and Gilman 1960).

 (iii) Children were addressed with *tu*.

 (iv) *Tu* was related to left-wing ideals, whereas *vous* had bourgeois connotations: in upper-class families, children might use *vous* to address their parents who might use *vous* to address each other.

 (v) There was non-reciprocal use between speakers in a position of higher status and those of lower status – for example, it was common for older speakers to address younger speakers with *tu* and in return receive *vous*; schoolteachers tended to use *tu* to younger pupils, who responded with *vous*.

(vi) There was a default set of honorifics – *Monsieur, Madame, Mademoiselle* – used when addressing strangers, which are accompanied by *vous*.

(vii) *Monsieur* and *Madame* could be combined with a professional title, as in *Madame la présidente* or *Monsieur le docteur*.

Many of these patterns still hold today (see Chapters 3 and 4), but the address pronoun system in French has undergone a certain cyclical evolution, in particular since the student and workers' revolts of the late 1960s, when changes in social attitudes and the spread of a utopian egalitarianism were reflected in the younger generation's greater use of informal *tu* than was the case among the older generation (Maley 1974). As the 1970s wore on (Coffen 2002: 235), the movement towards widespread use of *tu* turned out to be a temporary phenomenon and *vous* made a reappearance, due in the main to social hierarchies reasserting themselves. As social relationships have become more informal in France, use of *tu* has again become more widespread (Peeters 2004), in particular among the younger generation. The extent to which younger French speakers are a *tu*-generation is examined in Chapters 3 and 4.

The shift from adolescence and the early 20s to so-called adult life and entry into the workplace is often marked by a shift in the range of social relations that an individual maintains, which can in turn lead to a shift in address pronoun use towards greater use of *vous*. The workplace in France is thus a domain particularly worth exploring in relation to potentially evolving address practices, as will be seen in Chapter 4.

One of the areas where French differs not only from German but also from English and Swedish is in its use of a set of stand-alone honorifics, *Monsieur*, *Madame* and *Mademoiselle* (accompanied by the pronoun *vous*). These continue to be widely used when addressing adult strangers and in service encounters. There is currently some debate in France about the continuing relevance of *Mademoiselle* (see e.g. Crumley 2006, Peyret 2006); arguments against the term mirror those against the use of *Miss* in English (see above), although there is no equivalent replacement term for *Ms* in French. Current use of these terms is explored in Chapters 3 and 4.

1.4   German

German offers a number of unique perspectives to the study of address as well as some which are shared with one or more of the languages studied here but can be explored in a distinctive way for German.

The 'traditional' pattern of address pronoun selection – employed at least until the late 1960s – was as follows (Clyne 1995: 130–1):

  (i) *Sie* was the default pronoun of address (i.e. the form normally used in a
       first encounter with an adult interlocutor); *du* was the pronoun of solid-
       arity (Brown and Gilman 1960).
 (ii) Members of a family addressed each other as *du*.
(iii) *Du* was used to children under the age of 15.
 (iv) Young children tended to call everyone *du*.
  (v) *Du* was employed in prayer.
 (vi) People might, as a sign of friendship, decide (i.e. make a verbal agree-
       ment) to use *du*. Sometimes this was associated with a ritual drink
       (*Brüderschaft trinken*). The use of *du* was then reciprocal.
(vii) Older people (especially those of higher status) might asymmetrically
       address younger people, i.e. the older person used *du*, the younger one *Sie*.

As is the case for French, many of these patterns still hold. However, the current
study will show how a more progressive system has been developed but is often
juggled with the traditional one according to the roles which speakers and their
interlocutors choose to take.

German enables us to explore the limits of T and V contexts, and to differentiate between contexts which are clear-cut T or V territory or ambivalent ones
in which a great deal of choice is possible. There are people who can be
identified as *du* types or *Sie* types according to their use of address in these
ambivalent contexts, and in Chapter 3 we will consider whether they can be
described in terms of social indices. The existence of a plural T form *ihr* (see
Table 1.1) offers a third alternative pronoun enabling German to differentiate
between dyadic and multi-party communication and facilitating a focus on the
addressee's status as a member of a group. In addition, German enables us to
assess how much deviation there is from the link between T and first names and
between V and honorific + (title) + last name. Chapters 3 and 4 will discuss some
new developments in this regard.

As was the case with French, one of the big turning points in modes of
address in German was the student movement of the late 1960s and early 1970s,
which used universities as a first base to transform society and free it of its
bourgeois characteristics. Egalitarian nominal modes of address (honorific +
last name) between staff and students and egalitarian pronominal modes of
address (T) between students and, for at least some time, between junior staff
and students developed in universities and reciprocal T and first name spread
generally among the younger generation. The present-day situation will be
analysed in Chapter 4, but more conservative developments can be seen as
the result of anti-authoritarian changes often being perceived as imposed, that
is, implemented, in an authoritarian way. We will discuss in Chapter 4 how this
may extend to other domains, particularly the work domain.

German is a good testing ground for the spread and durability of the student
movement's role in address mode changes, especially since it did not affect

eastern Germany. While there was substantial variation in address modes between east and west during the 40-year division of Germany, some of the changes spread to eastern Germany via western Germany after the fall of the Berlin Wall in 1989. The perception of and attitudes to modes of address by eastern Germans can be assessed in an ambivalent context of the reception of western capitalist values and nostalgia for the collectivist mentality. Apart from the cultural variation brought about by the division of Germany and its aftermath, the longstanding cultural differences between Germany and Austria are also reflected in modes of address, especially in the workplace, with regard to both pronouns and titles (see Chapter 5).

German modes of address bear witness to the tension between collectivism and more dominant individualism, to globalisation and reactions to it, to the expression of national culture, present and past, in a pluricentric language, a language part-owned by different nations and cultures (see Chapter 5).

1.5   Swedish

Compared with German and French, Swedish offers a very different perspective on the study of address. While the Swedish address system looks very much like the French one – with an informal address pronoun (*du*) and a second-person plural form (*ni*) which can be used as a formal pronoun of address to one person – this is a superficial similarity, as the functions of the two pronouns are very different in Swedish. Swedish contemporary address practices are far more 'radical' than in German or French, and in reality the formal form of address has largely disappeared, leaving *du* as the default in almost all situations and to almost all interlocutors. This means that the Swedish address system is fast becoming similar in that respect to the English system. However, the current situation in Swedish is a relatively recent development and, in fact, the Swedish address system has undergone by far the most significant changes of the four languages in modern times. It is a compelling case of how a system can change from being characterised by a high degree of formality to extreme informality.

The traditional pattern of address usage in Swedish until the middle of the last century, when the system started to break down, was characterised by the following:

(i) *Du* was the pronoun of solidarity (Brown and Gilman 1960) and restricted in use to the family and other intimate relations. As a marker of solidarity, it was also used in the labour movement to emphasise equality and among friends, often after a ritual agreement to be on *du* terms, sometimes accompanied by a drink (*du-skål*, '*du*-toast'). Adopting *du* address was thus governed by several rules and it was the privilege of the older person or the woman to suggest it.

(ii) The pronoun *ni* had attracted negative connotations for many speakers as a result of having been used socially downwards, addressing a person who lacked a title, who in turn would have to give the title back to his/her interlocutor (Ahlgren 1978).

(iii) The lack of a neutral formal pronoun for addressing a stranger gave rise to a great deal of insecurity surrounding address use, leading to avoidance strategies such as the use of the third person, including the person's title if known, passives and other ways of avoiding direct address pronouns. Examples of such paraphrases are '*Önskas kaffe?*' ('Is coffee desired?'), '*Är det till att vara nöjd?*' (lit. 'Is it to be satisfied?', meaning 'Are you satisfied?') and '*Kan professorn komma i morgon?*' (lit. 'Can the professor come tomorrow?') addressing the professor directly in this way.

(iv) In the family it was not unusual for children to address their parents in the third person, e.g. '*Vill mamma ha kaffe?*' ('Does mum want coffee?'), avoiding the use of address pronouns.

(v) Similarly, children were expected to address older people in the third person, e.g. '*Vill tant Anna/farbror Sven ha kaffe?*' using the addressee's first name in combination with *tant* ('auntie') and *farbror* ('uncle'), no matter whether they were relatives or not. Teachers were addressed by *Fröken* (Miss) or *Magistern* (the equivalent of *Sir* in English).

The strong egalitarian movement in Sweden also worked as a catalyst for the introduction of *du* as a universal form of address. A contributing factor in the swift implementation of universal *du* was the cumbersome address system described above, in which Swedish lacked a polite pronoun to use with strangers.

The study will show that to older Swedes *ni* often has a negative connotation, a connotation that the younger informants are largely unaware of. Such differences between members of a speech community can potentially lead to misunderstandings. In Chapter 3 the social factors which govern the possible use of *ni* will be explored in more detail.

Workplaces, schools and universities (Chapter 4) are clear *du*-domains in Sweden today, which is a striking change from the situation around the middle of the last century. While *du* has become the default form of address, applicable in almost all situations, it has largely lost its role as a marker of solidarity or intimacy. Subsequently, other means must be employed to express such values and Swedish thus enables us to study what happens when the T–V distinction is eradicated (by the adoption of universal T) and how other means of expressing personal and social orientation to others through address come into play.

While Swedish is clearly different from both French and German, there are also very clear-cut differences between the two national varieties of Swedish – Finland-Swedish and Sweden-Swedish, to be discussed in detail in Chapter 5. In general the former has been described as more formal and more prone to V use than Sweden-Swedish, which has moved further along towards informal patterns of address. The national differences are addressed in some detail in Chapter 5 and allow us to also attribute some current variation to partly different past experiences in each country.

Few situations today call for the use of any other form of address than *du*, but as will become clear throughout the study, the situation is far from straightforward. Conflicting rules of language use are still in operation and the Swedish data in general clearly illustrate a great deal of variation, which further underlines the fact that the system is unstable. The controversial re-entry of *ni* into service encounters by young sales persons addressing the (very) old (see Chapter 4) is one case in point and one which has attracted much attention in the press since it was first observed more than two decades ago (Mårtensson 1986). Swedish thus enables us to address the question of cyclical movement in address, i.e. where a previously nearly extinct form re-enters the system but with new functions.

1.6   The research sites

The methodology used in this study combines both qualitative and quantitative techniques: focus groups, network interviews consisting of a questionnaire and an interview, participant observation and chat groups (see section 2.4 for details). We wanted to include national variation in our study, and we thus examine national varieties of German, Swedish and English. These three languages can be regarded as pluricentric languages, that is, ones with several interacting centres, each providing a national variety with at least some of its own norms (Clyne 1992: 1). We initially decided to include seven research sites: Paris, Toulouse (in the south of France), Mannheim (for western Germany), Leipzig (for eastern Germany, the former GDR), Vienna (Austria), Gothenburg (Sweden) and Vaasa (a town in one of the bilingual Swedish-Finnish-speaking parts of Finland). However, due to difficulties in recruiting and retaining research assistants, data for Toulouse comprise one focus group only, which will be referred to occasionally in the following chapters. For the purposes of comparison with English, one focus group each was held in London, Newcastle upon Tyne (in the north-east of England) and Tralee (in the south-west of Ireland, in a bilingual Irish–English area).

1.6.1   *Paris*

Paris was chosen as the main French language site, as it is the capital of France and a major urban and economic centre. All the 'Paris' participants in our study live and work in the Île-de-France region, which is made up of the city of Paris and the so-called 'inner ring' and 'outer ring' of *départements*. The total population of the Île-de-France region is 11,399,300, with a little over 2 million living in the city of Paris (2005 figures). Paris and its surrounding area exert a huge power of attraction on people both from other French regions and from other countries. One in every two Parisians – that is, inhabitants of the city of Paris – is in fact born outside the Île-de-France region, with nearly a third from other French regions and just under a quarter from other countries (based on 1999 INSEE figures, reported in *L'Express* 2006).

1.6.2   Toulouse

The choice of Toulouse was motivated by its position in the south-west of France in the border regions of the French state and in theory far from the influence of Parisian norms, a location therefore where distinct norms of address usage might be in operation. The inhabitants of the city and metropolitan area number 1,117,000,[2] which makes it the fifth largest city in France. Toulouse has the second largest student population after Paris and its university is one of the oldest in Europe. The city is the unofficial home of Occitan culture: the Occitan equivalent of the *Académie française* is situated there, as well as Radio Occitania, which promotes the language and culture. However, in the city proper, apart from a small number of street signs in Occitan, the language is almost never heard.

1.6.3   Mannheim

Mannheim was chosen because of its central location, just south of the centre of the old Federal Republic of Germany (West Germany). Situated at the junction of the Rhine and Neckar rivers in the state of Baden-Württemberg, it has a population of 390,000, but there are 1.7 million people living within a 25 km radius of Mannheim. It is not only an educational centre in its own right: Heidelberg, with its prestigious and historic university, is a mere tram ride away.

1.6.4   Leipzig

Leipzig was chosen because it is the largest city in eastern Germany other than Berlin (which had been divided). Leipzig has over 500,000 inhabitants and is in the state (*Bundesland*) of Saxony. It is both a trade centre with its annual trade fair and a traditional educational centre with a university and an annual book fair. The international contacts through the trade fairs and the relatively large percentage of international students kept Leipzig linked to the world, and the tradition of an educated and liberal middle class proved so strong in Leipzig that the city became one of the epicentres of the civil disobedience movement that ended communist domination of eastern Europe. In post-unification Germany, Leipzig has become one of the few economically strong regions in eastern Germany.

---

[2] These and subsequent statistics are from 2007.

1.6.5   Vienna

Vienna was chosen because with 1.9 million inhabitants in an Austria of 8.1 million inhabitants it is very much the urban centre of the nation. For five centuries the capital of a multicultural, multilingual empire, it looks both east and west, and a large part of the population, though Austrian citizens, reflect in their names and family history the ongoing relations with surrounding non-German-speaking countries. Ready contact with them is possible because Vienna is not far from Austria's eastern border. Past traditions and the long history of high culture and university education still motivate behaviour and the workings of Austria's institutions.

1.6.6   Gothenburg

Gothenburg was chosen because it is considered to be the capital of the western region of Sweden. It is also Sweden's second largest city (close to 900,000 inhabitants in the greater Gothenburg region). It is a significant trade and shipping hub of north-western Europe, with the largest harbour of Scandinavia. In general, large Swedish cities are characterised by a fairly high proportion of immigrants and Gothenburg is no exception to this. According to Sweden's statistical bureau (SCB), about 20% of the inhabitants in Gothenburg are of migrant backgrounds, with the largest groups coming from Iran and Finland.

1.6.7   Vaasa

Vaasa, on the west coast of Finland, is not a particularly large city (57,000 inhabitants) but nevertheless it is the regional capital of the province Ostrobothnia. Vaasa is officially bilingual, with a Finnish-speaking majority of 71.7% and a Swedish-speaking minority of 25.1% (Folktinget 2003). However, it is surrounded by municipalities, which are predominantly Swedish-speaking. Ostrobothnia as a whole has a slight Swedish-speaking majority (52.1%). Vaasa was chosen because of its large proportion of Swedish speakers.

1.6.8   London

London was chosen because it is the capital of England and the United Kingdom, an important financial, business and cultural centre, and a number of government departments are based there. London is, like Paris, a major global city and attracts people from other areas in the United Kingdom and from around the world. Greater London, which includes the 32 boroughs of Inner and Outer London and the City of London, has a population of just over

7.5 million; if we include the London metropolitan area, this figure rises to somewhere between 12 million and 14 million (Greater London Authority 2006a). According to the 2001 Census, nearly 2 million or just over a quarter of all Greater London residents were born outside the United Kingdom and a quarter of them were European-born (Greater London Authority 2006b).

1.6.9   *Newcastle upon Tyne*

Newcastle upon Tyne was chosen as it is considered the capital of north-east England, both economically and culturally, and has two universities. It is the 20th most populous city in England, with a population of 276,400 (2005 mid-year estimates). With the decline of the coal, engineering and shipbuilding industries, the service industry is now the largest local employer. The local variety of English is known as Geordie, the term also used to refer to people from Newcastle and surrounding areas who speak this variety.

1.6.10   *Tralee*

Tralee, at the head of the Bay of Tralee in the south-west of Ireland, is the largest city in County Kerry, with a population of about 22,000. It was chosen because the nearby Dingle Peninsula contains a gaeltach (Irish-speaking area) and so we were able to include informants who are childhood Irish–English bilinguals in our Tralee sample. The gateway to the Dingle Peninsula, it is an important tourist centre, but also an educational centre. Other industries include food ingredients and electronics.

1.7   Structure of the book

In this chapter we have introduced the grammatical resources available to each of our languages to address people. The chapter has also provided some background information on the research sites for this study. Chapter 2 discusses previous research on address in the four languages as well as more general literature on address, politeness, language and identity and other issues that might contribute to our understanding of address and to a model for the discussion of the phenomenon. This chapter also describes our project data, how they were gathered and the methodology we employed to analyse them.

Chapter 3 has two functions in the book. It discusses and compares the principles and practices of address choice – both pronominal and nominal – in the four languages. It also draws from the four languages the essential social significance of address mode in terms of social distance, inclusion and exclusion, and identity. These points are taken up again in Chapter 4, where we focus on address in each of the languages in the domains of family, school, university and work and the institutions associated with them. This chapter also considers address in a very formal and a very informal medium – formal letters to strangers and largely anonymous internet chat groups respectively. Chapter 4 again highlights the different ways in which the languages use their pronominal resources and the relationship between pronominals and nominals (including honorifics and titles) in address. It also demonstrates how a language such as English, without a binary pronoun system, goes about expressing social distance in address.

In the first four chapters the languages are generally treated as single entities. In Chapter 5 the focus is on national varieties of three of the languages: German, Swedish and (to a lesser extent) English. We discuss how sociopolitical and cultural history have left their mark on differential address practices in German in Austria and Germany, Swedish in Finland and Sweden and English in England and Ireland. We explore how in practices as well as in attitudes the division of Germany continues to influence address, two decades after the fall of the Berlin wall. At the same time, Chapter 5 discusses dilemmas and challenges resulting from contact between languages with different address practices. Finally, Chapter 6 presents a multidimensional, dynamic model of address that draws on the data and analyses presented in Chapters 3 to 5.

2 Multiple approaches for a complex issue

2.1 Introduction

The two areas of linguistics that are currently most concerned with comparisons between languages are typology and contrastive pragmatics. The first focuses on what can be ascertained about human cognition from the range of differences between languages, mainly at the morphosyntactic, semantic and phonological levels. The second relates to how different cultures utilise language as an instrument of action; there is an ever-increasing number of contrastive pragmatic studies, involving many languages. This study, exploring as it does the range of ways in which human relations are expressed through the choice of address terms over a number of languages, combines aspects of typological and pragmatic approaches. It also considers variation in the functions of modes of address in the context of social change. Among the issues that interest us are how speakers report on:

(i)   the ways in which they negotiate particular address choices;
(ii) variation and change in address practices across the generations;
(iii) the ways in which distinct address patterns develop in different domains and institutions;
(iv) modes of address in electronic communication, such as chat groups and email communication;
(v)   address practices in pluricentric languages, that is, languages which have several national varieties, such as German in Germany and Austria;
(vi) address practices in language contact situations.

This chapter provides the theoretical and methodological background for the subsequent chapters in which the results of our empirical study are outlined. First, we present background on research on address in general and in English, French, German and Swedish in particular (2.2). We then turn our attention to theoretical frameworks developed for the analysis and understanding of interaction and interpersonal relationships, and outline how these frameworks are relevant to the study of address practices (2.3). In the final section we describe the methodologies used in the study (2.4) before outlining the theoretical model that has guided our work on address (2.5).

2.2 Research on address

Although there have been many descriptions of address systems in many languages, relatively few have been comparative or empirical. The groundbreaking study on address pronoun usage from a sociolinguistic point of view is Brown and Gilman's 'The pronouns of power and solidarity' (1960). It provided subsequent research with two crucial dichotomies. The dichotomy of 'polite' V pronouns versus 'familiar' T pronouns, as Brown and Gilman labelled them (1960: 254), is linked to the macro-sociological dichotomy of 'power' versus 'solidarity'. In addition, non-reciprocal use of the V pronoun by one interlocutor and the T pronoun by the other is represented as a 'power semantic', while reciprocal use of either T or V is seen as a 'solidarity semantic'. Furthermore, Brown and Gilman predicted that the T pronoun would eventually prevail over the V pronoun.

The empirical basis supporting the far-reaching, even universal, theoretical assumptions of Brown and Gilman's study is rather limited, based on mainly male native speakers of French, German or Italian: 50 French, 30 Germans and 11 Italians visiting universities in the Boston area in the late 1950s. Both dichotomies presented by Brown and Gilman, as well as the assumptions underlying their research, have attracted criticism and stimulated new investigations. There are many languages of the world where pronouns of address are more numerous and varied than the simple Brown and Gilman T/V dichotomy. It is for this reason that Mühlhäusler and Harré (1990) criticise that binary system. However, this does not apply to any of the languages in our study. Braun (1988), adopting the Brown and Gilman model critically, collected data on pronouns of address from 30 languages. She mentions Polish, for example, which has one T pronoun (*ty*, second-person singular) and no less than three different V pronouns (*wy*, second-person plural, vs. *on/ona*, third-person singular masculine/feminine, vs. *oni*, third-person plural), and Japanese, with six address pronouns (1988: 304–5). Braun's analysis led her to question the universal validity of the dimensions of 'power' and 'solidarity' for the description of address and to emphasise the importance of including speakers' characteristics, such as age, profession, sex or dialect in any model of address practices (Braun 1988: 38–42, 306, 307). However, many of her findings rely on an extremely narrow empirical database, with only one or two informants per language.

The examples above from Polish and Japanese demonstrate the potential diversity in the linguistic expression of address. But what of languages of western European origin such as the ones that are the subject of this book? First, Brown and Gilman's predicted movement from non-reciprocal V/T to reciprocal T may be useful as a very broad generalisation, but the reality is far more complex. As an illustration, the pluricentric language Spanish shows great variation among its national varieties in terms of the number of pronominal forms and in the conventionalised social meanings that are attached to them. While most have a dichotomy of *tu* (T) vs. *vos/vosotros* (V), Columbian Spanish, for example, employs three pronouns of address, *tu*, *vos* and *usted*, while the T form is *vos* in Argentinian Spanish and *usted* in Chilean Spanish (Hughson 2005). Vanderkerckhove (2005) shows that colloquial Belgian Dutch employs a single pronoun of address *ge* (*gij* in stressed position) in contrast to Netherlands Dutch *jij/je* (T) and *U* (V).[1] In her study of Netherlands Dutch address patterns, Vermaas (2002) found substantial variation according to religion, with Catholics and atheists adopting the increased use of T and Orthodox Calvinists preserving and even accentuating V use in the younger generation. This demonstrates the significance of social stratification in variation in address and the problem of treating an entire speech community as a single unit.

Our data provide some evidence of cyclical developments in French, German and Swedish, thus going against Brown and Gilman's prediction of development towards universal T. However, it is English that provides the greatest challenge to the Brown and Gilman model, which limits address to pronouns. Historically, it is the V form *you*, not the T form *thou*, that has become the almost universal English pronoun of address, contrary to Brown and Gilman's hypothesis. But English address is far more complicated, for, as we shall demonstrate, some aspects of social distance (see section 2.3.3) expressed through pronominal distinctions in French or German are rendered by nominal forms of address such as *Sir/Madam* or *mate*.

As Brown and Gilman's study preceded the advent of modern sociolinguistics, issues of variation and language contact were not seriously considered. These issues play a key role in our study. The importance of variation was noted by Ervin-Tripp (1986: 219–20), who contributes to address research the insight that 'a shared language does not necessarily mean a shared set of sociolinguistic rules' but can operate according to a range of personal options, such as dispensation of particular rules. She formulates 'co-occurrence rules' for address term choice that determine 'the selection of alternates within the repertoire of a speaker in terms of previous or concomitant selections' (Ervin-Tripp 1986: 240).

Lambert and Tucker's (1976) study of French and Spanish address constituted a major advance in address research in a number of ways. The authors used detailed questionnaires with children (in most cases including teenagers) as the reference point to explore address modes and were the first to take into account variation, including national variation. Their research sites were French-Canada, France and St Pierre-en-Miquelon, a French territory in Canadian waters (French), and Puerto Rico and Colombia (Spanish). In some countries, comparisons are made between rural and urban informants, in some between isolated and

---

[1] Since the completion of the manuscript, Schneider and Barron (2008) has appeared. It contains eleven chapters on pragmatic variation in some pluricentric languages. One of these (Plevoets, Speelman and Geeraerts) is specifically on Dutch address in the Netherlands and Flanders.

neighbouring communities. Lambert and Tucker complemented their question-naire data with a psycholinguistic study of the social meaning of address forms, testing informants' perceptions (modern, old fashioned, more religious, more educated, rich, happy, affectionate) of families using different modes (reciprocal T, parents' T and children's V) in relation to favourable, unfavourable, ambiguous or neutral outcomes to a child's request. Other data collected were on reactions to inappropriate address modes and teachers' reports on their use of T and V with pupils. Despite considerable discrepancies in the size and range of samples and the distribution of the variables in the samples, the study brought a rich diversity to the study of address.

Social class seemed to be a very important factor in French-Canada, but age, gender and the urban–rural divide are also significant variables. Class played a less important role in France, where age, gender and solidarity and family reciprocal T were significant influences. Age and gender were particularly important in St Pierre-en-Miquelon, where variation was under young people's control and young girls extended more informal family address modes to the wider community. Puerto Rico had no stable, pervasive address norms except in the friendship domain, where reciprocal T predominated. In Colombia, where the interlocutor's gender was the most important factor, gender variation in address was strong among Catholic children but less so in the Jewish sample. Children there played an important role in acculturation.

In sections 2.2.1 to 2.2.4 we give a brief overview of language-specific studies that form the background to our own thinking. Given that English has a single address pronoun *you*, studies on address have quite naturally focused on other, nominal means of address. In the other three languages, which all have a T/V dichotomy, the focus of previous research has been on pronominal address practices. We will be using the terms T and V in what follows as if they were uncontroversial (cf. Agha 2007: 283), for ease of exposition; however, as we will show in Chapter 3 and subsequent chapters, the social meanings of T and V (and corresponding nominal modes of address) are by no means agreed and watertight.

2.2.1   English

Contrary to a popular belief among speakers of languages which have a prono-minal distinction, the existence of a single address pronoun in English does not make the English address system free from complexity. Indeed, there have been various claims about the ways in which English 'makes up for' its lack of a T/V distinction. Leech, for example, compares the use of first names on the one hand and title + surname (in our terminology, honorific + last name) on the other in English to that of T and V pronouns in European languages (Leech 1999: 112). Sifianou, for his part, argues that the richness and variety of politeness formulas and the use of indirectness in English can make up for the lack of pronominal distinction (Sifianou 1992, cited in Gardner-Chloros 2004: 7).

Nominal address forms in English are a particularly heterogeneous group, with a range of terms whose use varies according to factors such as domain, relationship between speaker and addressee, and various speaker characteristics such as age and sex. Leech, for example, divides nominals into various categories, on a scale from most intimate or familiar to most distant and respectful, naming them as follows: (1) endearments – *darling, sweetie*, (2) family terms – *mummy*, (3) familiarisers – *mate*, (4) familiarised first names – *Jackie*, (5) first names in full – *Jacqueline*, (6) title and surname (in our terminology, honorific + last name) – *Mrs Johns* and (7) honorifics – *Sir, Madam* (Leech 1999: 110–11). He also classifies them according to three functions: to summon attention, to identify one's addressee and, most importantly for our focus here, to 'establish or maintain a social relationship between the speaker and the addressee(s)' (Leech 1999: 108).

With respect to the use of honorifics (hon), last name (LN) and first name (FN), until recently the combination honorific + LN was considered the default address usage in British English. However, the use of FN is now becoming generalised, to the extent that honorific + LN 'is increasingly relegated to marking a more distant and respectful relationship towards an acquaintance' (Leech 1999: 112). Currently, in the English-speaking world, the expectation is a rapid shift to first names. However, this is a more recent phenomenon for speakers of British English and remains problematic for speakers over 50 (Bargiela *et al.* 2002: 4). The spread of first names is particularly noticeable in certain domains such as telephone sales (Gardner-Chloros 2004: 7), whereas the use of honorific + LN remains the norm in certain specific speech situations or domains, such as job interviews, doctors' surgeries and work situations where a degree of formality is required (Bargiela *et al.* 2002: 5). In their study of nominals in two English corpora – casual conversation between family and friends (British and Irish English) and radio phone-in calls (Irish English) – McCarthy and O'Keeffe (2003) show that in the radio data, the presenter and callers are immediately on first-name terms. This use of FN 'not only projects an intimate level of relationship, but appears to play a role in creating and sustaining such relations in the interaction' (McCarthy and O'Keeffe 2003: 154).

In the domain of service encounters, *Sir* and *Madam* retain their place in British English to address older male and female customers respectively (Leech 1999: 112). Leech's 'familiarisers' or Formentelli's (2007) 'terms of friendship' – terms such as *mate* and *love*, which we are calling 'T-like modes of address' – are used in complex ways in British English. To take *mate* as an example, in the past it was considered a marker of lower-class speech, particularly among men. Formentelli's study of the British National Corpus has shown that use of *mate* is expanding: he recorded its use by women, by speakers of different social backgrounds and in business settings among colleagues. He views this expansion as 'a signal of the increasing informality in social relationships' in Britain (Formentelli 2007). Furthermore, he found that *mate* is used as a term of endearment in close family relationships. It has also been noted that in the north of England, certain service providers (bus conductors, newspaper vendors, etc.) use *love* with clients, regardless of level of familiarity or the addressee's sex (Holmes 2001: 271).

In contrast with the other languages focused on here, there has been extensive discussion about replacing traditional honorifics referring to single or married women by a single, neutral term *Ms* in English (e.g. Pauwels 1998, Winter and Pauwels 2007). There is evidence that use of *Ms* is on the increase in English-speaking countries, but it seems that the relationship between *Mrs*, *Miss* and *Ms* varies from country to country (Pauwels 1998: 218). In British English, there is a tendency to merge *Miss* and *Ms*, at least on official forms, where *Mrs* contrasts with *Ms* (Graddol and Swan 1989). Thus, old inequalities are being perpetuated, in spite of the introduction of so-called 'new neutral terms' (Romaine 2001: 173). Romaine (2001: 158) presents findings from the British National Corpus, in which 'usage of Ms is still marginal as an address title in the UK. It accounts for only 5% of the occurrences of the titled forms used for women.' In this respect, British English is behind American English, perhaps because of a continuing British preoccupation with social status and consequently a lesser tendency towards social mobility (Romaine 2001: 159).

2.2.2   French

The student and workers revolution of 1968 in France (see section 1.1) marks a distinct shift in patterns of address in French. This change, which had echoes of the imposition of *tu* during the French Revolution of the late 18th century, was characterised by the 'egalitarian' use of *tu* and first names, above all among students and workers but also among those members of the bourgeoisie who were sympathetic to the cause. As Calvet remarked in the early 1970s, use of *tu* was spreading as a result of a long-established tendency and the cultural upheaval of May 1968, a change particularly evident in the universities (Calvet 1976: 16). However, the social movement symbolised by the spread of *tu* had well and truly lost momentum as the 1970s came to a close (e.g. Seidman 2004) and *vous* and more formal modes of address made a comeback (Coffen 2002: 235). There remain, however, pockets of so-called 'sixty-eighters' (*soixante-huitards*) who continue to prefer egalitarian *tu*, as well as tertiary institutions where *tu* is *de rigueur* among teachers and between teachers and administrators, part of a post-68 tradition.

Despite these changes from 1968 onwards, in the 1970s *vous* was still regarded as the neutral or default form. Roland Barthes, for example, observed at the time that 'signs have to be handled against a neutral background, and in French using *vous* is that background' (1971). This view of the neutrality of *vous* was still in vogue in the late 1990s, as noted by Halmøy (1999: 564). Currently, among the younger generation, *tu* has been described as the default form (Havu 2005, Peeters 2004), while *vous* retains its place among the older generations as the neutral pronoun (Havu 2005). It is not clear whether the use of *tu* by young people is evidence of a change in progress, or alternatively a case of age grading; in other words, as the younger generation grows older and moves through the life cycle, their use of *tu* may well decline (see e.g. Gardner-Chloros 1991, Havu 2005, Peeters 2004). Conversely, after people retire, they may use *tu* more widely, as they are no longer involved in workplace hierarchies (Gardner-Chloros 1991). For both older and younger generations, *tu* remains the pronoun of choice within the family and with close friends (e.g. Gardner-Chloros 1991, Hughson 2001).

There have been an increasing number of studies on address pronouns in French, particularly from the 1990s onwards, many of which are based on empirical data. Various factors have been identified as crucial in the choice of *tu* and *vous*, including relative age of speaker and addressee, whether the interlocutor is known to the speaker, the type of interaction, whether the interaction takes place at work or in a collective setting such as a sports club, and the degree of mutual empathy between speakers, often based on the outward appearance of one's interlocutor (e.g. Gardner-Chloros 1991, Havu 2005, 2006, Hughson 2001, Kerbrat-Orecchioni 1992). In addition, geographical variation within France has been studied: in a study on address pronoun use in Paris, Metz, Toulouse and Lyon, Havu found that, for example, the Parisian partic- ipants showed more hesitation over pronoun choice than speakers in the other cities (Havu 2006).

Morford (1997), in her study of address use by standard French speakers in the Paris metropolitan area, underlines the importance of context in determining pronoun use. She frames her analysis in terms of social indexicality, that is, the pragmatic functions of address pronouns. She argues that *tu* and *vous* can 'point' not only to the relationship between interlocutors but also to the setting. She gives the example of the use of reciprocal *vous* between two lawyers who know each other well and would normally use reciprocal *tu*. However, when they find themselves in court, they acknowledge the official setting by address- ing each other as *vous*.

In other recent work on *tu* and *vous*, there has been a growing emphasis on the identity and self-presentation strategies manifested in the choice of address pronoun. The notion that the application of basic T/V rules is 'a matter of individual appreciation' and 'negotiation' has been underlined by Kerbrat- Orecchioni (1992: 49–50). Further, different address forms can be used as boundaries 'to include or exclude an individual from the group to which the speaker belongs. This process of inclusion or exclusion allows [speakers] to establish and reinforce these boundaries and to build a collective as well as an individual identity' (Coffen 2002: 285; see also Coffen 2003). The importance of this identity function is echoed by Gardner-Chloros (2007: 107), who argues that 'the pattern of T/V use by a particular individual serves as an "Act of Identity" […], i.e. as a way of showing with which groups and which individuals one wishes to be identified and from which, on the contrary, one wishes to differentiate oneself'. The identity dimension of language choice is explored later in this chapter (see section 2.3.5).

2.2.3   German

As for French, the student revolt towards the end of the 1960s marks an important watershed in German address use. Bayer (1979), for example, describes how the anti-authoritarian upheavals in German universities in the late 1960s and early 1970s created two competing systems of address – the traditional one based on a neutral or an 'unmarked' V pronoun of formality vs. a 'marked' one for intimacy and a new one based on an unmarked T pronoun of solidarity vs. a marked V pronoun for social distance. The latter system was adopted by students and some university staff (largely younger and sub-professorial). There were misunderstandings between people using the two systems of address, as each group perceived the others' system as confrontational (suppressive or aggressive). There has, however, been a rollback of this development in the academic community since and a tendency to re-mark the boundaries between teachers and students by reciprocal use of *Sie* (see Amendt 1995). This relaxation of the *du* tendency was due to the resentment by some young people of the top-down imposition by professors of a pseudo-egalitarian address rule that did not reflect a lack of hierarchical structure. Overall, such developments have had only a moderate impact on the rest of society. However, one of the legacies has been a change in how the two competing systems are understood. The two systems have persisted, but their social meanings have shifted, creating confusion among speakers.

Hickey (2003) presents the German address system as both binary and scalar – binary because there are two pronouns of address and scalar because there are many linguistic devices that facilitate nuances that go beyond the binary system. The addition of first names to V, last names with T, phonetic reduction of *du* to *-ste* as in *Siehste!* (=Siehst du, 'See!') in V contexts, *ihr* in addressing a mixed group of T and V addressees and the generic *du* to address a dead person and in a eulogy creates a more differentiated system than a binary one, as does the use of more formal or more informal greetings and partings.

Apart from expressing social relationships, address pronoun choice can, according to Hickey (2003), denote a political statement or a work relationship. It can exclude people from a group, maintain social distance and even be used to insult. Hickey discusses permanent switches in both directions, who has the right to offer a T relationship and why it may be declined, the timing of a T relationship and interpretations of a change.

As ordinary people have become increasingly aware of the intricacies of their address systems, their interest has been stimulated by public discussion in the media and books on the topic directed at a wide readership. One example is Werner Besch's popular treatment of German address as a phenomenon of cultural history, which is a valuable background resource (Besch 1998). In Germany, periodic public opinion polls conducted since 1974 by the Institut für Demoskopie (Allensbach 2003) have shown the following about address practices:

- choice of *du* is increasing in most age groups in each survey;
- greater choice of *du* correlates with the younger age group, with some decline over time as people grow older;
- left-wing political views correlate with early adoption of *du*;
- *du* is used more freely by males and by those with university education or in apprenticeships;
- *du* is used more freely in western than in eastern Germany.

2.2.4   Swedish

Compared with many other European languages such as German or French, Swedish has experienced dramatic changes in the pronominal address system in the past 100 years. The complex historical development of the Swedish address pronouns *du* (T) and *ni* (V) is recorded by Ahlgren (1978) and is explained as a result of the earlier widespread use of titles, where *ni* was predominantly used to address somebody who lacked a title, but who in turn had to respond with the superior person's title (Ahlgren 1978: 78). Since *ni* had attracted negative connotations because of its use socially downwards, it could no longer be employed among the social elite to simply signal distance and the only possibility remaining was to use the interlocutor's title and consistently avoid direct address by pronouns altogether. Erik Wellander, a well-known language cultivator in the early 1900s, was a strong advocate for the (re)introduction of *ni* as a polite form of address (Wellander 1935), but the struggle to get *ni* socially accepted did not succeed. According to Paulston, it simply came too late (Paulston 1976: 365) as it was superseded by *du*, which had started to spread rapidly in the 1960s and 1970s. Ahlgren attributes this partly to the cumbersome use of titles and avoidance of *ni*, but he also interpreted it as a change from below, among ordinary people (Ahlgren 1978: 84–5). When Bror Rexed, the then director of the Swedish Health Department, pioneered the adoption of universal *du* among all staff at the department towards the end of the 1960s, this became known as the '*du*-reform' (see e.g. Teleman 2003). While it was not an officially sanctioned reform as such, Rexed's actions were a sign of the times. A democratic, no-nonsense form of address based on solidarity resonated with the egalitarian ideals of the social democratic hegemony of the late 1960s in Sweden. By the mid-1970s, a very formal system with avoidance of direct address, with mandatory use of titles, if known, had largely been replaced by *du* address.

However, this development was not without problems, as different groups of people tended to operate according to different norms of use (Paulston 1976). While Paulston's research confirms the rapid shift during the 1960s and 1970s towards universal *du*, Mårtensson (1986) describes the emergence of the V pronoun *ni*, in a new and much less hierarchy-related and deferential function, used particularly in service encounters to signal polite distance. However, two recent studies of reported address use (Norrby and Håkansson 2004) and actual use (Tykesson-Bergman 2006) in service encounters found no support for the re-emergence of the V form.

Mara and Huldén (2000) plot the development of address practices in Finland-Swedish. The historical development of address in Finland-Swedish was similar to that of Sweden, but *ni* lacked negative connotations and was therefore not as restricted in its use as was the case in Sweden. Although the '*du*-reform' led to a significant spread of the informal pronoun *du*, it was not as strong a movement as in Sweden. This also has been explained as a language contact phenomenon with influence from Finnish communicative patterns (Saari 1995). Finnish is characterised by a higher level of formality and indirectness (Saari 1995, Fremer 1998), leading to an impression of Finnish communication as being 'withdrawing and evasive' (Yli-Vakkuri 2005: 200). With regard to address practices, the V form (*te*) is more frequently used in Finnish than in Swedish, but more importantly, direct address tends to be avoided in Finnish, with more indirect reference to the addressee, e.g. through use of passives and third-person constructions (Saari 1995, Fremer 1998, Nyblom 2006).

2.3   Theoretical issues

Given that address is embedded in social interaction, in the following sections we comment on theoretical frameworks developed for the analysis and understanding of interaction and interpersonal relations and their relevance to address.

2.3.1   *Politeness*

Any investigation of the linguistic expression of social relations needs to take into account the notion of politeness. A great deal has been written about politeness, from a variety of perspectives (see e.g. Brown and Levinson 1987,

Fraser 1990, Holtgraves 2001, Watts, Ide and Ehlich 1992, Watts 2003, Lakoff and Ide 2005). Holtgraves (2001: 341–2) usefully divides approaches to politeness into three categories:

(a) a 'social normative view of politeness', in which being polite is considered as behaving according to a set of rules that is appropriate to the context;[2]

(b) a pragmatic view of politeness, in which politeness is one factor making up what is called pragmatic competence (e.g. Leech 1983, Lakoff 1973);

(c) a 'face management view of politeness', in which the principle underlying polite behaviour in interaction is attention to 'face' (Goffman 1967, Brown and Levinson 1987).

The notion of face is defined by Goffman as 'the positive social value a person effectively claims for himself by the line others assume he has taken during a particular contact' (Goffman 1967: 5). In other words, the presentation of self in an interaction is 'a claim to a particular social position' and the speaker seeks to meet the expectations of the position thus claimed (Svennevig 1999: 23). The self is thus a social construction that is performed or presented. For participants in a conversation, it is important to act in accordance with the face, or self-image, that they wish to project and to act in such a way that the face of other participants is not threatened (Goffman 1967).

Among those influenced by Goffman's model of face are Brown and Levinson (1987). Their politeness theory is based on three unrelated languages, English, Tamil (a Dravidian language) and Tzeltal (a Mayan language), and their respective cultures. This theory has as its underlying premise that speakers of a particular cultural background share assumptions about politeness, informing their choice of communicative strategies. Brown and Levinson distinguish between negative face, the 'want' not to be imposed upon by others, and positive face, the 'want' to be approved of by others. Brown and Levinson also distinguish between negative politeness, where a conflict is avoided through modesty, formality and restraint, and positive politeness, where a closer relation with the interlocutor is established through frank relations.

Brown and Levinson's theory has been criticised for its claims of universality. Ide (1989), for example, considers that the model is unable to deal with politeness in languages with honorific systems in which social conventions (such as the person's place in society) constrain interactional choice, as in the Japanese concept of *wakimae* ('discernment'). The model also fails to take into account the fact that choice of politeness strategies is closely linked to interlocutors' cultural background (see e.g. Ide 1989, Matsumoto 1989, Kasper

---

[2] See also Fraser and Nolen (1981) on the notion of 'conversational contract'.

1994): communicative principles vary across cultures and thus cannot be described within a single model.

Watts (2003) is also critical of Brown and Levinson, in particular their division of politeness into positive and negative politeness strategies and their conceptualisation of politeness as a speaker's rational choice from a pre-existing taxonomy of politeness options (Watts 2003: 87–8). The main argument put forward by Watts is that researchers interested in linguistic expressions of politeness need to rid themselves of a preoccupation with theory-driven model building in which they abstract themselves from actual negotiations of politeness in interactional contexts. Thus he argues for what he calls a radical shift in thinking about politeness, in which researchers need to focus on an everyday notion of politeness and 'find ways of looking at linguistic politeness as part of what happens in an interactional exchange' (2003: 255). In other words, politeness is not seen as a pre-existing, static concept or list of strategies but as something which is discursively constructed by interlocutors. 'Politic behaviour' within such a model is simply such behaviour – both linguistic and non-linguistic – that interlocutors perceive of as appropriate in the particular context. Polite behaviour, meanwhile, consists of actions that go beyond and are in excess of what interlocutors find contextually suitable (Watts 2003: 259; see also Watts 1989, 1991).

Applied to modes of address, we could say that the use of a particular form of address, e.g. *vous* in French, is merely politic behaviour if this is what interlocutors treat as normal and expected, while the same form could be polite in excess in another encounter. From such a point of view, address practices are relative and open to discursive negotiation. However, does adopting such an approach also mean that any research – into address or other forms of social practice – need only occupy itself with actual interactions? The answer to this question must be an unequivocal 'no': individuals enter into any interaction with a set of at least partly shared assumptions about what is appropriate behaviour in the situation at hand, based on their knowledge about the world, their partly shared histories and cultural experiences, i.e. a (partly) shared background context (e.g. Linell 1998, Morford 1997: 8).

These assumptions can be fruitfully explored, not only by examining actual interactions but also by asking people about their experiences and views on address practices, as members of particular speech communities or social networks. This is exactly what the present study sets out to do. Niedzielski and Preston (2000) discuss the historical tension between community beliefs about (a) language and (b) the linguist's claim to objectivity. We share their view that speakers themselves, through their comments on language use, provide an essential basis for the understanding of language and society. However, our study differs from many of those cited by Niedzielski and Preston in that we have included focus groups and not just individuals' perceptions (see section 2.4.1).

2.3.2   *Common ground*

It is worthwhile exploring further the role and nature of shared assumptions in social interactions. One way of thinking about such assumptions is through the notion of 'common ground' (e.g. Clark 1996), understood as 'mutual knowledge, mutual beliefs, mutual assumptions, and mutual awareness' (Svennevig 1999: 55) and governed by culturally informed, contextual constraints. Common ground can be established at two levels: personal and communal. The personal level relates to individuals' direct personal experience of one other and the communal level to their shared membership of a particular cultural community, that is, 'a set of people with a shared expertise that other communities lack' (Svennevig 1999: 56). How is this notion of 'common ground' relevant for an understanding of address practices? At the communal level, there is a common understanding of what the default address patterns would be within a particular cultural community. At the personal level, joint and direct experience of one another in a particular set of circumstances is the basis for decisions on which address forms to use. Both these levels can come together in establishing the common ground between individuals. If we take the example of a badminton club in Paris, the common ground is established through being members of a cultural community that plays badminton and through the personal relationships established and maintained through playing with a set of like-minded individuals, informally dressed in shorts and t-shirts, creating the conditions for reciprocal use of *tu*.

Furthermore, common ground is a useful concept in understanding how interactions between strangers function. Basically, 'strangers are people who have not established any personal common ground' (Svennevig 1999: 58). However, common ground can be determined through 'circumstantial' evidence or 'episodic' evidence (Clark 1996: 117–19; see discussion in Svennevig 1999: 59). The former refers to the physical elements of the situation, for example the appearance and dress of one's interlocutor; the latter has to do with the actions that speakers perform, for instance the kinds of conversational gambits that they employ. As an illustration, in first encounters it is common to engage in question-and-answer sequences about one another in order to establish some kind of common ground. Typical examples would be asking where someone lives and what they do for a living, categories which enable maximum inferences to be drawn about the extent of shared commonalities. There is, therefore, a kind of membership categorisation (Sacks 1992: 40–8) that takes place in initial encounters. The fundamental question is: 'Are you the same as or different from me?' With strangers, this membership categorisation is basically about trying to 'make sense' of the other person in terms of one's own set of membership categories. An initial categorisation can of course be renegotiated, as further information or 'evidence' comes to light. We will return to the question of membership categorisation in the choice of address mode in Chapter 3.

The importance of shared commonalities in address choice was noted by Brown and Gilman, back in 1960: 'The similarities that matter [in the use of mutual T] seem to be those that make for like-mindedness or similar behaviour dispositions. These will ordinarily be such things as political membership, family, religion, profession, sex and birthplace' (Brown and Gilman 1960: 258). This is echoed by Kallmeyer's *gemeinsame Lebenswelt* or 'perceived commonalities', which includes interests, affiliations such as being members of the same club, attitudes and place of residence (Kallmeyer 2003).

The notion of signalling sameness or difference is something that has informed the development of accommodation theory (see e.g. Giles 1984, Giles, Coupland and Coupland 1991). Through convergence with or divergence from the verbal and non-verbal patterns of their interlocutor, speakers can either 'index or achieve solidarity with or dissociation from a conversational partner reciprocally and dynamically' (Giles, Coupland and Coupland 1991: 2). Underlying convergence is a basic human drive to establish communion with others, whereas divergence underlines a drive to express individuality (Svennevig 1999: 24); people tend to be either self-oriented or other-oriented (Kerbrat-Orecchioni 1992).

From the above, we can posit three steps in encounters with strangers. First, there is a process of fairly instant membership categorisation. Second, a decision is taken on whether there is similarity or difference. In the case of enough perceived sameness, for example, the speaker may wish to express alignment or convergence with the other person. This relational work can be done in a variety of ways linguistically, including, of course, using the same address pronoun as one's interlocutor, or by exchanging first names. Third, as a consequence of the outcome of the two first steps, it can be established whether there is common ground, often an ongoing process of negotiation.

However, the notion of 'common ground' puts the emphasis on what is common, that is, sameness rather than difference, and in fact we need a model that enables us to distinguish not only degrees of sameness but degrees of difference. In the following section, therefore, we return to one of the parameters of politeness theory, as formulated by Brown and Levinson (1987), that is, (social) distance.

2.3.3   Social distance

The parameter 'distance', which was integrated into Brown and Levinson's (1987) theory of politeness, has been defined in a variety of ways in the sociolinguistic literature, as Spencer-Oatey has demonstrated (Spencer-Oatey 1996). According to her, researchers who have investigated the distance parameter and its effect on language use have applied varying terms to describe the phenomenon: 'distance', 'social distance', 'solidarity', 'closeness', 'familiarity' and 'relational intimacy' (1996: 2–3). For example, Brown and Gilman (1960) introduce the term 'solidarity' and regard it as an expression of like-mindedness, whereas Brown and Levinson (1987) employ the label 'distance' and further explain it as 'a symmetric social dimension of similarity/ difference' (Brown and Levinson 1987: 76). While the terminology differs, both these studies underscore the dimension of social difference/similarity perceived by interlocutors (see Spencer-Oatey 1996: 3–4 for further discussion). Social distance is usually conceptualised as a continuum, with extremes at either end of the scale. Typically a high degree of social distance exists between strangers, whereas low social distance characterises friendships and family relations. In the case of strangers, first encounters can become an opportunity for decreasing social distance and establishing common ground (see previous section). However, in a first encounter there is often no obvious need to decrease social distance, for example in fleeting contacts such as a service encounter or asking a stranger in the street for directions. Returning to Brown and Levinson's politeness framework, a high degree of social distance would typically lead interlocutors to use negative politeness strategies, e.g. using V and hon + LN. Conversely, a low degree of distance would lead to positive politeness strategies, where for example use of T and first names emphasises similarity between interlocutors (Brown and Levinson 1987).

2.3.3.1 Status

In addition to the social distance dimension – conceptualised as a non-hierarchical relationship leading to symmetrical language use (e.g. either recip-rocal T or V depending on the perceived degree of distance) – *power* has been introduced as a social factor to account for language practices which result from hierarchical relationships. Again, Spencer-Oatey shows that this dimension has been labelled in various ways, but 'power' and 'status' are the most common (Spencer-Oatey 1996: 7–8).

With particular reference to address, Brown and Gilman (1960: 256–60), for example, view difference in power as leading to non-reciprocal address practices, with the less powerful interlocutor using V 'upwards' but receiving T in return. However, the 'power semantic' works only in a static society in which everybody has a clearly defined place. In modern societies, charac-terised by social mobility, power is replaced by 'the solidarity semantic' (i.e. degree of social distance). Thus, the social distance dimension is hori-zontal, based on degree of similarity, whereas the power dimension is vertical and founded on degree of equality. While such a model conceptualises fundamental aspects of interpersonal relationships, the separation of 'social distance' and 'status' into two dimensions is not particularly helpful for our purposes. We see 'status' as one of the variables in a model based on social distance.

Table 2.1 *Dimensions of social distance*

Relation	Constitutive feature	Sphere
Affect	mutual attraction	emotional
Solidarity	mutual rights and obligations	normative
Familiarity	mutual knowledge of personal information	cognitive

Based on Svennevig (1999: 34).

2.3.3.2 *Social distance as a multidimensional concept*

Social distance has also been conceptualised as multidimensional. Svennevig (1999: 34–5) proposes a model of social distance relations that includes three factors or 'dimensions': *solidarity, familiarity* and *affect* (see Table 2.1). These three factors are usually, but not necessarily, interrelated and do not have to co-occur. Svennevig sets up his model by referring to three basic ways in which individuals present themselves: 'a set of feelings and attitudes (an emotional Self), a claim to a position in the social structure, involving certain rights and obligations (a social Self), and a model of the world (a cognitive Self)' (Svennevig 1999: 33). Bonding between individuals may take place on one or more of these levels of communication, 'involving emotional relations, normative or "moral" relations, and informational relations' (1999: 33).

The usefulness of Svennevig's model lies particularly in the fact that all three relations are scalar at the same time as they can be symmetrical or not. For the affective dimension, there is a continuum from attraction via indifference to rejection that can be reciprocal, but does not have to be so. Generally speaking a sense of (mutual) attraction is likely to lead to a rapid shift to T and first names, but the emotional dimension is also stronger for some people than others, leading them to claim a 'right' to use T or V (see discussion in Chapter 3 on emotional choice). The solidarity relation in Svennevig's model conflates the solidarity/social distance and power parameters in earlier models (see above); an asymmetrical distribution of rights and obligations leads to a power relation between interlocutors, while a symmetrical distribution leads to solidarity (Svennevig 1999: 34). As already mentioned, for our purposes it is useful to consider 'power' as an integral part of social distance. From our data we will show that these two parameters sometimes merge, i.e. some informants refer to differences in 'hierarchies' and 'status' when describing address choice, but from the focus group discussions it becomes clear that power difference is often considered one distancing factor among others, which will lead to a higher incidence of (mutual) V (see Chapters 3 and 4). Finally, 'familiarity' refers to the degree of shared knowledge (common ground) between interlocutors, where relationships vary along a scale from intimates to perfect strangers.

The three dimensions – solidarity, familiarity and affect – are dynamic in the sense that interlocutors explore their potential to minimise, maintain or augment social distance. Every communicative event is inherently relational and dialogic (Bakhtin 1986) and interlocutors negotiate their positions in various ways. As we will show in the chapters to follow, for some a move from V to T is a long and sometimes difficult process, while for others it is a shift that might take place in an initial encounter, based on the more or less instant recognition of similarity along one or more of the dimensions.

2.3.4   *Style*

Within a traditional sociolinguistic framework, stylistic variation has been interpreted as the level of attention that speakers pay to their own speech (Labov 1972: 70–109). From this point of view, style was not necessarily considered worthy of theoretical attention, the focus being on the importance of speakers' belonging to certain fixed social categories rather than on speakers' communicative purposes (Coupland 2001: 191). However, as Gardner-Chloros pointed out (2004: 10), more recent work by British and American scholars has focused on theorising the notion of style and in particular its place in the presentation of self (see e.g. Eckert and Rickford 2001). For example, Coupland views the selection of a particular style in an interaction 'as a special case of the presentation of self, within particular relational contexts – articulating relational goals and identity goals' (Coupland 2001: 187).

An added dimension in the choice of address term is the underlying social consensus on the meaning. Coupland argues that 'individuals, within and across speaking situations, manipulate the conventionalised social meanings of dialect varieties' (Coupland 2001: 198). The relationship between conventionalised social meanings and an individual's uptake of these meanings is also examined by Agha (2007) in his study of models of social conduct. Part of his study deals with registers of person deixis. Deixis basically refers to linguistic forms whose full meaning depends on the social context in which they are used, such as demonstratives *this* and *that*, adverbs *now* and *here* and, of course, address pronouns. In the past, person deixis was related to 'certain essentialising assumptions such as the view that (1) particular deictics have an inherent, unitary "social meaning" that is invariant for all speakers, that (2) such register formations constitute closed, internally structured "systems" of the language (e.g. an "address system") to which all language users are oriented' (Agha 2007: 278–9). If we apply this to address forms, the conventionalised social meanings attached to particular terms – for example, that German *Sie* is 'polite' – can be taken up, challenged and renegotiated by individuals in their situated identity work (see 2.3.5). Morford, in her study of French, underlines the importance of speakers' awareness of the social meanings of *tu* and *vous*. As an illustration, although *vous* is now used by people of different classes in all kinds of situations, it retains vestiges of its association with bourgeois status and in ideological terms can be considered as 'conservative', compared with a more 'left-wing' *tu* (Morford 1997: 16–17, 19).

2.3.5   Identity

Much of the current research on the relationship between language use and social categories places strong emphasis on the notion of *social identity* and what role language plays in shaping social identities. While an interest in identity is by no means new, social identity is arguably a crucial component in any sociolinguistic project. In identity research, the focus has shifted in the last few decades from an essentialist to a constructivist paradigm (Joseph 2004: 83–91). In early variationist sociolinguistic investigations, social categories such as age, gender, status and level of education were seen as relatively stable and unproblematic entities, which could be used to explain group behaviour (e.g. Labov 1972, Trudgill 1974). With the advent of interactional sociolinguistics and the ethnography of communication, which placed much more emphasis on qualitative data and the behaviour of individuals in actual speech events, the focus of identity research has also shifted (e.g. Gumperz 1982). A central point of much recent research in sociolinguistics, as in social psychology and in discourse analysis more generally, is that individuals are *agents* who negotiate identities in interaction.

For example, Le Page and Tabouret-Keller (1985), in their ethnographic study on language use and social identity in the Caribbean, set out to challenge existing stereotypes about linguistic and ethnic identities. They broke with the prevailing sociolinguistic paradigm at the time by viewing the linguistic behaviour of individuals not primarily as a reflection of their class, gender, race or any other pre-defined social group but as a series of acts of identities where 'individuals create the patterns for their linguistic behaviour so as to resemble those of the group or groups with which from time to time they wish to be identified' (p. 18). What is of interest for the present study is that social identities are dynamic and actively (re)created through language and are expressed or come to life as actual linguistic behaviour marking sameness or difference. These two dimensions are also present in Tajfel's work on social identity and the importance, according to the speech situation, of marking one's belonging to an in-group (the sameness dimension) or an out-group (the difference dimension) (Tajfel 1974).

A recurrent theme in much identity research at present is that identities are dynamic, fluid and multiple, which does not mean that 'anything goes'; according to Zimmerman (1998), a distinction between different levels of negotiability or stability is needed. In his model, *discourse identities* refer to the constantly changing roles we have in conversation, e.g. as speaker and listener, whereas *situational identities* deal with specific rights and obligations inherent in a particular situation, such as the behaviour of a doctor and patient in a medical consultation. While discourse and situational identities are variable throughout an interaction, *transportable identities* are more stable social categories that individuals carry with them from one speech event to the next. Examples of such transportable identities are age, sex, race and other visible signs, such as style of clothing. Even if transportable identities are viewed as more stable than the other categories, they are not static; they are valid only if interlocutors orient themselves towards them. In other words, identities have to be made salient within the interaction.

Pavlenko and Blackledge (2004) also distinguish between three types of identities: *imposed identities, assumed identities* and *negotiable identities* (2004: 21). An *imposed* identity is one that cannot be contested or negotiated (for example being identified as a Jew in Nazi Germany was not an identity open to any negotiation). An *assumed* identity is one which is accepted by many – typically dominant groups – in society. Finally, those identities that are *negotiable* typically involve such parameters as ethnicity, class, gender and status, which may be embraced, resisted or contested by individuals as well as groups. According to Pavlenko and Blackledge the negotiation of identities is grounded in 'positioning theory' (Davies and Harré 1990, Harré and van Langenhove 1999) and should be 'understood as an interplay between reflective positioning, i.e. self-representation, and interactive positioning, whereby others attempt to position or reposition particular individuals or groups' (p. 20).

Both Zimmerman's idea of layered identities in interactions and the concept of interlocutors positioning themselves in relation to one another resonate very well with Goffman's work on self-presentation and how the 'self' is constructed in interaction (Goffman 1959). For our purposes, the notion of positioning – of individuals as well as groups – is useful. An important point in Pavlenko and Blackledge's model is that all three types of identities are non-fixed in the sense that their level of negotiability can (and usually does) change over time. Forms of address can be used to signal affiliations and dis-affiliations with others, both individuals and groups, bringing us back to the notion of common ground discussed above. The social meaning of one such form or other develops over time and also varies in geo-spatial terms. The ways in which identities are expressed, or their expression avoided, is an area we will return to in the following chapters.

2.4   Methodology

The six main sites in our study are Paris (France), Mannheim and Leipzig (Germany), Vienna (Austria), Gothenburg (Sweden) and Vaasa (Finland) (see section 1.6). In each site, five sets of data were collected: two focus groups, network interviews consisting of two parts (a closed questionnaire and an open-ended interview), participant observation and chat groups. In addition, we conducted focus groups in London and Newcastle upon Tyne (England) and Tralee (Ireland).

2.4.1   Focus groups and participant observation

Focus groups are used extensively and successfully in market research (Greenbaum 1998) and there has been some positive experience with them in studies of language maintenance and shift (e.g. Kipp, Clyne and Pauwels 1995, Clyne and Kipp 1999, 2006). The focus groups for the present project were directed towards gaining information on who would address whom in which way in particular circumstances and the group dynamics led to spontaneous responses from one or more participants. This in turn resulted in animated discussion in which competing or complementary positions were strongly expressed concerning perceptions of, attitudes to and expectations of language use. Discussions such as these enable as true a picture as possible of the role of modes of address in human relations. Focus group meetings were held at each research site at the start and towards the end of the project. The first focus group meeting gave the project team insights into the current situation of address as perceived by members of the speech community and also helped with the selection of networks for the interviews. The second focus group meeting involved the participants in the interpretation of our data. They were presented with the findings so far and asked to comment on them. This applied especially to ambiguous and inexplicable findings. It also gave us an opportunity to debrief them on the project.

The focus groups were tape recorded and conducted by the local in-country research assistant, who took part in a training session conducted by the researchers at the Institut für deutsche Sprache in Mannheim.[3] The groups comprised up to 16 people, representing a fairly broad cross-section of the population in terms of age, gender and occupation, but with a bias towards the professional middle class and students. The age range was 16–83. Among leading questions initiated by the moderator were:

- How has the use of T and V pronouns changed?
- What has been the role of contact with other languages or with people using other languages in this change?
- How does a transition from a V to a T relationship occur?
- (For English-speaking groups) What in English corresponds to T and V use?
- How are pronouns used with titles and last names vs. first names?

---

[3]   We thank Ludwig Eichinger and Werner Kallmeyer of the Institut für deutsche Sprache for making this possible.

- How do people feel about being addressed in an 'unexpected' way?
- What are the differences in address usage between different countries and regions employing the same language?

The researchers conducted informal *participant observation* in the countries and places concerned and also informal fact-finding through conversations in their own networks while on extended visits to the countries. Participant observation took place, for instance, in shops, department stores, post offices, hotels, cafés and restaurants, government offices, churches, university departments, at social gatherings, in hospitals, doctors' and dentists' waiting rooms, at the hairdresser's, in taxis, in face-to-face situations and over the telephone. Quotations in the text from focus groups 1 and 2 and from participant observation are marked FG1, FG2 and PO respectively.

2.4.2   Interviews on address practices

A major part of our data comes from our network interviews conducted with informants from each research site, in total 72 for French, 144 for Swedish and 198 for German. In other words, 414 people have contributed their views on address and reported on their own usage of modes of address. The interviews were conducted by in-country research assistants using a questionnaire designed by the researchers. The research assistants selected 12 base participants[4] who were members of their own social network, including for example friends, family members, fellow students, work colleagues and neighbours. Each of these 12 base informants was asked to select 5 members of his or her own social network, resulting in a corpus of 72 participants per site (66 for German). All of them live either in the city in question or within commuting distance. Those who are in the workforce or who are studying do so in the city. The vast majority of the informants also grew up in the city or the greater metropolitan area.

All participants met with the local research assistant to fill out a closed questionnaire on address and to participate in a semi-structured interview on address practices. The questionnaire sought the informants' reported use of T or V and in some cases use of first name/last name + honorific and/or title or first name/kinship term when addressing somebody in a number of different situations. Several domains were presented: the public domain (e.g. how the respondent would address a stranger in the street, a shop assistant, a police officer, etc.), the private domain (e.g. addressing family members, friends) and the workplace (e.g. addressing colleagues, superiors, clients). In many of these scenarios informants were asked both how they would address the interlocutor in question and how they thought the other person would address them (for the full questionnaire, see Appendix A).

---

[4] For technical reasons 11 in German-language sites.

The questionnaire was immediately followed by the interview, which elicited responses to a series of questions regarding modes of address (see Appendix A), such as: How would you address your neighbour and how would they address you? From what age should someone be addressed by V? How would you start a letter to a person you don't know? Have you ever been addressed with a form you didn't expect? Have you noticed any changes in the way people address one other over the past 10 to 15 years? What do you think about companies that make their employees use the T-form, e.g. IKEA? The interviews were recorded and then transcribed. They varied quite considerably in length, from as little as 10 minutes to well over an hour in a few cases, providing a wealth of information and opinions on the issues at hand.

2.4.3   Chat groups

We had intended to set up chat groups in each language focusing on address so that we could obtain an additional source of information on attitudes and expectations through a different kind of debating culture from that of the focus groups. At the same time, the chat groups would enable us to observe address patterns between members within a new technological mode. However, we decided not to establish our own chat groups but tap into existing groups in each of the languages and thereby achieve all the intended goals. These groups ranged from forums on language and style to hobby-based chat groups for stamp collectors or *Simpsons* fans.

2.5   Concluding remarks

We would propose as our starting point for a model of address the concept of social distance, which we believe to be the overarching principle that guides interlocutors in their choice of address forms. Social distance is a multidimensional concept which involves degrees of affect, solidarity and familiarity (Svennevig 1999). Affect ranges from emotional closeness (as in an intimate relationship) to adversarial stance (as between enemies). Solidarity varies from perceived or stated similarity (as in being on the same wavelength, having similar experiences, rights or obligations) to dissimilarities (as in having different rights, etc. and therefore unequal status). Familiarity ranges from well-established relationships, as among intimates or close friends, to complete strangers with no personal knowledge of the other.

The concept 'common ground', which we can understand as 'low social distance', cuts across all three social distance parameters: a sense of attraction (affect) may occasion a search for traces of affinity, or commonalities between interlocutors, which might in turn help establish common ground. A sense of solidarity, for example between work colleagues, members of a sports club or political party, is clearly related to an established sense of common ground in that particular area or domain. Degree of familiarity is perhaps the dimension of social distance that is most obviously connected to common ground as it is based on mutual knowledge of background information about the other.

Both social distance and the expression of common ground are relational categories; in other words they are not stable, static categories, but are negotiated and renegotiated in the interactional context. This means that interlocutors – who of course change roles, so the addressor becomes addressee and vice versa – always position themselves in relation to the other and in doing so they make use of positive and negative politeness strategies which enhance the interlocutors' positive or negative 'face'. One way of claiming common ground, for example, is to employ positive politeness, which emphasises sameness and sharedness. Linked to the positioning of oneself in relation to the other is the 'reading' of the other. Many of our informants' descriptions of address choice can be interpreted as the ability to read the other person's (performed) identity and make a decision on whether to align themselves with the other person. Thus, address practices are about inclusion (of self and other), but also about exclusion (of self and other).

Finally, interlocutors bring their understandings of the conventionalised social meaning of the forms themselves to each interaction. We would argue, however, that there is a certain degree of shared social consensus about the meaning of a particular form – for example, in 'popular' discourse it is generally considered that French *vous* is 'polite'. These social meanings can be taken up or renegotiated by speakers in an interaction.

The literature survey in this chapter and the analysis and discussion of our data in Chapters 3 to 5 will lead to an inductive model (Chapter 6) based on properties of the languages, principles of address choice and linguistic and social factors.

3   Contextualising address choice

As we saw in Chapter 2 there has been a shift within sociolinguistic research from a view of social identity as a series of static categories assigned to an individual, such as age and sex, to a position of an individual's social identity being dynamic and contextually situated. Our German data, for example, demonstrate that speakers preferring *du* or *Sie* may have similar biographical and social characteristics, which underscores the need to search beyond static social variables to explain choice of address. In the present chapter we will mirror this shift in the way we approach our data. The chapter opens with a basic comparison of the linguistic resources available in the four languages, in order to highlight salient similarities and differences between them. We then consider the data through the prism of two traditional, static categories – age and status – given that they are fundamental elements used both to categorise others and to situate ourselves in the world, and examine their salience for speakers of each language in turn. Moving beyond these pre-defined categories, we take up the notion of 'perceived commonalities' as an explanatory category and highlight how 'sameness' and 'difference' are relevant in showing how address choices are contextually motivated. For the purposes of this chapter we are not differentiating between national varieties of German and Swedish, which is the focus of Chapter 5. The reader is reminded that our English data, which are intended as a point of reference, are limited to that from focus groups and also that the absence of the T/V differentiation puts pressure on first name/last name and/or honorific to fill the pronominal gap.

3.1   The basic address systems

In all our four languages, interpersonal relations may be expressed through modes of address. As we have shown in Chapter 1, there are two main ways of doing this in these languages: (a) pronominally and (b) nominally through first names, honorifics and/or titles and last names, or other vocatives. Each language, however, draws on a different inventory of terms.

Figure 3.1 provides a preliminary sketch for comparing reciprocal address terms to a single addressee in the four languages, placing forms along a 'social

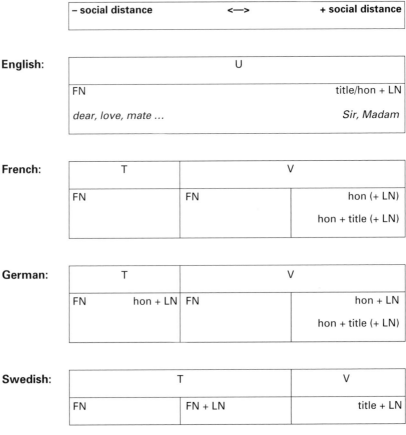

Figure 3.1 A basic continuum of reciprocal modes of address in English, French, German and Swedish (single addressee)

distance' continuum (see 2.3.3). We will come back to this sketch in more detail in Chapter 6. At this stage, the main aim of setting out the range of address possibilities in this way is to draw attention to what we are calling the default mode of address in each language. For English, we are using U to refer to the address pronoun *you*, as it fulfils the functions of both T and V without being the equivalent of either. In French and German, we consider V as the default pronoun, and in Swedish T is the default. Figure 3.1 also shows how the address pronoun(s) can combine with different nominal forms such as first name (FN) or last name (LN) and reflect different degrees of social distance. In the following sections, we discuss pronominal and nominal forms in turn.

3.1.1   Pronominal forms

Modern standard English has one single pronoun of address (U in Figure 3.1). One of the first things to note about English is in fact that use of U on its own can be considered the default, neutral address form, as the following discussion from London reveals (for transcription conventions, see p. ix):

(1)   I think that we go out of our way not to use nouns with people. You know, if I drop something in the street, I wouldn't use 'Sir' or 'Madam', I'd just go 'Excuse me! You've dropped something.'
(2)   Which avoids referring to them directly.
(1)   I think in this country we're all about avoiding referring directly to people.
(3)   But is that a conscious avoidance?
(1)   It's because we don't know. I think it's too difficult. Because you don't know strangers' first names so you can't do that. You don't want to make value or some kind of political judgement by going into the whole 'Mr', 'Mrs', 'Ms' thing. 'Mr' sounds terribly formal – it does to me, anyway. 'Sir' and 'Madam' sounds a bit archaic.

(London, FG, (1) male solicitor, 34; (2) female student, 35;
(3) unidentified female)

The moderator in the London focus group comments that *you* can be both formal and informal, sparking a discussion about how distance or formality are expressed in a language which lacks the pronominal distinction. Some of the discussion focuses on tone of voice, sentence structure and manner of speaking, all of which can convey the level of social distance that is much more immediately expressed in languages with a pronominal choice, for example:

(1)   You wouldn't say 'Are you alright?' to somebody you wanted to show a certain amount of respect to. Let's say your grandmother, you wouldn't go 'Are you alright?' you'd say 'How are you?' So there's a different manner, a different tone of using 'you'. There's also a different way of using 'you' as well, a different way of using it in a sentence. [...]
(2)   But the other thing, I think we all have the ability to change our role in voice, tone and in manner. And I think we do it sometimes very skilfully. But whoever we're with, we seem to tune in very quickly to the level that we should be at to be comfortable with them and to make them feel comfortable.

(London, FG, (1) male voluntary sector worker, 26; (2) male retired
secondary school teacher, 77)

While Swedish retains a pronominal dichotomy, the use of V is very restricted in contemporary usage and T is the default pronoun, as illustrated in the following quotation:

Är det någon som säger 'ni' idag? Man säger 'du'.
[Is there anyone who says *ni* nowadays? People say *du*.]

(Gothenburg, FG1, female IT designer, 40)

Thus we can say that English and Swedish are similar in that pronominal distinctions are either non-existent or very weak.

In spite of the widespread use of T, Swedish speakers still productively use the verbs *dua* and *nia* – meaning 'to address someone by the T or V form' – thus demonstrating that the topic of pronominal address choice remains relevant. This can be explained by the fact that the shift to a 'universal' T has been relatively recent and Swedish speakers continue to make reference to the use of V. In addition, different generations of Swedish speakers attach distinct social meanings to the two forms (see 3.2.3). Similar verbs exist in French and German: *tutoyer/vouvoyer* and *duzen/Siezen* respectively.[1] This is an indication that the speakers of the language are aware of pronominal distinctions and their social value and that pronominal use is a salient topic for them.

In French, V has traditionally been considered the default pronoun. In other words, in initial encounters with strangers, the most likely pronoun choice is V. However, there is evidence of a shift to T among the younger generation and of fluctuating patterns of pronominal use, resulting in what we call a 'grey area'. This is similar to German, where traditionally the default pronoun has been V in initial encounters, but our study also shows fluctuation in use of T and V, indicating a substantial 'grey area' where choice of default pronoun depends on a range of social and situational variables (see 3.4, 3.5, 3.6). German also has a specific pronominal form *ihr*, which is the grammatical plural of *du*, employed to two or more people addressed in the singular as *du*. However, it fulfils other functions in the address system, including unmarked plurality (see 3.2).

The choice of default pronoun for French, German and Swedish is exemplified in responses to our interview question 'Have you ever been addressed in an unexpected way?' Table 3.1 shows the differences between the three languages for this question. In French, the majority of those participants who answered 'yes' report on unexpected T (77%), which is also the case for German but to a lesser extent (58%), whereas Swedish participants who responded in the affirmative overwhelmingly report on unexpected V (96%). The point here is that the unexpected pronoun is precisely *not* the default: if the majority report that being addressed with the T form is unexpected, then we can conclude that V is the 'expected', or default, form. In addition, the number of people who recall instances of unexpected address of whatever form is higher among French participants (87%, 62/71) than among their German and Swedish counterparts (72%, 142/198, and 67%, 83/124, respectively), thus indicating the relative salience of address forms for these three different populations.

---

[1] Swedish does not mark person through verb endings (e.g. *Kommer du?, Kommer ni?* [Are you coming?], *Kom!* [Come!]), contrasting with French and German, where speakers have to choose the verb ending which corresponds to their pronominal choice (e.g. *Kommst du?, Kommen Sie?, Komm!, Kommen Sie!*; *Tu viens?, Vous venez?, Viens!, Venez!*).

Table 3.1 *Percentage of respondents reporting unexpected address in French, German and Swedish*

	French	German	Swedish
Unexpected T	77	58	4
Unexpected V	23	42	96
Unexpected address (T and/or V)	86	72	67
(N)	(66)	(155)	(83)

N – total number of informants who gave answers to a particular question.

Comments from our participants also indicate that V is the default pronoun for French, as the following quotation shows:

Si on sait pas, on vouvoie d'office parce que c'est plus facile. C'est neutre en fait. Le vouvoiement il est très neutre finalement, il est «on met une distance», «on se connaît pas bien», etc.

[If you don't know, you use *vous* automatically because it's easier. It's neutral in fact. Using *vous* is very neutral, it's 'we're establishing a certain distance', 'we don't know each other well', etc.] (Paris, FG1, male accountant, 29)

While this is less clear-cut in German, for most people in most situations V is the default pronoun, at least in first encounters:

Zunächst einmal geh ich überall hin und praktiziere das 'Sie', weil ich ja die Leute nicht kenne, wenn Sie auch gewisse Respektpersonen sind und dann wenn man [...] mehr zusammen arbeitet und wenn's noch im gleichen Büroraum ist, kommt auf längere Sicht automatisch das 'Du' zustande. Es wird dann angeboten. [Sie-Anrede] muss aber net heißen, dass man sich dann nicht leiden kann, [...] das kann trotzdem ein gutes Verhältnis sein.

[At first, I go everywhere and use *Sie*, because I don't know those people, particularly if they are people in positions of respect and then when you [...] have worked more together and particularly if that's in the same office, in the long run the *du* develops automatically. It is offered then. [Address with V] does not necessarily mean that you cannot stand one another, [...] it can still be a good relationship.] (Mannheim, FG2, male, home duties, 40s)

The status of *du* as default address pronoun in Swedish is illustrated in the following quotation, where the participant makes specific reference to the '*du-*reform' of the 1960s:

Det fanns en tid när du-reformen infördes och före det var det nog inte så vanligt med 'du' men efter det, och på ett sätt så kändes det ju lite främmande i början [att börja dua], man tyckte att det tog lite emot, men nu tänker man inte på det mera, i början nog när man inte var van. Det gick ju inte på en gång, men så där småningom utan att man märkte det, inte över en natt men några år.

[There was a time when the '*du*-reform' was introduced and before that it wasn't that common to use *du* but after that, and in a way that felt a bit strange in the beginning [to start to use T], you thought that it felt a bit odd, but now you don't think about it any more, it was in the beginning when you weren't used to it. It didn't happen right away, but gradually without you thinking about it, not overnight but after a few years.] (Vaasa, Q3, female retired school teacher, 67)

3.1.2   Nominal forms

In English, address variation is manifested in a range of nominal forms, from 'T-like' terms such as first name, *mate* and *dear* to 'V-like' hon + LN, *Sir/Madam* and title + LN. Until recently, hon + LN was the default. The following excerpt from our London focus group exemplifies how the use of FN is increasingly common, even in domains or institutions viewed as bastions of tradition such as the law (see also Chapter 4):

I find it's the norm to use the Christian name. But I work in quite a traditional, hierarchical environment – a law firm – and we address all the clients by their first names. (London, FG, male solicitor, 34)

This use of FN is commented on by other participants in the same focus group, some indicating that FN has become their default nominal address form:

<How do you think it would feel to speak to everybody on first-name terms? Would you feel comfortable with that?>

(1)   *Personally, I can't remember the last time I didn't.* [general murmur of consent]
(2)   *I would agree. [...] I strive to call everybody by their first names. Sometimes I feel almost like I'm bulldozing over formality in calling people by their first name.*
       And if someone really takes umbrage to it and is going to go 'Oh, I can't be – you're not calling me Mr,' then that's their problem.
                 (London, FG (1) male student, 23; (2) male housing support officer, 28)

Terms such as *pet, love* and *dear* are typically mentioned by participants in focus group discussions in relation to service encounters, often used by women; *Sir* and *Madam* are also used in the transactional domain (see 4.5.4 for further discussion). *Mate* tends to be used between men, for a variety of purposes (see 3.6.3).

    In Swedish, honorifics and titles are used sparingly and in formal contexts FN + LN is more common. In French and German, the default nominal form that accompanies the T pronoun is FN; the default form for the V pronoun is honorific (title) + LN in German (*Herr (Professor) Müller*) and honorific (hon) + LN (*Madame Chirac*) or honorific alone (*Madame*) in French. However, the combination V + FN is also used in certain contexts and can be considered an intermediary form. In French, for example, the combination is used with a partner's parents and in the workplace (see 4.1.1 and 4.4.1). In German, older

people use V + FN to younger people they have known since the latter's childhood (see 4.1.2). In addition, another intermediary combination in German is T +
hon + LN. The traditional default mode of address in German and French for
people with titles (such as professor, doctor, minister of state, judge and clergy)
was hon + title (+ LN) – *Herr Professor* or *Madame la Présidente*. But in
Germany and France, and to a lesser extent in Austria, the use of titles has
declined substantially (see Chapters 4 and 5).

3.2 Social meanings of pronominal address forms

In what follows, we concentrate on pronominal forms for French, German and
Swedish. Given that 'you' is the pronominal address form in English, as we
have seen in the previous section, we will not be discussing English here.

3.2.1 French

In French, our focus group data show that there are (a) situations in which *tu* is
the default form of address – that is, with family and close friends – and (b)
situations in which *vous* is the default form – that is, with strangers and in
particular hierarchical work relationships (see also Chapter 4). In general, our
participants attach the following basic social meanings to the two pronouns:
- *vous* is equated with notions of respect, politeness and neutrality, as well as
  distance and the maintenance of barriers;
- *tu* is equated with notions of conviviality, proximity, affection and affinities.
These meanings are summed up by a young Parisian lawyer:

*Le 'tu' [...] fait tomber toutes les barrières qu'impose le 'vous', c'est-à-dire la distance,
la courtoisie, le respect, le monsieur avant, peut-être, les choses comme ça. Et il est
certain que quand on passe sur le 'tu', [...] c'est une relation beaucoup plus directe. Et
donc comme on a un fil qui est beaucoup plus direct, on peut le raccourcir à mort et
mettre ce qu'on veut dedans. Alors qu'avec un 'vous' le fil est beaucoup plus long et il est
parsemé de nœuds.*

[*Tu* [...] drops all the barriers that *vous* imposes, that is, distance, courtesy, respect,
monsieur first, perhaps, things like that. And it's clear that when you move to *tu*, [...] it's
a much more direct relationship. And so as you have a much more direct line, you can
shorten it like mad and put what you want in it. Whereas with a *vous*, the line is much
longer and full of knots.] (Paris, Q3, male lawyer, 32)

These conventionalised meanings are reiterated in the following example, but
the participant goes on to observe that *tu*, just like *vous*, can be used to mark
respect in certain circumstances. This demonstrates that contextual factors can
determine how the pronoun is interpreted, illustrating the potential multifunc-
tionality of the pronominal forms:

'Tu' c'est convivial, 'vous' c'est mettre une barrière. Voilà. 'Tu' c'est: ça dépend, dans certains cas c'est convivial, dans d'autres ça peut marquer le respect et 'vous' c'est aussi marquer son respect. Ça dépend du contexte.
[*Tu* is convivial, *vous* is about putting up a barrier. *Tu* is: it depends, in some cases it's convivial, in others it can mark respect and *vous* is also about marking respect. It depends on the context.] (Paris, Q5, female manager, 47)

The potential of each form to take on qualities of the other is underlined by other participants: *on peut vouvoyer quelqu'un et ne pas le respecter* ('you can use *vous* with someone and not respect them') (Paris, Q12, male estate agent, 33); *on peut très bien respecter quelqu'un en utilisant le 'tu'* ('you can perfectly well respect someone by using *tu*') (Paris, Q10, male managing director, 60).

A minority of participants indicate that they do not have a preference regarding how they are addressed. However, the underlying conventionalised social meanings of the two pronominal forms remain, even as the use of *tu* is extended into new domains:

Ça ne me gène pas. Il y a des amis des grands qui viennent des fois, il y en a qui me tutoient tout de suite, il y en a qui me disent 'vous'. Ça ne me dérange pas. Quand ils me tutoient je me dis 'Ils me prennent de leur génération, c'est bien.' Mais quand on me dit 'vous', pour moi c'est une marque de respect aussi, donc ça ne me dérange pas. Pas de préférence.
[It doesn't bother me. There are friends of my grown-up children who come over sometimes, some of them use *tu* with me straight away, some of them use *vous*. It doesn't bother me. When they use *tu* with me, I tell myself, 'They take me for someone from their generation, that's good.' But when they use *vous*, for me it's a mark of respect as well, so it doesn't bother me. [I've] no preference.] (Paris, Q4, female nurse, 53)

Focus group discussions also highlight the extension of *tu* into previously exclusive *vous* domains. Several participants explicitly state that *tu* is becoming more frequent. One participant considers that *tu* and *vous* are no longer so codified and that *tu* is encroaching on the 'public sphere':

J'ai l'impression qu'avant c'était beaucoup plus codifié, quoi, le 'tu' et le 'vous'. [...] Tu avais 'vous' pratiquement tout le temps et 'tu' dans le cercle privé. Maintenant, le 'tu', j'ai l'impression qu'il s'est élargi [...] beaucoup sur le cercle public. Sauf les gens qu'on connaît absolument pas qui, eux, seront dans le 'vous', quoi.
[I have the impression that before it was much more codified, *tu* and *vous*. […] You had *vous* practically all the time and *tu* in the private sphere. Now, I have the impression that the use of *tu* has extended […] a lot into the public sphere. Except for people who you don't know at all who would still be *vous*.] (Toulouse, FG, male education counsellor, 29)

The idea that *tu* is becoming more prevalent is underlined by other participants. A 32-year-old woman employed in the Paris fashion industry considers that young people use *tu* with each other more easily; however, as soon as questions of hierarchy or respect come into play, young people still use *vous*:

Je crois que c'est une erreur de croire que les jeunes ne vouvoient plus. Entre nous on se tutoie beaucoup plus facilement [...]. Mais dès que c'est dans un lieu différent, dès qu'il y a un coup d'hiérarchie, un coup de respect, on va vouvoyer toujours.

[I think that it's an error to think that young people no longer use *vous*. We use *tu* with one another much more easily [...]. But as soon as it's in a different place, as soon as there's a question of hierarchy or respect, we are going to always use *vous*.] (Paris, FG1, female fashion designer, 32)

Thus she considers that the traditional social meanings of *tu* and *vous* are still drawn upon by younger French speakers, even though *tu* use is on the increase among her generation.

3.2.2   German

German is similar to French in that there are contexts in which T is the default pronoun of address – among family members (see 4.1) – and contexts in which V is the default pronoun of address – among strangers and people whose 'outgroupness' needs to be marked. The majority of informants do not nominate specific words to describe the social meanings of the German address pronouns, but those who do use words like *Nähe* ('closeness'), *persönlich* ('personal'), *privat* ('private') and *vertraulich* ('intimate') to describe *du*, and *Distanz* ('distance') and *Respekt* ('respect') for *Sie*.

In both languages there is a grey area, where either V or T may be the default pronoun. Most usually V is the default pronoun in first encounters and there is either a swift transition to T or V remains the default pronoun for ever or at least for a long period. This variation may be due to individual preference, to a network preference and/or to the interplay, weighting and interpretation of different social variables (see 3.4 and 3.5, and Chapter 4).

The grey area is more extensive in German than in French, given the greater use of T in German, as well as the wider variety of social meanings attached by different German speakers to the role of address in human relations. This variety of social meanings came out in our German focus groups. One of our Mannheim participants cautiously expressed what we could call the 'traditional' position: since a *du* relationship is generally unretractable (in the absence of a complete termination of the relationship, cf. Kretzenbacher 1991: 59–60), it represents a lifelong commitment that cannot be taken lightly:

Das ist mitunter vielleicht ein sehr großer Schritt aber das ist teilweise der größte Schritt, den man manchmal tun könnte, tun sollte und die weiteren Schritte danach sind unter Umständen leichter.

[It [using *du*] is perhaps sometimes a very big step but it's partly the biggest step you can sometimes take or should take and the next steps after that are possibly easier.] (Mannheim, FG1, male, home duties, 40s)

However, there were other participants in the Mannheim focus group who considered T and V almost interchangeable:

Wenn man Leute mag oder auch gut kennt, ist das 'Sie' oder das 'Du' nicht unbedingt der große Unterschied.

[When you like people or know them well, *Sie* or *du* doesn't necessarily make a big difference.] (Mannheim, FG1, female arts teacher, about 30)

While this view was not universally accepted by the focus group participants, it was regarded as the majority position, especially among the younger generation. For example, a Mannheim secondary school teacher reported a discussion with her students in which one of them proposed a dichotomy of a *ganz herzliches, freundliches, warmes 'Sie'* ('a totally cordial, friendly, warm *Sie*') and a *ganz interesseloses 'Du'* ('completely indifferent *du*'). In this example, the 'traditional' social meanings attached to T and V, which place them on a continuum of social distance, are reversed.

There are still clearly rules that are applied to the choice of address pronoun and we will be discussing them in this chapter. But the grey area described above, as well as variation patterns, have created a large measure of insecurity among German speakers, something that some take up as a challenge:

Das ist ja das Spannende an der Kommunikation, weil du sagst, es gibt ein missbräuchliches 'Du' [...] du meinst vielleicht [...] du kannst jemandem mit nem 'Du' Respekt entgegenbringen, jemand anders nutzt es vielleicht aus, also es ist ja immer beidseitig ja, und ich einfach kann leider nicht immer voraussetzen, dass der das so versteht, wie ich das sage.

[That's the exciting thing about communication, since you are saying there is an abuse of *du* [...] you probably think [...] you can show someone respect with a *du*, another person might perhaps take advantage of that, so it's always mutual, isn't it?, and unfortunately I can't always predict that my opposite number will interpret the *du* the way I use it.] (Leipzig, FG1, female psychologist, 30)

Man muss vielleicht mehr Fingerspitzengefühl entwickeln wie das früher war, wo's denn gut ist und wo nicht [...] früher war das einfacher geregelt.

[Perhaps you have to develop more intuition than used to be the case before, where it is a good thing and where it isn't [...] that used to be laid down more simply in rules.] (Leipzig, FG1, clergyman, 50)

In contrast to French, German has the informal plural form, *ihr*. Apart from being the plural of *du*, *ihr* is also used when addressing two or more people, some of whom are addressed in the singular as *du* and others as *Sie*. *Ihr* is also employed collectively in a friendly informal way to people with whom one is on *Sie* terms. A dialogue betweeen two of our Viennese focus group members links the use of *ihr* as an intermediate form with less encroachment on sensitivities:

(1)   Vielleicht ist auch die persönliche Empfindlichkeit etwas geringer, wenn ich: jemand per 'Sie' angesprochen werden will und der redet mich nicht per 'Sie' an, bin ich empfindlicher als wenn ich dann mit 'Ihr' angesprochen werde.

(2)   Es wird als Zwischenstufe empfunden.

(1)   Ich seh das als eine Zwischenstufe. Da steckt Unverbindlichkeit drin.

[(1) Maybe one's personal sensitivity is somewhat less strong, if I: someone wants to be addressed with *Sie* and the other does not address me with *Sie*, I will be more sensitive to that than to being addressed with *ihr* in such a case.
(2)   It is being perceived as an intermediate form.
(1)   I see it [*ihr*] as an intermediate form. There's something noncommittal in that.]
(Vienna, FG2, (1) male high school teacher and administrator, 57;
(2) male retiree, 77)

Ihr is also employed when it is not the person being addressed as an individual but the collective entity to which the addressee belongs which is being referred to, e.g. *Wie viele Bücher habt ihr in der Bibliothek?* ('How many books do you have in the library?'), referring to the addressee's university library, not his personal one (PO).

3.2.3   Swedish

What comes out from participants' comments in the Swedish data is that *du* is the neutral, expected form and *ni* is the special case, whose use can lead to people interpreting the communicative situation as problematic:

Är det nån som tilltalar mig med 'ni', så tar jag avstånd, tar ett steg tillbaka, blir på min vakt. [...] Någonting är tokigt om nån tilltalar mig med 'ni'.
[If somebody addresses me with *ni*, then I distance myself, take one step back, I'm on my guard. [...] Something is wrong if somebody addresses me by *ni*.] (Vaasa, Q2, female illustrator, 27)

The social meanings of the T and V pronouns are clearly linked to generational differences. According to the Vaasa focus group participants, people who are above 40 years of age have been brought up to use V with unfamiliar people in general, whereas comments from the younger focus group participants demonstrate great insecurity about which pronoun to use in such contacts. They have grown up in a time of frequent and spreading use of T and contrary to the older generation who were taught in school to use V to unfamiliar people, they have never had any formal guidance as to what pronoun to use:

Jag tillhör en generation som alltid sagt 'du', när man blir äldre och ringer mera officiella telefonsamtal kan det vara jobbigt att veta om man ska nia eller dua [...] funderar emellanåt på vad jag ska säga. Vissa tar illa upp om man säger 'du'.
[I belong to a generation who have always said *du*, [but] when you get older and make more official phone calls it can be a real problem to know whether you should say *ni* or *du* [...] you wonder now and then what you should say. Some people take offence if you say *du*.] (Vaasa, FG1, female sales manager, 29)

In Sweden, the situation is more complicated. The oldest generation (participants above 60) are the most ardent supporters of general T and also report strong negative feelings towards the V pronoun. The following quotation illustrates the negative connotations that many older people in Sweden have towards *ni*, since it used to be employed asymmetrically and downwards:

Jag tar inte illa upp om någon säger 'ni', men tycker inte om det [...] Det var nedlåtande att kalla folk för 'ni' när jag var ung [...] Det var 'ni' till hembiträden.
[I don't take offence if somebody says *ni*, but I don't like it [...] It was condescending to call people *ni* when I was young [...] It was *ni* to maids.] (Gothenburg, FG1, female retired journalist, 67)

The oldest generation are the only ones who have experienced the cumbersome use of titles and avoidance of pronouns altogether if the title of the interlocutor was not known, so it is hardly surprising that they are supporters of general T use. Among the youngest focus group participants (20–27 years old) the fact that *ni* could be regarded as anything but a polite form is a revelation, as a 27-year-old female journalist states: *Jag visste inte att 'ni' kunde vara nedlåtande* ('I didn't know that *ni* could be condescending'). Finally, in the middle generation (36–53 years) there is variation in address use, with some participants reporting that they would never use V, while others would possibly use it in certain circumstances (particularly in addressing a much older person; see also 3.4.3). Overall, the focus group discussion points in the same direction as our interview data, except that the youngest generation in the focus group reported that they would not use V themselves as it was simply considered a 'foreign' form that they had not come in contact with. This underscores how ubiquitous the T form is in Swedish today.

## 3.3		Transition

How do people go about moving from one mode of address to another? There are explicit ways of signalling this transition. In French one can say, for example, *On peut se tutoyer* ('We can say *tu* to each other') or *On se tutoie?* ('Shall we say *tu* to each other?'):

<Quand est-ce qu'on passe du 'vous' au 'tu' dans une relation?> *Quand on se connaît et qu'on est sur pied d'égalité, quand on a l'impression d'appartenir au même groupe. A chaque fois que j'ai dit 'On se tutoie?' ça s'est passé. Je l'ai dit après avoir spontanément dit 'tu', d'une manière naturelle.*
[<*When do you go from* vous *to* tu *in a relationship?*> When you know each other and you're on an equal footing, when you have the impression of belonging to the same group. Every time I've said 'Shall we call each other *tu*?' it's been fine. I've said it after having spontaneously said *tu*, in a natural way.] (Paris, Q3, male retired teacher/lecturer, 62)

In German, the expressions are *Sollen wir uns duzen?* ('Should we use *du*?') or *Wir könnten uns ja duzen* ('We could say *du* to each other, couldn't we?'). The transition to T was traditionally accompanied by a drink ('Brüderschaft trinken' ('to drink to a fraternal relationship')) or, between the sexes, a kiss, though that is rarely the case today.

In both French and German, some of our participants indicated that there does not have to be a formally marked transition:

<Est-ce que vous utilisez souvent une expression comme 'on peut se tutoyer', ou est-ce que c'est plus implicite?> *'On peut se tutoyer' je pense que c'est plus dans le cadre du travail. Au début je vais vouvoyer et généralement assez vite on va se tutoyer. Ça arrive moins à l'extérieur.*

<Do you often use an expression like 'We can say tu to each other', or is it more implicit?> 'We can say *tu* to each other', I think it's more within the workplace. At the beginning I will use *vous* and generally pretty quickly we'll say *tu* to each other. It happens less outside [work].] (Paris, Q9, male accountant, 33)

Im Laufe der Zeit, wenn man mit jemand öfter was zu tun hat, man kommt mit dem klar, irgendwann, ohne lang zu reden, sagt man 'du' und dann ist es auch in Ordnung, das hab ich zig Mal praktiziert.

[By and by, if you are dealing with someone, you get along well with them, at some stage, without long discussion, you use *du* and that's OK then, I've done that dozens of times.] (Mannheim, Q6, male office worker, 61)

In German, sometimes one interlocutor will slip into T or first names and see whether the other falls in line. If not, it can be regarded as a slip of the tongue:

Ich mach das [duzen] dann einfach, die Reaktion ist dann oft etwas erstaunt, aber oft auch irgendwie angenehm überrascht und nehmen das gerne dann an.

[I simply do it [use *du*] then, the reaction is often a bit amazed, but also often somewhat positively surprised and they happily accept it then.] (Mannheim, Q11, female psychologist, 45)

The German focus group discussions revealed that in some contexts the transition from a *Sie* to a *du* relationship is still generally a rite of passage offered at the end of a hierarchical relationship – examples cited were at the end of a PhD by supervisor to student and at the end of school to a former pupil by a secondary school teacher. Some participants upheld the traditional rule, whereby only the older person, the more senior or the woman in an asymmetrical dyad is entitled to initiate a *du* relationship.

Das ist einfach vom Gegenüber abhängig, denk ich doch [...] Alter einfach, auch der Bekanntschaftsgrad. Auch bei Kollegen, wenn man sie schon kennt, dann sagt man, duzen wir uns doch [...] nach einer gewissen Zeit und dann sagt man, 'Mensch, duzen wir einander', aber nicht von Anfang an. Es gibt gewisse Regeln, dass der Ältere dem Jüngeren das 'Du' anbietet, der Mann der Frau, das würde ich als überholt bezeichnen. Der Jüngere würde dann das 'Du' nie ablehnen, das ist klar. Da freut man sich dann auch drüber. Das ist ein Kompliment.

[Well, I should think that depends on your opposite number... one's age, also the degree of mutual acquaintance. With colleagues, too, when you know them already, you say 'Hey, let's use *du* with each other' [...] after a while, 'Come on, let's use du', but not right from the start. There are certain rules, that the older one offers the *du* to the younger one, or the male to the female, I would call those obsolete. The younger one would never decline the *du*, that's obvious. You are happy about it. It's a compliment.] (Mannheim, Q9, female housekeeper, 43)

However, generally many in the German focus groups felt that the tradition was breaking down, as cautiously expressed by the following participant:

Zum Beispiel wenn der Jüngere dem Älteren das 'Du' anbietet, mein Gott. Es geht um professionelle Zusammenarbeit und respektvollen Umgang.
[For example when the younger person offers a *du* relationship to the older one, who cares?]. It's about professional cooperation and respectful interaction.] (Leipzig, FG1, male civil servant, 32)

As we will discuss in section 4.2.2, another rite of passage that is breaking down in German is the use of V by teacher to pupil after a certain age.

In contemporary Swedish, there is no formally marked transition, as T is the default form. In Swedish, the verbs *dua* and *nia* are used not to introduce a change from one form of address to another but to refer to how someone has been addressed (expressions in bold):

*Jag kan bara komma på kungafamiljen som undantag mot **duande**. Jag har frågat runt på jobbet, ingen **niar** där. Min generation **niar** inte.*
[I can only think of the royal family as an exception to using *du*. I've asked around at work, but no one uses *ni* there. My generation doesn't use *ni*.] (Gothenburg, FG1, female IT designer, 40)

In the recent past, however, up to and including the 1950s, the transition to greater intimacy was marked by expressions such as *Ska vi lägga bort titlarna?* ('Shall we drop titles?'). Such expressions cover the shift from hon or title + LN and third-person address to T and FN. This was sometimes accompanied by a formal drinking ritual *du-skål* ('the *du*-toast'), as in German. The actual move to T and FN was a complicated affair, in particular if it involved a man and a woman. In the following quotation, a focus group participant tells an anecdote about a male doctor who had to engage the help of his wife in order to move to T with a female member of staff in a socially acceptable way at the time:

En äldre bekant, hon var kurator – Fröken Andersson – jobbade ihop med en läkare och hans sekreterare. Läkaren och sekreteraren var 'du' med varandra. Sekreteraren var ledig en dag, läkarens hustru kom till arbetsplatsen och lade bort titlarna med kuratorn. Läkaren lade sedan bort titlarna med kuratorn. Kuratorn undrade mycket över det här men läste sedan att en gift man inte fick lägga bort titlarna [med en kvinna] med mindre än att hans fru gjort det innan.
[An older acquaintance, she was a counsellor – Miss Andersson – worked with a doctor and his secretary. The doctor and the secretary were on *du* terms. The secretary had a day off, the doctor's wife then came to the workplace and dropped titles with the

counsellor. The doctor then also dropped titles with the counsellor. The counsellor wondered a lot about this but later she read that a married man was not allowed to drop titles [with a female] unless his wife had done so earlier.] (Gothenburg, FG1, female retired writer, 67)

In the examples from French, German and Swedish, it can be noted that the transition involves a shift from V to T. If one wants to reduce social distance in a language such as English, similar conversational moves can be made, which can involve explicit invitations to use first names, as the following example shows:

Yes, if I was to ask someone, such as yourself [said to Jane], *who I'd met in London or somewhere, then I'd say, 'Oh, by the way, my name's Dorothy', and I would expect you to reciprocate and I would use your name. And I wouldn't use any kind of other title or any other kind of replacement for your name.* (Newcastle, FG, female retired nurse, 63; Jane: mother, 44)

3.4   Social variables: age

We have seen in section 3.2 that although we might expect an underlying social consensus about the meaning of T and V in the different language communities under study, the reality is that the social identity of the speaker plays a role in fluctuating and evolving social meanings attached to the different forms. In what follows, we begin by examining our data through the prism of more traditional social categories such as age and status, before exploring how address choices are in fact contextually and pragmatically motivated.

As we have already foreshadowed in some of the discussion in 3.2, age is one of the most salient social categories. It has been shown in sociolinguistic research that age is fundamental in explaining linguistic variation. In previous address research in French, German and Swedish, for example, age, and particularly relative age, has emerged as a significant category (e.g. Gardner-Chloros 1991 for French; see 2.2.3 on the Allensbach surveys and Besch 1998: 10 for German; Mårtensson 1986 for Swedish). In western societies, it is generally recognised that there is a growing preoccupation with the concept of age, particularly with youth and the importance of being youthful. As one of our participants in Paris joked when asked about being addressed as 'Madame' rather than 'Mademoiselle', 'c'est des rides' ('it's about wrinkles'; female, nursery assistant, 53). The following example from our London focus group illustrates the same point. The discussion centres on the use of honorifics in service encounters and one of the participants makes the comment that the female equivalent of *Sir* has the added complication of age, reflected in the choice between the honorifics 'Miss' and 'Madam':

Isn't the thing though, [that] 'Sir' is universal but there is this bit where you have the 'Miss' versus 'Madam'. Which is when you're first addressed as 'Madam'... (laughter).

Table 3.2 *Percentage of population in each age group according to language (French, German and Swedish)*

	French	German	Swedish
under 31	33	40	27
31–50	42	34	43
51+	25	26	30
(N)	(72)	(198)	(144)

But there is this thing about, at what age does it turn to 'Madam'? You have this formality but then you still have the dilemma about 'Miss' or 'Madam'. (London, FG, female finance director, 39)

In our French, German and Swedish interview samples, the age range of participants spans 18 to 82 years.[2] For ease of comparison, Table 3.2 shows participants divided into three main age groups.

People's opinions on the relationship between address use and informants' age in German, French and Swedish were sought in various ways. First of all, the questionnaire included two basic questions explicitly asking participants to comment on age as a variable in pronominal address choices: (1) how they would address a stranger (older, younger, same age) when asking directions, and (2) how they would address a police officer (older, younger, same age). It should be noted that it is usually relative rather than absolute age that is the variable in social distance determining choice of address mode. The first of these questions is discussed in this section and the second will be examined in the section on status. However, we were also interested in stimulating more reflective responses from our participants about the age variable. We did this by asking them in the interview at what age someone should be addressed by V, a seemingly innocuous question that in fact generated among some participants a great deal of discussion. In what follows, we will present the responses elicited from our French, German and Swedish participants and then turn our attention to English.

3.4.1   French

From French responses to the question about addressing a stranger, we can see that the age of the addressee is a major variable in determining address pronoun choice (significant at $p < 0.005$). Table 3.3 shows that the only context where there is 100% use of V is with a considerably older stranger, while between a quarter and a fifth of our participants report using T and not V with a stranger of

---

[2] In terms of the sex variable, our sample of participants is slightly biased towards women: in French, women make up 51% of the sample; in German, the figure is 53% and in Swedish 59%.

Table 3.3 *French: use of V* with a stranger when asking directions*

Address choice with:	% informants using V
Stranger, considerably older, same sex	100
Stranger, considerably older, opposite sex	100
Stranger, same age, same sex	79
Stranger, same age, opposite sex	82
Stranger, younger, same sex	76
Stranger, younger, opposite sex	75
(N)	(72)

* includes participants who report using T or V.

the same age or younger. This variation in address choice to older strangers and same-age strangers is statistically significant ($p < 0.025$) and the difference between older strangers and younger strangers is even more so ($p < 0.005$). Nevertheless, the general trend is *vous* with strangers: with considerably older strangers, all participants use V and the characteristics of the speaker do not matter. Examining the data more closely, it is clear that the younger age group – those aged 30 and under – use significantly more T with same-age addressees than the other two age groups: over half (58%) use T, compared with only 10% of those aged between 31 and 50 and none of those aged 51 and above.

Turning now to our qualitative interview data and the age at which someone should be addressed by V, 28 participants offered an immediate response and gave an age between 11 and 40 years (with an average age of just over 18 years) or mentioned adolescence or coming of age: *on va dire vers quatorze, quinze ans* (let's say around 14, 15 years old) (Paris, Q2, female switchboard operator, 28). It should be taken into account, however, that informants may be reacting to three different situations – school, public life and social life – all of which might generate a different response. After leaving school or at the age of 18, young people will generally be addressed by V in their interactions with the wider community. However, in social life, peers of about the same age will automatically employ T for much longer.

There are also other variables suggested by an additional 29 participants, who find it difficult to pin down straightaway a specific age that would automatically trigger V address. From their final answers, the age range for this group of participants is between 10 and 33 years, with an average of nearly 19 years. The following example illustrates one participant's difficulty in giving a straight response and she begins by saying 'It depends':

Ça dépend qui on a en face. <De 'manière générale', on va dire.> Parce que si c'est un – il y a pas une manière générale. Par exemple, un petit jeune qui va me vouvoyer, je vais le *reprendre et lui dire 'Non, tu me tutoies' parce que je suis encore jeune! Ça donne l'impression d'être vieille. [...]* <Par exemple, tu rentres dans une boutique, jusqu'à quel âge ça te semble normal qu'on te dise 'tu'?> *Ah oui, d'accord. Jusqu'à seize ans peut-être. Quatorze ans. Oui, quatorze, quinze ans.*

[It depends on who you have in front of you. <*In general, let's say.*> Because if it's a – there's no 'in general'. For example, a youngster who's going to use *vous* with me, I'll correct him and tell him 'No, you use *tu* with me' because I'm still young! It gives me the impression of being old. [...] <*For example, you go into a shop, until what age does it seem normal for people to say tu to you?*> Oh right, OK. Up to 16 maybe. 14. Yes, 14 or 15.] (Paris, Q2, female pharmacist, 31)

In this example, there is a great deal of hedging from the participant and only when pushed by the interviewer, who gives the specific context of an encounter in a shop, is the participant finally able to give a precise age.

For a further ten participants, age does not enter into pronoun choice at all; the choice is entirely dependent on personal affinities:

Je regarde même pas l'âge. C'est la personne, le physique quoi. <Même les enfants tu pourrait les vouvoyer?> *Oui.* <Donc pour toi c'est pas tant l'âge, c'est plus ce que la personne dégage?> *Oui.*

[I don't even look at age. It's the person, their appearance. <*You even use vous with children?*> Yes. <*So for you it's not so much age, it's more what the person gives off?*> Yes.] (Paris, Q4, female janitor, 42)

So, even with a category that initially seems as watertight as age, some people can offer a direct response, others need a degree of contextualisation in order to arrive at an answer and yet others reject age as a variable determining address choice. Nevertheless, in spite of the hesitation and hedging displayed by some interviewees, overall the responses point to a general transition age for *vous* use around adolescence or coming of age.

Age is also signalled through forms other than pronouns. The shift from *Mademoiselle* to *Madame* is one in which age is the most salient variable. In the following extract, the participant points to a subversion of normal rules for using *Mademoiselle* and *Madame*, as part of a flirting technique. This consists of addressing older women with *Mademoiselle*, thereby signalling that they have a youthful appearance, and of addressing younger women with *Madame*, signalling respect and thereby creating the opportunity to start a conversation without one's intentions being manifest:

J'ai un ami qui a une théorie amusante là-dessus. Pour aller aborder des filles, une femme qu'on aurait normalement appelée 'madame', il faut l'appeler 'mademoiselle'. Du coup elle va être contente, ça fait jeune. Au contraire, une jeune qu'on veut aller aborder, on l'appelle 'madame', elle est surprise, et c'est plus facile [...] d'enchaîner la discussion parce qu'après elle est surprise, c'est comme une marque de respect. C'est flatteur.

[I have a friend who has an amusing theory on that. To chat up women, you have to call a woman who you would normally call *Madame*, *Mademoiselle*. She'll be instantly happy, it

Table 3.4 *German: use of V* with a stranger when asking directions*

Address choice with:	% informants using V
Stranger, considerably older, same sex	100
Stranger, considerably older, opposite sex	100
Stranger, same age, same sex	59
Stranger, same age, opposite sex	61
Stranger, younger, same sex	42
Stranger, younger, opposite sex	42
(N)	(198)

* includes participants who report using T or V or avoiding address altogether.

makes you feel young. On the other hand, a young woman who you want to chat up, you call her *Madame*, she's surprised, and it's easier […] to keep the discussion going because she's surprised, it's like a mark of respect. It's flattering.] (Paris, Q9, male accountant, 33)

Some (male) participants also discussed the shift from *jeune homme* to *Monsieur*, reflecting a similar age-based transition:

De plus en plus les jeunes m'appellent 'monsieur', c'est horrible. C'est inattendu parce qu'il y a quelques années ils ne m'auraient pas dit 'Monsieur'. A un moment on m'appelait 'jeune homme' et j'appréciais assez peu, je ne sais pas pourquoi. Ça m'est arrivé jusqu'à vingt, vingt-cinq ans. [...] Quand on emploie 'jeune homme', j'ai l'impression qu'il y a une responsabilité qui pèse. Vous n'êtes plus vraiment un enfant, plus vraiment un adolescent, mais vous n'êtes pas encore un 'Monsieur'. Vous êtes quelqu'un en devenir.

[More and more young people call me *Monsieur*, it's horrible. It's unexpected because a few years ago they wouldn't have called me *Monsieur*. At one point they called me *jeune homme* and I didn't appreciate it very much, I don't know why. It happened around 20, 25 years. […] When you use *jeune homme* I get the impression that it's a responsibility which weighs on you. You are no longer really a child, no longer really an adolescent, but you're not yet a *Monsieur*. You are someone in the making.] (Paris, Q3, male lawyer, 32)

3.4.2 German

The German questionnaire data show the same pattern as the French: considerably older strangers are addressed categorically with V. Likewise, the differences are statistically significant, for age overall ($p < 0.005$) and for address choice between older strangers and same-age strangers ($p < 0.005$) and same-age strangers and younger strangers ($p < 0.025$). A striking difference, however, between the two languages is the much greater use of T with same-age or younger addressees (see Table 3.4), which reinforces the picture we already have of T being more common in German.

If we examine the data more closely, age of the speaker is the variable determining greater T use with same age and younger addressees. For example, 78% of speakers aged 30 years and younger use T to someone of the same age, compared with 22.7% of those aged between 31 and 50 years. None of the participants aged 51 years and over used T to an addressee of the same age. Thus, age of speaker has a more pronounced effect on the choice of T in the German data than in the French.

The interview question on age for German shows that for the majority of participants, the age for addressing a person with V ranges from 13 to 30 years, with a median age of 18. Just as for French, there are three dimensions to the age of transition in German: the age at which school teachers' traditionally start to call their students V, the legal and perceived age of adulthood and the period during which young people perceive themselves and their peers as young and thus are automatically inclined to exchange T.

However, 44 participants are unable to give an explicit age and 34 say 'it depends'. The reasons why some participants find it difficult to give an explicit age for V, mirroring those given by French participants, are illustrated in the following examples:

Wenn sie halbwegs einen erwachsenen Eindruck machen, [das ist] schwer an einem Alter festzumachen, hängt auch von der Situation ab.

[When they make a more or less grown-up impression, [that is] difficult to tie to a particular age, it also depends on the situation.] (Leipzig, Q2, female psychologist, 30)

Man weiß ja meistens nicht, wie alt das Gegenüber ist. [Ich finde,] von dem Moment an, in dem man jemanden als erwachsen empfindet, aber das ist wieder eine individuelle Sache. Ich glaube nicht, dass es da eine Formel gibt.

[In most cases you do not know how old your opposite number is. [I think] from the moment one feels the other is an adult, but that again is an individual thing. I don't believe there's a fixed formula for that.] (Mannheim, Q4, male student, 26)

Others also mention the importance of context in determining the salience of age when choosing address terms, as the following quotation shows:

Wenn ich den Eindruck habe, dass derjenige eben erwachsen ist oder mir im Kontext begegnet, wo er selbständig agiert sozusagen, als selbständige Person, da würde ich den eben siezen. Wenn mir jemand im Geschäft was verkauft, auch wenn das der Lehrling ist, der fünfzehn ist oder so, dann ist der mein Geschäftspartner in dem Moment und dann siez ich den.

[When I have the impression that this person just is a grown-up or when I encounter them in a context where they act in an autonomous way, to put it that way, as an autonomous person, then I would use *Sie*. When someone is selling me something in a shop, even if it is the apprentice and 15 years or so of age, then this person is my partner in a commercial transaction and I address them with *Sie*.] (Mannheim, Q11, male manager, 61)

3.4.3   Swedish

In Swedish, where the T form is the default pronoun of address, one would expect age not to play any significant role in determining pronoun choice.

Table 3.5 *Swedish: use of V* with a stranger when asking directions*

Address choice with:	% informants using V
Stranger, considerably older, same sex	53
Stranger, considerably older, opposite sex	58
Stranger, same age, same sex	4
Stranger, same age, opposite sex	3
Stranger, younger, same sex	2
Stranger, younger, opposite sex	2
(N)	(144)

* includes participants who report using T or V or avoiding address altogether.

However, as is evident in the initial focus group data from both Gothenburg and Vaasa, pronoun choice in addressing a considerably older unfamiliar person appears to be problematic:

Det är svårt att säga 'du' till någon i åttioårsåldern.
[It is difficult to say *du* to somebody in his/her 80s.] (Gothenburg, FG1, female nurse, 52)

Nutidens äldre vill ju vara unga och det finns faktiskt de som tar illa upp om man niar, så det är inte så entydigt.
[Nowadays, older people want to be young so there are actually those who take offence if you say *ni*, so it is not so clear-cut.] (Vaasa, FG1, female social worker, 59)

Similarly, our questionnaire data also point to age being a significant variable for address pronoun choice; when participants were asked how they would address a stranger, a surprising number opted for V to address a considerably older stranger (see Table 3.5). This result is statistically significant for age overall ($p < 0.005$) and, in addition, there is a statistically significant difference between address choice to older strangers and same-age strangers ($p < 0.005$).

Just as with the French and German data, age is an important variable in address choice, but the effect in Swedish is clearly more substantial and more independent. As Table 3.5 illustrates, over 50% of the participants report that they would address a considerably older stranger with V, while less than 5% report V use with same-age or younger addressees. Some comments by our participants indicate that the use of V is restricted to the extremely old: *'du' automatiskt om det inte är till en döende 98-åring* [*du* automatically unless it's to a dying 98 year old] (Gothenburg, Q4, male journalist, 32).

The responses to the age question in the interview point to three important trends. First, about a third of the participants find it impossible to pin down a certain age from which it would be generally acceptable for V to be used (48/ 144, 33%). Second, many (29/144, 20%) are of the opinion that there are other variables that are more important than age. Third, for those informants who do give an age boundary for V address (49, or 34%) there is substantial variation, with a range from late teens to 100 years old. Most informants who select an age for V mention 70–80 (23 informants) while 13 informants opt for 60–65. A further 14 informants simply state 'older person' without giving a specific age. Another trend, already noted in the French data, is the fact that many informants argue that it depends on other factors, such as the situation, or what impression the speaker gets of the addressee:

Svårt. Om nån är väldigt mycket äldre. Men det hänger också på vad det är för person man ser. Jag säger 'du' till en hejig nittioåring som säger 'du' och 'tjohoj'. Men jag säger 'ni' till en person som man känner förväntar sig att bli tilltalad på ett annat sätt. Det hänger på om man känner personen väl eller om det är en främling. Det varierar efter situation.

[Difficult. If somebody is very much older. But it also depends on what type of person it is you see. I say *du* to a easy-going 90 year old who says *du* and 'howdy'. But I say *ni* to a person who you feel expects to be addressed in a different way. It depends on whether you know the person well or if it is a stranger. It varies with the situation.] (Gothenburg, Q4, female teacher, 30)

For those Swedish-speaking participants who do state an age boundary for V address, the median is 67.5 years. Compared with the other languages this is clearly a much higher age. It is also interesting to note that the likelihood of addressing an older person with V (*ni*) is fairly evenly distributed across the ages of the informants and includes both the youngest (18-year-old) and oldest (83-year-old) informant.[3] It is striking how many construct images of the very old as worthy of V address. According to a young waiter we talked to, a 'walking-stick factor' exists in Sweden today. He maintained that he addressed patrons as *du* but that he would hesitate if they were very old and frail. This explains why some elderly people perceive *ni* as a marker of exclusion from mainstreamness.

The salience of age is further illustrated in the responses to the question on how to address police officers of differing ages. Once again, the results are statistically significant for age overall ($p < 0.005$) and between address choice to older police and police of the same age or younger ($p < 0.025$). If we compare the data for use of V with a stranger (Table 3.5) and with a police officer (Table 3.6), distinct patterns emerge. A police officer of the same age or younger

---

[3] This is in contrast to the results from the initial focus group in Gothenburg, where the oldest participants reported not to use V themselves and were clearly against use of V and commented on the negative connotations traditionally associated with the V pronoun in Sweden. (For a fuller description, see Clyne *et al.* 2006: 298–302.)

Table 3.6 *Swedish: use of V* with a police officer*

Address choice with:	% informants using V
Police officer, considerably older, same sex	37
Police officer, considerably older, opposite sex	38
Police officer, same age, same sex	15
Police officer, same age, opposite sex	15
Police officer, younger, same sex	11
Police officer, younger, opposite sex	11
(N)	(144)

* includes participants who report using T or V or avoiding address altogether.

receives more V than would a stranger of the same age or younger. This indicates that the authority invested in the function of police officer overrides what would normally be an automatic T situation in Swedish for some (between 11% and 15%).

A considerably older police officer, however, receives *less* V than a considerably older stranger.[4] This seeming anomaly could be linked to the median age boundary for V address set at 67.5 years. It is likely that our participants would think of a police officer still in active service, and since retirement age in both Finland and Sweden is about 65, this places the considerably older police officer in an age bracket where a large number of respondents find T address the natural choice. In regard to the older stranger, on the other hand, which triggered a much higher incidence of V, it is quite possible that the participants who indicate V address have conjured up an image of a very old person, thus worthy of V address.

3.4.4   English

In French, German and Swedish, age is a major variable in the choice of address terms and more particularly the choice of address pronoun. In these three languages, discussion has centred around the pronominal distinction, whereas when we move to English, discussion in the focus groups necessarily shifts to nominal address forms. However, these nominal choices reflect similar concerns with situating oneself in relation to one's interlocutor. It is simply that in English, the choice is between forms such as *Mrs Jones* or *Irene*, rather than between V and T. Age is a salient category and people explicitly raise age as an

---

[4] There are clear differences between the two Swedish sites with regard to the use of V with the police officer, a question we will return to in Chapter 5.

important variable in their social relations. One example is a discussion in the London focus group on the use of FN and hon + LN in a doctor's surgery. A nurse in her early 30s comments on her use of FN with younger patients and hon + LN with patients in their 50s and older. The grey area for her are those patients in the intermediate age group and she would explicitly ask for their preference:

I think it depends on what situation you're in. I mean, in my job, if I have younger patients then I would assume that they want to be called by their first name and I'll probably use that without asking them. If they're a bit older, if you can't quite judge what sort of person they are, then I would ask them what they would want to be called. Um, if they're older, you know, getting into their late 50s and 60s, then I would probably use 'Mr' and 'Mrs' out of respect and then take it from there. (London, FG, female nurse, 33)

What this example points to is that for this particular participant, there is a clear age at which the use of hon + LN is triggered, the late 50s. In this respect, English is much more akin to Swedish than to French and German. Furthermore, even though age is salient, the participant feels the need to raise other parameters, prefacing this need by the phrase 'it depends'.

Another participant comments on this usage from the patient's perspective, noting the shift in the way he was addressed, from FN + LN to hon + LN:

I'm just thinking back, when I was young, in the doctor's surgery, when it was my turn to see the doctor she would call out 'Charles Livingstone'. But now she calls out 'Mr Livingstone'. I don't know when that changed. I can't think. It's the same doctor's surgery. (London, FG, male mortgage broker, 34)

Just as in the French data, the shift from *Miss* to *Mrs* is about the physical signs of aging:

(1)   *(...) if someone got it wrong and called you 'Mrs' when you're a 'Miss' or the other way around by mistake, how offended would you actually be? Would it matter at all? Would you actually be offended?*
(2)   *Not offended, you just instantly think of your mum, that's all.* [laughter]
(3)   *You usually think, 'Do I really look that old?'*
                    (London, FG (1) male student, 23; (2) female financial manager, 39;
                                    (3) unidentified female participant)

The choice of honorifics to address a female interlocutor (*Miss, Mrs, Ms*) has been the topic of much debate, particularly with regard to feminist language planning and the introduction of *Ms* as a neutral form (e.g. Pauwels 1998, Winter and Pauwels 2007). This issue was discussed in all our English-language focus groups. Our data are limited, which precludes a more detailed discussion of the current use of *Ms*, but they do support the current view that *Ms* is not widely used in British English (see 2.2.1). In the following exchange from Tralee, one (female) participant makes the statement that some women do not like being called *Mrs*, but prefer *Ms*. This is followed by partial agreement by two other (female) participants, both of whom consider *Ms* suitable, but only in writing:

(1)   I think some women don't like to be called 'Mrs' so they prefer 'Ms'.
(2)   I always write out Ms on my letters but I would not like to be called 'Ms'.
(3)   Me too. When they ask you in a form or something to give your title, I don't like 'Miss' so I say 'Ms'.
       (Tralee, FG (1) female librarian, 35; (2) female student, 25; (3) female student, 19)

Yet another participant takes a negative view of *Ms*, regarding it as outmoded, both in the written and oral form: *I'd still hate to be called or my name written with Ms. I think it's old-fashioned, going back to the days of women's lib and all that. The world is different now.* (Tralee, FG, female teacher, 30)

In the London focus group, one student said she would not use *Ms* to refer to herself, on a form for instance, while another female participant insisted: *I don't see why I should have to declare my marital status when the males of the species aren't expected to.* (London, FG, female sign language interpreter, 35)

This view was shared by several of the female members of the Newcastle focus group, though some agreed it was stigmatised: *I think most people do think 'Ms' is a term referring to a divorcee although it's not meant to be.* (Newcastle, FG, female student, 27)

3.4.5   Summary

Our overview of the four languages shows that in French and German what we could call the onset of 'mature adulthood' is clearly marked as a transition to V, with fairly similar age ranges reported (10–40 and 13–30 years old respectively). It may be that our informants have different interpretations of the question, focusing on either rites of passage, legal adulthood or the end of young adulthood, that is, the end of the age where young people would automatically exchange reciprocal T. As one informant puts it:

Niemand will alt werden und drum wird bis in die 30er nicht akzeptiert, dass man älter wird und gesetzter wird.
[No one wants to get old and so up to their 30s they don't accept that they are getting older and becoming staid.] (Mannheim, Q10, male researcher, 29)

This contrasts with Swedish, and to a lesser extent English, where the age at which there is an explicit shift in address terms occurs at another momentous period in life, namely the transition towards retirement, or later. In the Swedish data, the median age for V address is 67.5 years; in the English data, there are indications from some participants that 'older' can be translated as late 50s and 60s.

3.5   Social variables: status

Another aspect of marking social distance through modes of address relates to hierarchical differences. Within sociolinguistics, participants have traditionally been categorised according to socio-economic status, which has been defined according to various criteria or combinations thereof, including profession and education (e.g. Labov 1972, Trudgill 1974). In the case of our sample, participants tend to belong to the highly educated professional groups: for example, if we take the criterion of education, 78% of the Swedish-speaking participants, 67% of French participants and 70% of German-speaking ones have undertaken studies beyond secondary level. This is a reflection of our technique of using network interviews, where we enlisted graduate students as data collectors in all our locations who drew base informants from their respective networks. Although the samples are not necessarily accurate reflections of educational and professional profiles within the society at large, the distribution of the categories is comparable in the different data sets. As far as the English data are concerned, our participants are also mainly from highly educated professional backgrounds.

In the French, German and English data, discussions around status focus predominantly on workplace hierarchies, whereas in the Swedish data there is little discussion of address in the workplace. The workplace in general is discussed in more detail in Chapter 4, which deals with networks and domains; here, the emphasis is on how status is indexed or codified through address practices. In French or German, for example, where both T and V are in current use, status can be expressed through pronoun choice. In Swedish, meanwhile, where T is nearly universal, status relationships are rarely indexed through address pronouns.

For comparative purposes, in each language we begin with data from the questionnaire, which give an overview of pronoun use with work superiors and colleagues. We then discuss for each language the interview questions in which issues relating to status are explicitly discussed. In French the following interview question gives rise to status-related comments: 'How do you feel about companies which prescribe the T form, e.g. IKEA?' In the Swedish interviews, status comes up in responses to the following questions: (a) 'Would you like to be addressed more formally or less formally?' and (b) 'In radio and on television, especially in talk shows, T is sometimes used by the interviewers regardless of who they are interviewing. Do you think that such an address usage is impolite or is it appropriate and polite? Why/why not?'

3.5.1   French

The hierarchical nature of the French workplace is evident in the responses of our participants to questions about how they would address colleagues and superiors,

Table 3.7 *French: address pronoun use at work (speaker–addressee)*

	T–T (%)	T/V–T/V (%)	V–T (%)	V–T/V (%)	V–V (%)
Superiors	24	6	16	6	49
Colleagues	84	13	0	0	3
(N = 68)					

Table 3.8 *French: opinion of companies such as IKEA prescribing* tu

Opinion	No informants	%
Positive	24	33.8
Negative	32	45.1
Other/no opinion	15	21.1
(N = 71)		

as Table 3.7 shows. Nearly half of the participants (49%) report reciprocal V with their work superiors, whereas reciprocal T is reported by fewer than a quarter (24%). The total number of participants who report using V, in both reciprocal and non-reciprocal use, is 71%. Among work colleagues, in contrast, 84% report reciprocal T and only two participants report using reciprocal V.

Also of note is that 16% of participants report non-reciprocal use, addressing their superiors with V and receiving T. Non-reciprocal use in French extends beyond pronouns and includes honorifics and first names. Participants were asked to indicate whether they used FN, hon, or hon + LN with work superiors and colleagues. Even in cases where reciprocal V is reported, a third (11/33) of our participants indicate that hierarchical status is underlined by using a combination of V + hon or hon + title to their superior who uses V + FN in return (see Chapter 4 for further discussion).

The notion of hierarchies is firmly anchored in participants' conceptualisations of the workplace, as their responses to the question on what they think of companies that prescribe the T form show (see Table 3.8). In the French context, the participants understood the imposition of T as being between employees in the company and not between employees and customers.

Nearly half of the participants (45%) are negative about the imposition of universal T, as they consider that workplace hierarchies cannot simply be eliminated by a superficial change in pronoun:

C'est comme si on utilisait la langue pour essayer d'effacer les inégalités sociales, des inégalités qui par ailleurs sont réelles. [...] Chacun a sa place. C'est comme ça que les conflits peuvent se régler aussi. Quand on est trop impliqué, et c'est ce que le tutoiement peut faire, il me semble que c'est plus, ça peut etre plus dangereux toujours pour celui qui est inférieur dans la hiérarchie.

[It's as if language was being used to try to efface social inequalities, inequalities that are in other respects real. [...] Everyone in their place. That's how conflicts can be sorted out as well. When you are too implicated, and that's what using *tu* can do, it seems to me that it's more, it can always be more dangerous for the person who is inferior in the hierarchy.] (Paris, Q1, female French teacher, 31)

Those who are negative also consider that imposing *tu* is hypocritical, as the same conflicts are to be found behind an appearance of equality and friendliness:

Je pense que c'est hypocrite. Parce que c'est fait comme si on se connaissait alors qu'en fait on se connaît pas plus que ça. C'est une apparence, il y a quand même une atmosphère de confiance, d'amicalité [...]. Mais en fait, derrière ça c'est toujours les mêmes conflits avec tous les gens.

[I think it's hypocritical. Because it's done as if we knew one another when in fact we don't know each other that well at all. It's about appearances, there is an atmosphere of confidence, of friendliness [...]. But in fact, behind that it's always the same conflicts with everyone.] (Paris, Q11, male student, 23)

Of the minority (34%) who are positive about T imposition, this is primarily because it creates a more equitable, collegial and open environment:

Il y a plus de convivialité. Surtout que ce soit du plus haut gradé au moins haut. Au moins ils se disent tous 'tu' et comme ça il y a pas de: tous pareil, en fait. C'est plus équitable.

[There is more conviviality. Above all if it's from the highest rank to the least high. At least they say *tu* to each other and in that way it isn't: everyone [is] the same, in fact. It's fairer.] (Paris, Q2, female switchboard operator, 28)

In terms of titles and honorifics, one of our participants explicitly remarked on the changes she had noticed in her workplace, a bank, where she had been employed over the last 30 years (Paris, Q5, secretary, 49). The use of *Monsieur* and *Madame* to hierarchical superiors was common practice when she first started at the bank, but these days FN is much more widespread, even when used with V. She also commented on the disappearance of hon + title combinations, such as *Monsieur le directeur*, in direct hierarchical relations.

Participants also mention the use of address to signal lack of status. This is primarily the case in encounters with police, either through participants' own experience or in reported accounts: *On peut tutoyer de façon méprisante aussi, comme le fait souvent la police avec les personnes d'origine arabe* ('You can use *tu* in a contemptuous way, as police often do with people of Arab background') (Paris, Q3, male, computer engineer, 43). The racist connotation of T use is further emphasised in the following extract:

Si je croise un gamin de dix-sept ans, Maghrébin, il m'adresse la parole, je vais lui dire 'vous'. Je dois absolument lui dire 'vous'. Parce que si je lui dis 'tu', un, il va me prendre

Table 3.9 *German: address pronoun use at work (speaker–addressee)*

	T–T (%)	T/V–T/V (%)	V–T (%)	V–V (%)
Superiors	34	6	0.1	60
Colleagues (N = 198)	67	21	0	13

pour un policier, ce qui me ferait mal, et puis deux, il va considérer [...] que lui-même est considéré comme un citoyen mineur.

[If I meet a youngster of 17, North African, and he speaks to me, I'm going to say *vous* to him. I absolutely have to say *vous* to him. Because if I say *tu* to him, one, he's going to take me for a police officer, which would hurt me, and two, he's going to think [...] that he is viewed as a second-class citizen.] (Paris, Q3, male historian, 69)

3.5.2 German

In the German workplace, a person's status within the institution generally determines the address patterns. According to Table 3.9, 60% of our participants use V with their work superiors and are addressed by them with V, approximately the same number who use T with same-level work colleagues (67%). Thus workplace hierarchy plays a significant role in German address pronoun choice. It is worth noting that there is hardly any non-reciprocal pronoun use in German, contrasting with the results for French above. However, fewer German participants report using T with work colleagues than do French participants.

In German, titles, an important status symbol, are employed much less in face-to-face communication than was the case 40 years ago (PO). As we will see in section 5.4.1, they are far more prevalent in Austria than in Germany, where the use of titles has become controversial. Titles are still employed in formal address, in speeches, on envelopes and sometimes in official letters. Nowadays they are no longer transferred to the wife of the title holder (*Frau Pastor, Frau Professor*).

Generally, German participants viewed non-reciprocal choice of address pronouns between adult strangers as inappropriate, but in certain settings, such as the university, there is limited non-reciprocal use (see Chapter 4). While V is the default pronoun in interactions with strangers and authorities, there are exceptions to this rule. Several participants report disapprovingly that immigrants are often denigrated by being addressed with T, as exemplified by the following quote from the Vienna focus group:

Mein polnischer Freund wurde von der Polizei und so fast automatisch geduzt; das fand ich dann, das hat mich dann sehr schockiert.

[My Polish friend was almost automatically addressed as *du* by police; I found that that shocked me very much.] (Vienna, FG1, female student, 23)

Table 3.10 *Swedish: address pronoun use at work (speaker–addressee)*

	T–T (%)	V–T (%)	V–V (%)	avoid (%)
Superiors	90	6	1	3
Colleagues	98	1	0	1
(N = 140)				

It should be pointed out that the use of T to migrants per se is not necessarily racist. It can even be used to express solidarity, as in interviews in the asylum seekers' support group magazine *Pro Asyl*: *Yildiz, du lebst seit 14 Jahren geduldet in Deutschland* ('Yildiz, you (*du*) have been living in Germany on a temporary protection visa for 14 years') (*Pro Asyl*, 28 September 2007, p. 2).

3.5.3   Swedish

In Sweden and Finland, and in Nordic societies in general, egalitarianism is ranked very highly. This is evident in the fact that status difference can be actively resisted, as the following quotation from the first Gothenburg focus group shows:

Skulle aldrig falla mig in att säga 'ni' till någon chef på grund av rang. [It would never enter my mind to say *ni* to some boss because of rank.] (Gothenburg, FG1, male manager at government department, 27)

In the Swedish questionnaire data there is almost unanimous T among colleagues and superiors alike, as Table 3.10 shows.

The interview question seeking comments about radio and TV presenters' habit of using T with everybody reveals some interesting results about status.[5] Recalling that T is the default Swedish address pronoun, it is not surprising that the majority (91/144, 63%) claim that universal T is suitable. In the following quotation the participant takes the explicit view that it is wrong to treat people differently, thereby ranking them:

Jag vet inte om det är artigt men jag tycker att det vore direkt olämpligt att kalla vissa för 'ni' och vissa för 'du' för det skulle ju bara rangordna människor.
[I don't know if it is polite but I think it would be quite inappropriate to address certain people with *ni* and other people with *du* because that would just rank people.] (Gothenburg, Q10, female journalist, 29)

---

[5] For French and German, this question did not give rise to any comments on status.

However, over a third (51/144, 35%) argue that this practice is not always appropriate. Here, the majority (36/51) mention people of elevated status, such as the Swedish king and the Finnish president, followed by the elderly (15/36) as exceptions to universal T address. This is illustrated in the quotation below:

Jag tycker nog det är ganska lämpligt, förutom då om det är presidenten eller statsministern som är lite högre, annars tycker jag nog att man kan dua helt fritt.

[I think it's quite suitable, except if it is the president or the prime minister who are a bit higher, otherwise, I think that you can use *du* quite freely.] (Vaasa, Q4, male student, 21)

Whether somebody would like to be addressed more formally or less formally could also indicate an awareness of status hierarchies in society. Presumably, a wish to be addressed more formally might reveal a wish to enjoy more respect and status. In our Swedish data, a large majority (109/141, 77.3%) say that they are content with the way they are addressed, while a small number of participants wish to be addressed less formally (13/144, 9.2%) and more formally (12/144, 8.5%) respectively. For those who would like to be addressed more formally, the reason is sometimes linked to a sense of difference and an increase in status, as illustrated in the quotation below:

Det är en boost för självförtroendet, för min ålder betyder 'ni' att du är viktig. Det är som att leka bal på gymnasiet, man spelar en roll. Det känns inte äkta, men det är spännande med 'ni'. <'Ni' är artigt?> Ja, aldrig nedsättande eller att man skiljer ut sig. 'Du' går att använda överallt, det mest neutrala och minst personliga även om det används personligt också.

[It's a boost for your self-esteem, at my age *ni* means that you are important. It's like playing going to the ball in high school, you play a part. It doesn't feel genuine, but it is exciting with *ni*. < 'Ni' is polite?> *Du* can be used everywhere, the most neutral and least personal even if it used personally too.] (Gothenburg, Q9, male laboratory assistant, 20)

There is also evidence that participants reject or resist status-marked honorifics. The following example shows how one participant makes fun of the use of the honorific *min herre* ('Sir') in a service encounter:

Nån i Östermalmshallen som sålde chokladpraliner, nån pralinör, kallade mig för 'min herre' för att jag skulle köpa praliner, det tyckte jag var urlarvigt.

[Somebody in Östermalmshallen [a fresh food market of snobbish appeal in Stockholm] who was selling chocolates, a chocolatier, called me *min herre* because I was about to buy chocolates. I found that really silly.] (Gothenburg, Q8, male author and translator, 61)

However, there are some examples, albeit not many, where participants display some sensitivity towards status-related differences. In a society where T is the norm, it is through first names that status distinctions can be expressed:

Har jobbat på ganska formella arbetsplatser [domstol]. Trots att jag backat lite för att använda förnamn till höga chefer, har jag alltid tilltalat dom 'du'. Däremot förnamnet känns lite obekvämt. <Kan du använda efternamn i stället?> Nej, undviker det.

[[I] have worked in quite formal workplaces [court of law]. Despite having had doubts about using first names to high-up superiors, I have always addressed them with *du*. But using first names feels a bit uncomfortable. <*Can you use last names instead?*> No, [I] refrain from that.] (Gothenburg, Q8, male prosecutor, 33)

The following participant, when asked if she would use V with an older person, replied:

Om de på något sätt uppvisar ett sånt beteende att de vill bli tilltalade på det sättet, om de visar en högre klass.
[If they in some way display such behaviour that they want to be addressed like that [with V], if they show a higher class.] (Vaasa, Q6, female project manager, 32)

This example indicates a mix of several social variables: the participant was asked about age and responded with class. But more importantly, and this will be discussed in section 3.6, it is a question of gauging how the interlocutor wishes to be addressed.

3.5.4   English

English, with its single pronoun *you* (U), does not mark address pronoun choice. This does not mean, however, that status cannot be signalled through other address terms. In the London data, the notion of class is evoked on several occasions. The following participant refers explicitly to class differences in use of the V-like *Sir* and *Madam*:

I can remember my experience with 'Sir' and 'Madam' being quite class-based because I grew up in a very working-class environment but I speak fairly well, which was quite lucky because it meant when I was seventeen I could get a job on reception at a five-star hotel in Central London, which none of my classmates would have had a hope in hell of getting. But what it meant was that I ended up speaking to people who I considered to be of a much higher class than myself and I started calling them all 'Sir' and 'Madam', and they loved it. They thought it was great. You know, they thought I was the most polite thing, the shiniest little button. (London, FG, male housing support officer, 28)

Status can also be marked through use of hon + LN:

<Can you think of any circumstances where you'd use 'Mr' or 'Miss' and the surname? Or where you would use anything else rather than the person's first name? In formal situations?> *I work for a local authority and if I'm speaking to a member of the public, making an enquiry or something like that, you tend to be quite formal when you approach them because you want to be represented as some kind of professional and you want to treat them with respect as a taxpayer. So you go to every length you can to try and be as formal as possible.* <So you always use 'Mr' or 'Mrs'?> *Yes.* (Newcastle, FG, male graffiti coordinator, 30)

The following example, on the other hand, shows how first names can be used to break down traditional notions of status between teachers and students in school:

I had an interview at a school once, it was quite a middle–upper-class school, and they wanted the students to address their teachers by their first names, to sort of break down the traditional sort of teacher–student roles. Because the teachers all used first names, they wore jeans to school, everything like that. But I think that was a very middle-class ideal of being politically correct by addressing the teachers – and I'd be Mary, I wouldn't be Miss Smith. So I don't know whether it's a class thing. (Newcastle, FG, female secondary school teacher, 34)

3.5.5   Summary

The French and German data show that one's position in the work hierarchy can have an effect on address choices (see also 4.4). Among German-speaking participants, pronominal reciprocity is clearly the norm, whether between same-status colleagues or between workers at different levels in the hierarchy. Reciprocity is also widely reported by French participants. However, over 16% of French participants report non-reciprocal address in hierarchical relationships, compared with only 0.1% of German speakers. It is not clear to what extent reciprocal V in German between workers and their superiors denotes a more 'equal' relationship than the use of non-reciprocal address in French. This could simply be the result of conventionalised workplace practices.

In Swedish, in contrast, there is obvious resistance to status-marked address use. Despite the overall similarities in the pronoun system in Swedish and English, there is a clear difference in how hierarchy is marked, or not, through the address system. English makes much more use of honorifics to mark status- or class-based difference, whereas this is not the case in Swedish. This sets Swedish apart from the other languages and in this respect English functions much more like French and German.

Neither of the categories examined so far – age and status – is persuasive enough, either alone or in combination, to fully explain participants' address choices. In the next section, we therefore turn to the question of perceived commonalities in establishing common ground.

3.6   Perceived commonalities

The use of T in French and German, or first names in English and Swedish, is often an indication of an affinity between two or more people. This reduction of social distance is what Kallmeyer (2003) has termed '*gemeinsame Lebenswelt*', that is, perceived common experiences and perceived affinities among individuals. Our focus groups and interviewees have identified as facilitating factors common background, interests or attitudes, such as sharing political and ideological affiliation, playing sport together or membership of a close-knit church congregation. In German, particular situations, such as being on holidays in the mountains (but not sitting next to each other on an aeroplane), may produce enough (temporary and reversible) commonalities to release people from normal address rules; as was reported in both Mannheim and Vienna, at 2000 metres above sea level, anyone can use *du*. Kallmeyer's concept of 'perceived commonalities' is not dissimilar to Brown and Gilman's (1960) 'likemindedness' and to Clark's (1996) notion of 'common ground' (see 2.3.2). In what follows, we will discuss French and German together, as they demonstrate similar patterns, and Swedish and English separately.

3.6.1   French and German

In French and German, belonging to the same group is a significant factor in using reciprocal T, either in first encounters or after a brief period of V. Group membership can be something more or less stable over time, as in belonging to the same sports club:

Ça m'arrive souvent quand je vais au sport, [...] parce que on est tous dans la même situation, on partage un truc, notre intérêt pour le badminton, tout le monde se tutoie. Il y a jamais personne qui se vouvoie, ce serait infaisable, impossible. Et on est de tous les âges, depuis l'adolescent jusqu'à soixante ans. Donc tout le monde se tutoie.

[It often happens to me when I play sport, [...] because we are all in the same situation, we share something, our interest for badminton, and everyone uses *tu*. No one ever uses *vous*, it's unthinkable, impossible. And we're all different ages, from adolescent to 60. So everyone uses *tu*.] (Paris, Q3, female academic, 39)

The participant goes on to say that a student of hers joined the club and when the student found out that she was a university lecturer, the student immediately went back to V, although she was then urged to use T. For this student the V environment of the university domain (between staff and students) dominated other variables (see 4.3.1).

There are also examples of the importance of being part of a club in the German data. The following example in fact shows a German participant's astonishment at being addressed with *Sie*, in spite of his perception of commonalities. In this example, the overriding variable for the participant's interlocutor is age:

Ich fand's eher etwas belustigend und zwar war das in der Jugendarbeit wo ich eigentlich in einer Jugendgruppe war [...], die zwar eine gewisse Bandbreite des Alters abdeckt, aber man war so genau so Gruppenmitglied wie der etwas Jüngere und der hat mich dann gesiezt.

[I found that a bit humorous; it was in youth work, where I was actually in a youth group [...] which does, however, cover quite a broad range of ages; in any case, you were just as much a member of the group as someone who was a bit younger, and that person then addressed me as *Sie*.] (Mannheim, Q2, male manager, 33)

A second example from French shows that being part of a group can take the form of a spontaneous coming together over a common purpose, as in taking part in a demonstration:

Il y a même un tutoiement spontané [...], le jour où je participe à une manifestation. D'abord, on est 120 mille dans les rues de Paris, je peux aborder des gens que je ne connais pas en les tutoyant, ou être abordé par des gens qui me tutoient. Parce que le seul fait d'être impliqués dans une manifestation, donc on sait qu'on s'en va [...] dans le même sens, aussi bien la démarche que la démarche politique, et le tutoiement est complètement légitime.

[There is even a spontaneous use of *tu* […], the day I take part in a demonstration. First of all, there are 120,000 of us in the streets of Paris, I can go up to people I don't know using *tu* with them, or I can be called *tu* by people. Because the simple fact of being part of a demonstration, so we know that we're all going […] in the same direction, on the march as well as politically, and using *tu* is completely legitimate.] (Paris, Q3, male historian, 69)

A third French example takes the concept of group membership one step further. It constructs a chance encounter with a stranger as a temporary and contextually situated sense of community, marked by the spontaneous use of reciprocal T. The participant is talking about meeting a stranger of around her age in a shop:

Si je suis dans un magasin, je regarde un article, et qu'il y a quelqu'un à côté de moi qui regarde le même article, et qu'on finit par échanger nos impressions, il est possible qu'à [cette personne] je lui dise 'tu' à ce moment-là. [...] Ce sera perçu comme simplement, nous partageons un moment, une situation, et nous échangeons autour de cette situation. Je crois qu'il faut qu'il y ait partage de situation, que ce soit des touristes à l'étranger, on est dans la même galère, que ce soit dans un commerce, que ce soit dans un moyen de transport quelconque. Effectivement, il y a communauté d'un instant, autour de quelque chose.

[If I'm in a shop, I'm looking at an item, and there's someone next to me who's looking at the same item, and we end up exchanging our impressions, it's possible that I'll say *tu* to the [person] at that moment. […] It will be perceived as simply, we are sharing a moment, a situation, and we are exchanging around this situation. I think that there has to be a sharing of situation, whether it's tourists abroad, we're in the same predicament, whether it's in a shop, whether it's on public transport. There is in fact a community of an instant, around something.] (Paris, Q3, female academic, 39)

There are other parameters that create a sense of perceived commonalities: for example, external indices of various types, such as haircut or style of clothing. These indices provide a key to reading the other person (cf. Joseph 2004: 36–7 on how language enables individuals to 'read' one another) and then making an appropriate selection of address forms. The following two examples illustrate exactly this point:

L'apparence, quelqu'un à qui je vais demander mon chemin, quelqu'un qui a des dreads comme moi, voilà, cette personne va le prendre mal si je le vouvoie, à mon avis. Et quelqu'un qui est vachement bien sapé, même s'il est même un peu plus vieux que moi, mais pas énormément, je vais peut-être le vouvoyer.

[Appearance, someone who I'm going to ask directions from, someone who has dreadlocks like me, well that person is going to take it badly if I use *vous* with them, I reckon. And someone who is really well dressed, even if they're only a little older than me, not a lot, I'm maybe going to use *vous* with them.] (Toulouse, FG, male student, 21)

Einen Punker in meinem Alter würde ich nicht siezen, einen Banker schon.
[I wouldn't address a punk my age as *Sie*, but I would a banker.] (Mannheim, Q1, male linguist, 37)

These examples from French and German also point to the lack of commonalities as a reason for *not* exchanging T. In the French data, about a third of participants mention the expressions '*on n'a pas élevé les cochons ensemble*' (literally 'we have not raised pigs together') or '*on n'a pas gardé les vaches ensemble*' ('we have not looked after cows together'), meaning 'don't get so familiar with me', used in situations where one's interlocutor has wrongly assumed common ground.

In German, the existence of *ihr* offers German speakers additional possibilities for marking inclusion and exclusion. An ambivalent example comes from the television news at the time of the G8 summit in Heiligendamm in June 2007. A spokesperson for the German dissenter group, ATTAC-Deutschland, which had been conducting a peaceful and orderly demonstration, sent a message on TV to the *Autonomen*, a far more radical political group. The latter hijacked what was a peaceful demonstration, turning it into a violent protest: *Wir wollen euch nicht dabei* ('We don't want you to be involved in this') (Sven Gienholt, ARD Tagesschau, 3 June 2007). The spokesperson is thus addressing ATTAC members using *euch*, the object form of *ihr*, thus marking them as fellow dissenters, while at the same time delivering a message that excludes them.

The moderator of the first Paris focus group sums up the group's ideas about commonalities and this summarises what we have found in both the French and German data:

À partir du moment où on se reconnaît un peu dans la personne, ou on reconnaît certains codes, ou on se dit, il y a de grandes chances pour que je partage quelque chose, qu'on vient du même univers, on a peut-être plus de facilité à tutoyer.
[The moment you recognise yourself a little in the other person, or you recognise certain codes, or you say to yourself, it's very likely that I share something, that we come from the same universe, you will perhaps find it easier to use *tu*.] (Paris, FG1, female moderator)

3.6.2   Swedish

In contrast to the situation in French and German, where perceived commonalities are a trigger for T address, in Swedish, due to T being the default form of address, the reverse is the case: a perceived *lack* of commonalities, i.e. increased social distance, can lead to V address. Our data show that the decision to address a person (usually older) with V is guided by a sense of the addressee being different. In the following example, the appearance and behaviour of one's interlocutor are the prime motivating variables in choice of address pronoun:

Det är ju så relativt och individuellt. Om vi går upp till sjuttio- åttioåringar så kan det ju finnas personer som är hur ungdomliga som helst och då ser man ju genast att där är ingen farbror eller farmoraktig, farfaraktig fast vederbörande har åldern inne för det, men man får vara finkänslig så att inte vederbörande känner sig stött.
[It is so relative and individual. If we go up to 70 to 80 year olds there might be persons who are as youthful as anything and then you see immediately that it isn't an old man or grandmother type or grandfather type, even if the person in question is the right age for it, but you have to be sensitive so that the person doesn't feel hurt.] (Vaasa, Q7, male expert advisor, 63)

The most salient feature is a person's general appearance, displayed by style of clothing and other accessories:

Snäppet under mina föräldrars ålder, femtiofem till sjuttio år, då kan man fundera, det beror på vilka signaler de ger. En dam med hermelinpäls och bijouterier kan man ana skulle gilla det, snarare än nån med Fjällrävenryggsäck. De yttre attributen kan skvallra om vad man vill.
[Just below my parents' age, 55 to 70 years, then you might consider it [V address], it depends on what signals they give. A lady with an ermine fur coat and jewellery you can sense would like it, rather than somebody with a Fjällräven rucksack. The external attributes can reveal what you want.] (Gothenburg, Q2, female university student, 24)

Det är mer personlighet. Är man en fisförmäm person så vill man bli niad. Man märker om han eller hon vill vara fin eller vanlig. Till en gammal tant som går på NK kan man säga 'ni'.
[It is more personality. If you are a toffee-nosed person then you want to be addressed by *ni*. You can tell if he or she wants to be better or like everybody else. To an old lady who shops at NK [expensive department store] you can say *ni*.] (Gothenburg, Q9, male student, 20)

It is interesting to note that several informants construct images of women dressed in fur coats (see quotation above), or men wearing hats, which is quite unusual to see nowadays: *hatt och rock och var verkligen farbror* ('hat and overcoat and was a real old man') (Gothenburg, Q3, female cleaner, 25). A young waiter told us that he would address customers with T, except for *affärsmän i tredelad kostym med väst* ('businessmen in a three-piece suit with a vest') or somebody really old, with a walking stick. Such representations of rare – expensive or outdated – styles might also be an indication of the actual infrequency of V address in Swedish today.

Swedish, then, with its overwhelming majority of situations with default T and its extreme reliance on relative age as a social distance variable, is very different from both German and French with respect to the role of perceived commonalities as a variable in determining social distance. However, the fact that many of our Swedish informants (about 20%) say that it is not age as such which determines choice of address, as well as the quotations above, make it evident that in Swedish, as in German and French, age often interacts with other variables such as general style, or a perception of the addressee expecting a more formal or respectful treatment. In Swedish, it is the perception that the addressee is different from the speaker, i.e. there is a lack of commonalities, which creates enough social distance to make V address relevant.

In a language such as Swedish, in which T is the natural choice in almost all contexts, it cannot therefore be used to signal commonalities, for example friendship, political affiliation or collegiality at work. It is thus the use of first names that signals low social distance and familiarity, and there is evidence, as we saw earlier, that for some people in hierarchical relationships use of T is considered quite normal, whereas the use of first names is viewed as too familiar. Another example from participant observation within the Swedish university context concerns an academic newly arrived in a Swedish department who found it strange to be greeted not simply with *hej* ('hello') but also with her first name, thus indicating the familiarity attached to first names. Furthermore, in recent years, it has become more common to be addressed with first name by strangers such as sales people or business contacts. Participants who comment on such use of FN resist this trend strongly:

När man blir tilltalad med förnamn av en obekant har det slagit över.
[When you're addressed with your first name by a stranger, it's over the top.] (Gothenburg, FG1, female writer, 67)

Fruktansvärt obehagligt med förnamnstilltal – förnamnet är privat.
[Extremely unpleasant with first-name address – your first name is private.] (Gothenburg, FG1, female cashier, 20)

3.6.3   English

Our discussion so far has focused mainly on pronoun choice as the way of signalling common ground. However, as we have just seen in Swedish, first names play an important role in languages where pronoun distinctions are weak or non-existent. In the Irish English focus group, there was some discussion of the move from hon + LN to the use of first names. This move is similar to the shift from V to T in French and German:

Well if someone addresses you by your first name it means they want to get to know you and if you address someone as Mr so and so and he says call me Paul, for example, [it] shows that he is on your side. (Tralee, FG, male college lecturer, 45)

The assumption underlying first-name use is that the two interactants share some kind of commonalities. However, this use of first names can also be exploited in certain transactional relationships, particularly those conducted on the phone. In the following example, the participant's response shows that her interlocutor has violated what she considers as her personal space. She does

not want to establish any common ground with her interlocutor and there is no
reason for establishing any kind of intimacy:

<Has anybody been speaking to anybody from their mobile phone company? [...] there's
a tendency to, you know, 'Hello Mr Samuels. Is it OK if I call you Peter?' [...] How does
it feel if they speak to you using your Christian name without checking with you first?> *I
instantly don't trust them because they're being over-familiar if they use my name and
they don't know me.* (London, FG, female nurse, 33)

Even in a situation where many variables remain constant, such as in a workplace environment in interactions between an employee and their customers, all
relationships may start with hon + LN, but some will shift to the use of first
name, while yet others will shift to use of terms of endearment. Such grading
can be explained through the notion of personal affinities between speakers,
which override the workplace conventions, as in the quote from the London
mortgage broker in section 3.7.

As with French and German, where 'groupness' is signalled through T (and
first name), group membership in British English, particularly among men, can
be marked through nominals such as *mate*:

*I'm a West Ham supporter and if I go to the football and I meet someone there, he would
have a very strong East End accent and I would find myself immediately talking similar to
that, 'cos that's how I spoke when I was younger. And I would be referring to him as
'mate' immediately.* (London, FG, male journalist, 30)

From the following Newcastle example of an encounter in a music shop, we can
see that *mate* also functions in a very similar way to French *tu* in that it creates a
sense of instant, temporary community between two like-minded individuals:

*If I bump into someone looking at the same music section as me, it could be a long time
before I found out what his name was. It could be a long time, we'd be talking for hours
before we ever got to that point. [...] So, it'd be quite a while. So we'd call each other
'mate' but it would be a long time before we made our formal introductions.* (Newcastle,
FG, male English teacher, 25)

As Formentelli (2007: 11) points out, 'the vocative *mate* can [serve] the function
of identity marker, i.e. claiming common ground, sharing feelings and wants,
stressing membership in the same group or category'.

However, our data from both London and Newcastle point to an additional
function of *mate*, what our participants describe as a 'leveller', a 'diffuser' or a
'disarmer'. In the following example from London, in response to a question
about using familiar forms with strangers, the participant explains that *mate* can
be used to maintain a certain distance in an encounter between two male
strangers:

*I'd use 'mate' in that situation because it's quite a disarming thing. You know, if you want
to make it clear that you're not threatening, you want to make it clear that you don't want*

to… But also you keep that distance because you don't really want to get that involved. If you go, 'Yeah, cheers mate', it kind of ends things easily. (London, FG, male journalist, 30)

3.7   The individual as variable

Underlying the notion of perceived commonalities is some kind of shared group membership, however enduring or temporary this may be. What our data also show is that the basis of choice of mode of address can vary according to individual. The role of the individual in address choice is illustrated in the following comment from a Parisian participant:

Je pense que nous aurons beaucoup beaucoup beaucoup de mal à expliciter dans quelles conditions un locuteur francophone en France utilise […] le 'tu' et le 'vous'. Je pense qu'il y a des règles de base mais c'est vraiment très très différent selon chacun. Il y a du ressenti là-dedans et c'est son histoire personnelle qui joue.
[I think that we will have lots and lots of difficulty explaining under what conditions a francophone speaker in France uses […] tu and vous. I think that there are basic rules but it's really very very different according to each person. Feelings come into it and each person's own history plays a role.] (Paris, Q1, female student, 30)

Some participants in the French data stated that they found it difficult to use T: *Je tutoie pas facilement* ('I don't use *tu* easily') (Paris, Q12, male estate agent, 33), whereas others classified themselves as a T person, particularly outside the work environment: *Je suis de nature à tutoyer tout le monde* ('I'm the kind of person who uses *tu* with everyone') (Paris, Q5, male bank employee, 27).

In the English data too participants mentioned the importance of the individual in address choice and the kind of relationship that evolves:

<I mean, in your work as a mortgage broker, when do you know it's OK to stop addressing someone as 'Mr Smith'?> *When I've developed a relationship with that client.* <And how do you know…?> *I can't explain. You get a feel for it. There will be some people now who I've had a relationship with for many years and I'll still talk to them formally: 'Mr', 'Mrs'. Most I have on first-name terms and some I call 'mate'. I can say 'Right mate, how are you?' So it depends. It really depends. You have to gauge, maybe that's more the skill of it.* (London, FG, male mortgage broker, 34)

There is a consensus in our German-speaking focus groups that some people are more likely to use T and others V. Participants differentiate between *du-Typen* and *Sie-Typen* (*du* and *Sie* types). In the interviews, a number of people characterised themselves as using *du* or *Sie* as the default pronoun unless there was some compelling reason (such as workplace hierarchy) to depart from this. Also, some of our German-speaking participants describe their choice of address form as based on rational principles; for instance:

Man ordnet ja bestimmte Leute irgendwo ein für sich, in der Funktion, in der Wertschätzung, in der Hierarchie, alles Mögliche.
[You do classify particular people somehow, according to their function, esteem, hierarchy, in all sorts of ways.] (Mannheim, FG1, male police officer, about 40)

This contrasts with others, such as a student in the Mannheim group, who insist that theirs is an emotional choice:

Ich habe die Regel – entweder ist mir jemand sympathisch oder nicht, ich glaube, mein Herz gibt mir die Berechtigung jemanden, den ich das erste Mal sehe, mit Sie oder Du anzusprechen nach meinem Gefühl.
[I have this rule – either I like someone or I don't, I believe my heart gives me the right to call someone I meet for the first time *Sie* or *du* depending on my feelings.] (Mannheim, FG1, female student, 24)

The intersecting of the affective and professional domains was explicitly commented on by some French participants, whose use of address pronouns at work reflects personal affinities with their interlocutor and not address practices dictated by the work setting:

Les gens avec qui j'ai une affinité, je les tutoie. Et les gens avec qui je n'ai pas d'affinité, je les vouvoie, quel que soit l'âge. [I use *tu* with people who I feel an affinity with. And I use *vous* with people I don't feel an affinity with, whatever their age.] (Toulouse, FG1, female accountant, 41)

    The examples above show how an individual can determine address patterns in an interaction, prescribing or imposing their own set of norms, be they rationally or emotionally determined. We could classify such people as 'givers'. The question of who initiates the choice of address pronoun is taken up further by two Toulouse participants. Both in their late 20s, they make a distinction between those who 'give', those who 'receive' and those who do both:

(1)   *Il y a des personnes qui le donnent et des personnes qui le reçoivent.*
(2)   *Et les deux aussi.*
(1)   *Oui. Donner et recevoir, pareil.*
(2)   *Tu l'impose ou tu le suis, quoi.*
[(1)   There are people who give it and people who receive it.
(2)   And who do both as well.
(1)   Yes. Giving and receiving.
(2)   You either impose it or you follow it.]
    (Toulouse, FG1, (1) male education counsellor, 29; (2) male bookshop assistant, 27)

A female participant, a philosophy student in her early 20s, would be classified as a 'receiver'. She said that whether she is called *vous* or *tu* does not bother her; what is important is the person facing her and their expectations. It seems that, for her, the choice of address pronoun is related not to respect or marking distance but rather to accommodating to her interlocutor's address pronoun choice:

J'ai vraiment l'impression que c'est quelque chose qui, enfin, vient pas de moi, que je veux pas vouvoyer ou tutoyer les gens. Et c'est vraiment plus que c'est l'autre et pas moi. Par exemple, ça me dérange pas qu'on me vouvoie dans le travail ou qu'on me tutoie. Pour moi, ça n'a pas une valeur particulière, mais par contre, celui d'en face, il attend un vouvoiement et c'est pour ça que je le mets, parce que c'est la forme. Mais pour moi c'est plus une forme que vraiment un choix personnel. Peut-être c'est parce que pour l'instant, je n'ai pas eu trop à me poser la question.

[I really have the impression that it's something that doesn't come from me, that I don't want to use *vous* or *tu* with people. And it's really more that it's the other person and not me. For example, it doesn't bother me if people use *vous* or *tu* with me at work. For me, it doesn't have a particular value, but the person facing me is expecting *vous* and that's why I use it, because that's the expectation. But for me it's more a convention than a personal choice. Perhaps that's because up till now I haven't really had to think about it.] (Toulouse, FG1, female student, 22)

This notion of being a 'receiver' was also mentioned by a Swedish-speaking participant, who emphasises the importance of address choice and how it is related to reading the interlocutor's preference. In other words, the participant in question positions himself primarily as a 'receiver' who waits for the other person's move:

Jo, det funderar man ju nästan alltid på när man kommer i kontakt med okända människor, är det här en du- eller ni-människa? Speciellt i gränsfallen är det alltid svårt att hur ska jag tilltala den här personen och då måste man ju känna sig fram lite och man märker ju responsen sen från den andra.

[Yes, you think about that almost always when you come in contact with unknown people, is this a '*du*-person' or a '*ni*-person'? In particular in the borderline cases it is always difficult to know how to address this person and then you have to go on feeling a bit and then you notice the response from the other.] (Vaasa, Q4, male tertiary teacher and project leader, 46)

We can construct individuals as givers or receivers based on their orientation towards their interlocutors in terms of their active or passive participation in verbal exchanges. Receivers converge to the speech patterns of their interlocutor, whereas givers impose their own patterns and can thus diverge from the interlocutor's address choices. Just as there are T people and V people, there are also networks that employ T or V within their group. Inevitably some people will belong to both T and V networks and their use of T with members of a T network may be misread by members of their V network as an indication of a very close relationship. Such an overreading has the potential of face loss.

In summary, the individual's sense of identity can influence how and which address choices are made, a dynamic nicely summed up by one of our London focus group participants:

It's how much do we own what we are called? Because you have a right to tell me what to call you but I actually have a right to call you what I want as well. Because you are part of my life and part of my identity, your identity is part of my life as well. (London, FG, male housing support officer, 28)

3.8   Concluding remarks

Address is an important way of managing interpersonal relationships. Each of the four languages enables its users to express a degree of social distance, common ground and group boundaries through pronominal and/or nominal modes of address. The decision as to what mode(s) of address to employ can be determined by rational choice or spontaneous emotional reactions.

Variables impacting on the degree of social distance, such as age and status, clearly play a role when our participants try to pin down what makes them choose one address form over another in a particular instance. However, as seen from the quotations in this chapter, these social categories are not stable entities and their relative importance is negotiated in the particular situation at hand. Often, participants take note of visible attributes to guide them in how to address someone whom they are meeting for the first time. For most participants, it is a question of reading the addressee's identity, waiting for the other person's initiative and searching for indices of how to address them.

For French and German, we have argued that, in encounters with strangers, *sameness* is the salient category, which, when recognised as such, promotes use of T. Sameness in our data, expressing common ground and a sense of common identity, is reflected in various kinds of group membership, ranging from belonging to a club to the kind of instant, temporary community that can be established between individuals over a common purpose, and to recognising oneself in the presentation of one's interlocutor. Although English does not offer a distinction between T and V, the dichotomy of FN versus hon + LN fulfils similar functions as those of T and V in French and German. We have seen that low social distance modes of address such as *mate* and *love* and the high social distance forms *Sir* and *Madam* are comparable to T and V respectively. However, *mate* can also act as a 'T-like distancer' in its role of disarming an aggressive interlocutor through what is in essence an in-group marker. We will see in Chapter 4 that *Sir* or *Madam* can act as a 'V-like distancer'.

In contrast, although in Swedish sameness can also motivate a switch to first names, it is *difference* that is the salient feature and is the trigger for V. This is to be expected, given how little V is used. Difference is reflected in the physical presentation of the other, including not only clothing and other apparel but, we could argue, also the physical manifestations of extreme old age, where Swedish expresses negative politeness towards the elderly through the special use of V.

In most respects, French and German handle address in similar ways. Both languages have a choice of address pronouns in the singular. Choice of nominals, first names or last names, titles and other honorifics is strongly associated with one or other of the address pronouns: in general, FN in French and German goes hand in hand with T and hon + LN with V. However, compromise forms – T and hon + LN and V + FN – are not uncommon. For example, V and FN is used non-reciprocally in cross-age, cross-status communication in German and in family and workplaces in French (see 4.1.1, 4.4.1). T and hon + LN also occurs in German in some workplace situations (see 4.5.2).

To a large extent V is the default pronoun used with strangers in both French and German. There are, however, important differences in address use in the two languages, including the greater use of compromise forms in German that we have just discussed. Moreover, German employs T more than French does. The two variables that we have examined in this chapter, age and status, condition to a certain extent speakers' address choices in French, although individual preference plays a role. In German, in contrast, there is a strong element of individual preference in choice of address forms (both pronominal and nominal), with some individuals denying the social significance of the T–V distinction. Variation in modes of address is therefore very common in German, leading to considerable insecurity. Also, plural *ihr* is utilised as an intermediate form to express plurality or collectivity in mixed groups, where different inter-locutors exchange T and V, and even among groups of V users.

In all of the languages, many of the participants' responses are qualified by the words 'it depends'. When we asked participants to nominate the age at which people should be addressed in a particular way, those who started their responses 'it depends', or who hedged and sought clarification of situational elements, were focusing on contextualising their response. These participants situate themselves in relation to their interlocutor and his or her needs. In other words, they have an awareness of the self in relation to others. Some partic-ipants, meanwhile, readily nominate an age – for them 'this is how things are' – with no reference to any contextual factors. However, variation may be due to the transition from V to T (or from hon + LN to FN) being associated with a rite of passage that may be age related or linked to a particular professional or other attainment.

Social variables are always embedded in particular domains and the medium of communication is also highly relevant for choice of address forms. These areas are discussed in the following chapter.

4   Institutions, domains and medium

In the previous chapter, we discussed the principles and variables that lead to the choice of one mode of address over the other, especially in spoken language. Differences between French, German and Swedish became evident. It was also possible to sketch the situation in English, which has to use modes of address other than pronouns to mark differences in social distance. The reader is reminded that the English data, intended for comparison, comprise only focus group discussions. In other words, these data do not investigate address practices in various domains in the same structured way as our questionnaire and interview data for the other languages. In this chapter, we will turn our attention to how address actually works in institutions and domains – the family, workplace, university, school and the transactional domains – and what the social significance of these address practices is. We will also consider address in letters and chat groups.

4.1   Family

4.1.1   French

Communication within the family adds kinship terms to the set of modes of address in all our languages. In French, our Paris interview data show that T is used 100% of the time between parents and children and around 95% of the time between grandparents and grandchildren. The overwhelming majority of parents are addressed by a kinship term – *maman, papa*. However, just over 10% of our Paris informants address both or one of their parents by their first name: all but one are in their twenties or thirties, which indicates that this tendency to use parents' first names is found among the younger generation. From Table 4.1 we can see that use of address forms with a partner's parents shows much greater variability (with an overall statistical significance of $p < 0.025$ and $p < 0.1$ for the difference between reciprocal T use and non-reciprocal T use). These members of the family may not necessarily be considered part of the inner family circle.

The majority of partners' parents are addressed by FN (72%), followed by *Monsieur/Madame*, with or without LN (17%). Of those participants who report

Table 4.1 *French: pronoun used to/by partner's parents*

	%
Reciprocal T	22
Reciprocal V	36
Gives V/receives T	36
Gives V/receives T or V*	2
Reciprocal V(T)	2
V/nothing	3
n/a	11
(N)	(72)

* The speaker usually uses V, but occasionally uses T.

using FN, over three quarters combine FN with V (78%), a combination that marks both respect and familiarity. There is considerable use of V, both reciprocally and non-reciprocally in combination with T, with nearly three quarters of our informants using either combination. It is within these family relationships that the greatest use of non-reciprocal address in French is to be found: over a third of participants report non-reciprocal use (T by the older relative, V by the younger one), which is slightly more prevalent among people aged 30 and under (10/23, 44%) and among women (14/23, 61%). One of the Paris interviewees who uses V + FN with her partner's parents, who use T + FN to her, explains that she prefers to use V out of respect and that it doesn't make the relationship unequal in any way:

Mes beaux-parents, je les vouvoie, alors que ça fait cinq ans maintenant que je suis avec mon petit ami, donc je les connais depuis longtemps. Mais j'arrive pas à les tutoyer. [...] <Tes beaux-parents t'ont invité à les tutoyer?> Non. Eux, par contre, ils m'ont pas proposé mais à la fois ils connaissent un petit peu comment je fonctionne et ils savent que j'ai du mal à tutoyer. Donc ils ont même pas essayé en fait. Et ça les dérange pas de toute façon parce que, outre le 'tu' ou le 'vous', après on peut avoir quand même une facilité, une aisance à parler avec les personnes qui nous sont proches. Et le fait que ce soit un 'tu' ou un 'vous', ça change pas les relations derrières en fait. [...] C'est juste que moi [...] par respect pour eux je préfère les vouvoyer parce qu'ils sont plus âgés que moi. C'est simplement ça en fait.

[I use *vous* with my parents-in-law, although I've been with my boyfriend now for five years, so I've known them for a long time. But I can't manage to use *tu* with them. [...] <*Have your parents-in-law asked you to use* tu *with them?*> No, they haven't asked me to but at the same time they have an idea of how I work and they know that I find it hard to use *tu*. So they actually haven't even tried. And it doesn't bother them anyway because, apart from *tu* and *vous*, you can find it relatively easy to talk to people who are close to you. And the fact that it's *tu* or *vous* doesn't actually change the relationship underneath. […] It's just that I […] prefer to use *vous* with them out of respect for them because they're older than me. That's all it is, actually.] (Paris, Q5, female bank employee, 24)

Another interviewee explains the relationship from the other side, that is, from the point of view of the 'mother-in-law'. In this case, her son-in-law over time moved from using *vous* to *tu* with her and she now finds this perfectly normal:

Bon, dernièrement une de mes filles s'est mariée. C'est vrai que mon gendre me vouvoyait et j'ai remarqué que de plus en plus il me tutoyait mais ça me choque en rien du tout. […] <Et vous préférez qu'il vous tutoie?> Oui, peut-être aussi, dans la mesure où – je sais que le vouvoiement pour beaucoup de personnes est une marque de respect mais effectivement, le fait qu'il se soit marié avec ma fille, il est devenu mon fils. Donc, ça me choquerait plutôt que mon fils me vouvoie. Donc qu'il me tutoie maintenant pour moi est la normalité.

[Well, just recently one of my daughters got married. It's true that my son-in-law would use *vous* with me and I noticed that more and more he was using *tu* with me, but it doesn't shock me at all. […] <*And do you prefer him to use* tu *with you?*> Yes, perhaps as well, to the extent that – I know that using *vous* for many people is a mark of respect but actually the fact that he's married to my daughter means that he's become my son. So, it would rather shock me if my son used *vous* with me. So it's normal for me now that he uses *tu* with me.] (Paris, Q4, female nurse, 53)

In her relationship with her own parents-in-law, however, she uses V + FN and receives T + FN, marking her as part of a transitional generation. The following example shows how in family relations that are less central, such as those between an aunt and the parents-in-law of a niece or nephew, the choice of pronoun can be difficult, giving rise to fluctuation, and time is required for the final choice to be made to employ a mode of address expressing full inclusion:

Dans le cadre de la famille, j'ai des nièces qui viennent de se marier. Avec les beaux-parents de l'une d'entre elles, je ne sais pas trop quoi faire. On ne se connaît pas beaucoup, on n'a pas encore trouvé, quelquefois on se dit 'tu' et quelquefois on se dit 'vous'. On appartient un peu à la même famille maintenant, mais on ne trouve pas tout de suite le juste milieu.

[Within the family, I have nieces who have just got married. With the parents-in-law of one of them, I don't quite know what to do. We don't know one another very well, we haven't yet settled on a choice, sometimes we say *tu* to one another and sometimes we say *vous*. We sort of belong to the same family now, but we haven't struck the right balance straightaway.] (Paris, Q2, female educator, 57)

4.1.2   German

German traditionally based its T relationships on the family (Brown and Gilman 1960). Our interview data show close to 100% use of T in German between parents and children and between grandparents and grandchildren. With very few exceptions, parents are addressed by their kinship term *Vater*, *Vati* or *Papa*, or

Table 4.2 *German: pronoun used to/by partner's parents*

	%
Reciprocal T	74
Reciprocal V	7
Gives V/receives T	17
Gives V/receives T or V	<1
Gives T or V/receives T	<1
Avoids address/receives T	<1
Gives *ihr*/receives T	<1
(N)	(198)

Mutter, *Mutti* or *Mama*, and grandparents are addressed by *Oma* ('grandma') or *Opa* ('granddad'), with FN sometimes added to differentiate them, e.g. *Oma Frieda* and *Oma Luise*. Children (and grandchildren) in turn are addressed by FN. However, knowledge of earlier patterns is still transmitted through oral tradition. Some of our German informants reported that their grandmother's generation was the first to say *du* to their own grandmothers or that their grandfather's comrades in World War I were disgusted that he said *du* to his parents.

Only two participants from our German-language sample, both in Vienna, address their parents by their FN or are addressed this way by their children. One Viennese university professor (Vienna, Q2, male university professor, 54) reports that his children employ FN in about 70% of instances and that this is frequently commented on by friends and his mother-in-law. A Viennese researcher in her mid-20s reports using FN more than the kinship term in addressing her father. Her younger sisters do this habitually. She also notes that this does not ever occur in her friends' families. No indication is given as to the conditions for variation. In addition, three people in their 20s, one in each research site, were aware of people addressing their parents by their FN although they did not practise this themselves.

However, what constitutes family membership is not completely clear-cut. It is the partner's parents and siblings around whom family membership and concomitant modes of address may become blurred. Table 4.2 shows that in German, in contrast to French, reciprocal T predominates in communication with one's partner's parents (all combinations are statistically significant ($p < 0.005$)).

Nevertheless, over a quarter of our German informants do not employ reciprocal T with a partner's parents, with 17% using non-reciprocal V–T address. These patterns are sometimes identified with child–adult communication. Reciprocal V with a partner's parents occurs in 7% of instances. The non-reciprocal mode is most prevalent in the 21–30 age group – 34% as opposed to 56% reciprocal T. This is possibly because of the many de facto relationships in that age group, which some parents may consider not completely within the family. A partner's parents are most likely to be addressed by FN (in 54% of cases) followed by a kinship term, *Vater* or *Mutter* (in 17% of cases).

The dilemmas of transition loom large in the minds of many German speakers. A Mannheim mother reflects on how address with her daughter's boyfriend developed:

Am Anfang, das erste Mal hab ich dann 'Sie' gesagt, [...] und auf einmal war ich dann beim 'Du', obwohl, ich weiss nicht, korrekt ist das von meiner Seite her auch nicht [...] wenn er noch länger mit ihr zusammen ist, werd ich vielleicht auch sagen, 'Sag du zu mir', aber damit warten wir noch ein bissel.

[At the start, the first time I said *Sie* [...] and suddenly I was saying *du*, although I don't know, that isn't quite proper of me [...] if he is with her for a long time, I might say 'Say *du* to me' but we'll wait a while for that.] (Mannheim, Q5, female secretary, 52)

Younger members of our first Mannheim focus group exchanged anecdotes in which they were persistently quizzed by their parents concerning the seriousness of their current relationship with their girl- or boyfriend so that the parents could decide whether the time was opportune to address them as T. This would signal the lowering of social distance that included people within the in-group of the family. For instance, a 28-year-old female ethnologist in the first Mannheim focus group reports that she and her partner had to pass the test of staying together after a trip to India before T was offered to her partner. A teacher and disk jockey, about 30, reports on a discussion initiated by his partner's parents and his reactions:

Das ist lustig, das ist genau wie bei mir gewesen mit meinen Eltern, die da eben mal mit dem 'Sie', da haben sie mich dann auch gefragt, mit meiner Freundin irgendwann, waren wir zwei Jahre zusammen oder anderthalb, ich weiß es net mehr, dann haben sie gefragt, also schon in die Richtung gehend, 'Ja bleibt ihr jetzt länger, also, dann würden wir nämlich das "Du" mal anbieten'. Also als würde man sich, also da haben dann wir ne richtige Diskussion gehabt, weil ich gesagt hab, 'Also, ich mein, macht was ihr wollt, aber ich bleib net länger mit ihr zusammen, nur weil ihr euch jetzt duzt', also schon fast wie ein ja so in den Kreis aufgenommen, den Kreis der Familie aufgenommen zu werden.

[That's funny, it is exactly the same as with my parents, who asked me at a particular point of time about my girlfriend, when we had been together for two years or one and a half, I don't remember how long, they asked something like 'If you're going to stay together longer, then we would suggest we exchange *du*'. Then we had an actual discussion because I said, 'Well, as far as I am concerned, do as you please, but I won't stay with her longer just because you are on *du* terms', practically like admitting her into the circle, into the family circle.] (Mannheim, FG1, male teacher and DJ, 30)

Not only should the initiation of the T relationship not be too hasty, it should also not be tardy either, for this can lead to guilt feelings on the part of the parents, as a 29-year-old Mannheim student reports:

Aber noch zu der Situation mit den Eltern, bei mir war das gerade anders rum. Meine Eltern hatten Bedenken, dass sie nicht rechtzeitig das Du angeboten haben, dass sie außen vor sind. Also dieses Du war nicht das Angebot hineinzukommen, 'du gehörst jetzt dazu', sondern die haben sich tierisch geärgert, 'Mist, wir haben was verpasst, das hätten wir ja schon längst machen müssen, wie kriegen wir das hin', und wochenlang, sogar monatelang überlegt zu welcher Situation, wie, wann und wo sie jetzt am besten das 'Du' für meine Frau anbieten können, also damals Freundin, jetzige Frau anbieten können.

[But on the situation with my parents I should add, in my case it was the other way around. My parents were worried that they hadn't entered into the *du* ritual early enough, that they were left out. So this *du* was not an invitation to come in, like 'you're part of it now', but they were terribly angry. 'Damn, we missed the opportunity, we ought to have done that ages ago, how do we get this straightened out?' and for weeks, even for months they were reflecting on the situation, how, when and where they could offer my wife, then my girlfriend, now my wife, a *du* relationship.] (Mannheim, FG1, male student, former carpenter and workplace tutor, 29)

These are just some indicators of the anxiety which commitment and obligation cause in German, especially since T relationships in German, as in French, are generally not retractable and may have to survive longer than marriages and de facto relationships. This is reminiscent of the quote in section 3.1 about the move from V to T being perhaps the greatest step you can take.

One extension of the family boundaries we have observed in Germany and Austria is friends of the parents being addressed by children and young people, under parental encouragement, as *Onkel* ('uncle') or *Tante* ('aunt'). There is even a name for such relationships, *Nennonkel* and *Nenntante*, someone you call uncle or aunt without being related to them (Wahrig 1977: 2638).

4.1.3   Swedish

Among our Swedish participants, children and parents almost always use reciprocal T (with fathers: 94%, 132/141; with mothers: 95%, 136/143). Those few participants who report not using T with their parents are from the oldest generation and use third-person address,[1] i.e. the kinship term – for example, 'Vill mamma ha en kopp te?' ('Would mum like a cup of tea?'). This is a practice which historically was rather common; in order to show one's parents respect, they were addressed in the third person. It should be emphasised that addressing close relatives is the only situation in our questionnaire data where the level of T use is actually lower in Swedish than in German or French: in the latter two languages, use of T was 100%. Four fifths of our participants use a kinship term with one or both of their parents (82%), with 12% using FN and 6% using both kinship term and FN, the latter a combination that was not reported by the French or German participants. In Swedish, therefore, there is a higher use of FN to address parents than in either French or German.

---

[1] These older participants are referring to practices of the past.

Grandparents are usually also addressed by T (and kinship term), but somewhat less so than parents. There is a range from 85% reciprocal T (paternal grandmother) to 89% (paternal grandfather), but this can perhaps be explained by variation in the total number of responses – 130 for maternal grandmother, 99 for maternal grand-father, 111 for paternal grandfather and 91 for paternal grandfather. The majority of those who do not use T with their grandparents report addressing their relative indirectly by using the kinship term '*Är farmor trött?*' (lit. 'Is grandmother tired?', meaning 'Are you tired, grandmother?'). Moving away from the immediate family to address practices with one's partner's parents, 95% of our participants report reciprocal T (compared with 22% in French and 74% in German). The fact that reciprocal T is so dominant in Swedish underscores the position of T as the default address pronoun. Despite the strong move in Swedish society towards addressing everybody with *du* and first name if known, there are some pockets of older address practices left. Until the 1960s (the time of the '*du*-reform', see 2.2.4), it was common practice for children to address their friends' parents as well as somewhat older family friends by *tant* ('auntie', but not a relative) and *farbror* ('uncle', father's brother, and used in general to a non-relative) + FN. Addressing a stranger, children tended to use *tant* or *farbror* and third-person address (i.e. avoiding the use of T or V). Although these practices have largely disappeared, some of our participants report incidents where they have been addressed as *tant* or *farbror* by small children, whose mothers have encouraged such a use. The reaction is generally one of acceptance, but a number of people from both Vaasa and Gothenburg expressed their dismay the first time this happened:

Jo, jag har blivit tilltalad med, då just när jag jobbade som ung sommarjobbare på bank, med 'tant'. Ska du ge det där åt tanten. Och det tycker jag var väldigt otrevligt, den gången, i dag bryr jag mig int i det, i dag kan jag acceptera det, men int då.
[Yes, I was addressed as *tant* when I worked as a young person in the summer relieving staff in a bank. And I found that very unpleasant. That time. These days I don't care, these days I can accept it, but not then.] (Vaasa, Q4, female teaching centre pedagogue, 41)

En mamma sa till sitt barn 'Ge det till tanten' och jag var väl runt tjugo då och då blev jag lite förvånad, men det är ju klart – barnet var väl mindre/yngre än mig. Många kvinnor skulle bli upprörda om de blev kallade för tant därför de känner sig inte som tanter eller inser inte att de är tanter.
[A mother said to her child 'Give it to *tant*' and I was around twenty then and I got a bit surprised, but sure, the child was a lot younger than me. Many women would be upset if they were called *tanten* because they don't feel like *tanter* or do not realise that they are *tanter*.] (Gothenburg, Q3, female cleaner, 25)

4.1.4   English

In English, as in the other three languages, communication between parents and children is generally non-reciprocal in that parents generally address their children by first name and the children respond by kinship term. This may be the full form – *Father* or *Mother*, *Christopher* or *Christine* – or the diminutive form, such as *Dad/Daddy* or *Mum/Mummy* or *Chris*. In some families, however, children call their parents by their first name, for example:

I call my mum and dad by their first names. I don't know when it started or why. I still call them mum and dad sometimes. (London, FG, male solicitor, 34)

I grew up with a friend at school who called her mum 'mum' and her mum called herself 'mum' and called her father 'David' and Amber called him that right from day one. (London, FG, female student nurse, 29)

Others address their parents by their first name to irritate them. Still others, observing their friends using first names with their parents, interpret it as lack of respect. It has not been possible to find social indices to differentiate these people. Grandparents are called by their kinship terms *Grandpa*, *Grandma/Gran/Nan*.

Where the diminutive form of the child's name is preferred, the full name may be indicative of a marked situation such as reproach:

But if I was ever called Christopher when I was growing up it was because I was being told off or something. Because it carries more weight. (London, FG, male voluntary sector worker, 26)

A number of our London focus group members remark that, as people get older, they no longer call their uncles and aunts by the kinship term but by their FN. However, no indication of the age threshold can be generalised from the data. In Newcastle a differentiation was reported in that the blood relative is addressed by kinship term + FN, the relative by marriage by FN:

(1)	*'Aunt' always seemed really formal to me. So I use 'auntie'. If I'm talking to them it will be 'auntie' and then the name. But then I don't call my uncle 'uncle', just his name.*
(2)	*Is he the blood relative?*
(1)	*No.*
(2)	*Because if it's the blood relative you tend to speak with the – 'My Auntie Maureen' or 'My Auntie Wendy' because they are my parents' siblings. Whereas their husbands are just Maurice and Trevor.*
Moderator	*Is that coincidental do you think or is it deliberate?*
(2)	*Deliberate on my part. I wouldn't feel right calling my auntie who I've called that from that big. But the blokes, who aren't my family... It wasn't a conscious decision, it's just what's happened. Neither of us engineered it.*

(Newcastle, FG, (1) female law lecturer, 29; (2) male IT project manager, 45)

Yet there is a consensus in the Newcastle focus group that older friends of the family are called 'Uncle' and 'Aunt(ie)' (cf. Swedish older usage). Among the experiences related is the following:

I call my Irish neighbours 'uncle' and 'aunt' because we grew up in the same house for the past 25 years. (Newcastle, female student, 27)

In London this is reported especially for members of certain ethnic groups, such as Indians and Pakistanis.

4.2   School

4.2.1   French

The overwhelming majority of interviewees report that they used V to address their teachers at school (96%, 68/71). Of those that give the title they used with their teachers, most indicate 'Monsieur' or 'Madame' (75%, 39/52), or 'M/ Mme' + LN (21%, 11/52). At primary school in France, teachers use T when addressing their pupils (PO). The reported age at which teachers start to use V with schoolchildren shows great variation, ranging from 6 to 20 years, with an age being given by 49 out of 72 participants. The two most cited ages are 12 and 14 years (by 10 participants each), the first marking the transition between primary and secondary school and the second occurring as children approach the switch between *college* and *lycée*, which begins at age 15. Four of our participants continued to be called T by their teachers throughout their schooling.

Six of our interviewees are secondary school teachers. They report that in general they use T with other teachers and V with the school principal or vice-principal and with administration. The following example is from a teacher in her early 30s who works in a *collège*, the first part of secondary schooling (age 11–15), and she reports reciprocal V use between her and her pupils:

Les seuls adultes que je vouvoie c'est, en fait, le proviseur et le proviseur-adjoint. C'est-à-dire vraiment les gens qui sont mes supérieurs hiérarchiques et qui sont en haut de l'échelle. Parce que, eux, ils sont vraiment détachés de tout corps enseignant. Mais les collègues je tutoie tous, sans qu'il y ait de distinction de sexe, d'âge [...]. <Et tu vouvoies les élèves?> Je vouvoie les élèves qui me vouvoient en retour.

[The only adults that I use *vous* with are in fact the principal and the vice-principal. In other words, really the people who are my hierarchical superiors and who are at the top of the ladder. Because they are really detached from the whole teaching body. But I use *tu* with all my colleagues, whatever their sex or age [...]. <*And you use* vous *with the pupils?*> I use *vous* with the pupils who use *vous* in return.] (Paris, Q1, female secondary school teacher, 31)

The use of reciprocal V between secondary school teachers and students is common practice nowadays. However, four of our participants, who are in their 60s, talk of their experience of first starting to teach at the end of the 1960s and the early 1970s, when there was a general increase in T use (see 4.2.1). In the following extract, a teacher aged 62 at a *lycée* in Paris (age 15–18) talks about using T with his pupils, a spontaneous choice when he first started teaching and something he continued until he retired in 2006:

J'ai commencé à enseigner en 1971, c'était peu de temps après 68, j'étais encore bien jeune. Et je n'ai pas beaucoup réfléchi, c'est venu spontanément. Je me sentais suffisamment proche des élèves pour les tutoyer. J'ai même le souvenir qu'à cette époque-là, au début des années 70, il est arrivé que les élèves me tutoient aussi [...]. Par contre, les générations suivantes, que j'ai continué à tutoyer jusqu'à l'année dernière, m'ont vouvoyé [...]. Là, la différence d'âge s'était creusée aussi, mais les temps avaient changé peut-être.

[I started to teach in 1971, it was just shortly after 68, I was still very young. And, I hadn't really thought about it, it just came spontaneously. I felt close enough to the pupils to use *tu* with them. I even remember that at that time, at the beginning of the 70s, it happened that the pupils used *tu* with me too [...]. On the other hand, the following generations, who I continued to use *tu* with until last year, used *vous* with me [...]. There the age difference had grown as well, but the times had changed perhaps.] (Paris, Q15, male secondary school teacher, 62)

Later in the discussion he expands on his reasons for using T – he considers it to be part of his conception of teaching, being close to his students and open to discussion – and he also acknowledges that the period itself could well have played a role. Finally, he notes that he was in the minority at the two schools he taught in during his career:

Je pense que j'étais dans une minorité. Beaucoup de collègues vouvoient les élèves, vouvoyaient déjà à l'époque, vouvoient encore aujourd'hui. [...] Je me permettais de tutoyer les élèves dès le premier jour et de les appeler par leur prénom en classe parce que je savais qu'on allait passer l'année ensemble, voire trois ans de suite, pour beaucoup. [...] Donc on allait devoir vivre ensemble.

[I think that I was in a minority. Lots of colleagues use *vous* with the pupils, were already using *vous* at the time, still use *vous* today. [...] I permitted myself to use *tu* with the pupils from the first day and to call them by their first names in class because I knew that we were going to spend the year together, even three years in a row, for lots of them. [...] So we were going to have to live together.] (Paris, Q3, male secondary school teacher, 62)

Another secondary teacher also mentions the changes that took place in the late 1960s, when he started teaching in the provinces, where not only were teachers using *tu* with pupils but also pupils were using *tu* with their teachers. This shift did not last and the teacher describes what he calls '*reconquête de la tradition*' ('reconquest of tradition'). He views this resurgence of V as in part the resurgence of old traditions both at the university and schools levels, and also points out that the use of *tu* by teachers is influenced by social class:

Je crois que c'est lié à une évolution sociologique qui fait que, on a progressivement tourné le dos à ce que je vais appeler les acquis de 68. [...] Et puis, j'ai envie de dire, la vieille tradition de l'université française, de l'école française, a repris le dessus. C'est-à-dire que la génération de jeunes profs qui est arrivée en, on va dire en 80, elle avait été formattée pour abandonner ces pratiques qui étaient des pratiques choquantes pour une

partie de la société. Et encore, ça c'est certainement pas fait partout, le tutoiement. Je
suppose que dans les lycées de Neuilly autour de Paris il était peu probable qu'on ait
jamais tutoyé un élève.

[I think it was linked to a sociological evolution that meant that people progressively
turned their backs on what I am going to call the achievements of 68. [...] And, I want to
say, the old tradition of the French university, of the French school, took the upper hand.
That is to say, the generation of young teachers who arrived in, let's say 1980, had been
trained to abandon these practices, which were shocking practices for part of society. And
even so, it certainly wasn't the case that *tu* was used everywhere. I suppose that in the
lycées in Neuilly [upper-class suburb] around Paris it was very unlikely that anyone ever
used *tu* with a pupil.] (Paris, Q3, male historian, 69)

4.2.2   German

Of our 198 interviewees, 188 (95%) addressed their teachers with *Sie*, 6 (3%)
with *du* and 4 (2%) with *du* or *Sie*. Of our informants, 125 (67.6%) used hon +
LN, 53 (28.6%) title + LN, mainly from Vienna, 4 (2.2%) FN and 3 (1.6%) FN
or hon/title + LN. The age at which teachers started to use V with students was
reported as being from 14 upwards, but many (58 in total, or 29.3%) report that
T was used until the end of schooling.

In the nine or ten compulsory years of schooling in German-speaking
countries, there is non-reciprocal communication between teachers and students, with teachers employing T and FN and the children responding with V
and hon + LN (*Herr/Frau Schmidt*). The practice of reciprocal T between
teachers, which was ushered in by the student movement in the late 1960s/
early 1970s in some schools, is now very unusual. There has been a tradition of
children being addressed as V by their teachers at the age of 16 (or 14, the age of
Jugendweihe (secular confirmation) in the GDR). Generally the transition now
occurs by the start of the second-last year of secondary school, if at all.
However, we have observed Year 13 (matriculation) classes in Berlin and
Bonn in which non-reciprocal address has continued following agreement
between the parties. Most of our interview data from all the German-speaking
locations indicate a continuation of non-reciprocal address to the end of schooling. One former teacher from Vienna reports:

Ich habe die Erfahrung gemacht, dass Schüler sehr gern per 'du' angesprochen werden
und das 'Sie' als seltsam empfinden.

[It has been my experience that school students like to be addressed as *du* very much
and regard *Sie* as strange.] (Vienna, Q11, male school inspector (former teacher), 54)

This concurs with the wide range of ages at which German speakers locate the
transition between T and V (see 3.4.2).

Another issue was introduced by a trainee teacher in her 30s, now an editor,
from Mannheim, who during a teacher training placement at her 'old' school
found that teachers who had known her as a student had misgivings using V +

Frau R. and offered a T-relationship which she couldn't refuse but which in turn led to her having trouble addressing them with T and FN.

Yet in junior classes, especially in Austria, pupils are now increasingly addressing their teachers as T. This is reported by teachers and ex-teachers, a parent, a religious instruction teacher and a special school educationist, all from Vienna.

4.2.3   Swedish

In the Swedish questionnaire data, 93 of 144 (65%)[2] of the informants report that they used T with their teachers, and of those, 66 (71%) report that they would have employed T in combination with the teacher's FN. However, the practice of addressing female teachers as *fröken* ('miss') and male teachers as *magistern* ('Sir'), in combination with T, continues to some extent: 18% (17/93) report using T in combination with a title. A teacher in the second focus group in Gothenburg reported that his students always addressed him by his first name, but that on occasion a child has called him *fröken* in class by mistake.

Another of our Gothenburg informants, also a teacher, recalls the practice of using titles in his schooldays:

Det skulle ha varit på skolan för länge sen för det var viktigt att man använde magistern och fröken och så, inte namn och så där.
[It would have been at school a long time ago because it was important you used *magistern* and *fröken* and not names and that.] (Gothenburg, Q3, male teacher, 34)

The inter-generational variation is evident in the debate below between two younger and two older focus group members in Vaasa, with the younger ones favouring closeness of relationship with one's teacher and the older ones the maintenance of respect for one's superiors:

(1)   *Och lärare i skolan det är en respektfråga. Jag tycker int att det är riktigt naturligt att eleverna, än i denna dag, duar lärarna, för jag anser att respekten lider av duandet i skolan. Jag har själv varit lärare på finska sidan vid Kurssikeskus [Kurscentrum] och det var elever mellan fjorton och arton år och jag tyckt int riktigt om när de ropade 'sinä' ['du'] då när de tilltalade. Det är nog precis samma sak i Vikingaskola [en svenskspråkig lågstadieskola i Vasa] också, där tycker jag nog att barnen duar lärarna. Respekten tror jag lider av duandet, så därför la jag av lärare.*

(2)   *Jag tror att jag och Maria (4) kanske hör till den generationen som har duat lärarna i skolan i alla tider.*

(3)   *Det är en generationsfråga det här.*

---

[2] This level of T address might seem low given that T is the default address pronoun, but it is explained by the fact that the participants who report not addressing their teachers with T are older and are referring to address practices that predate the '*du*-reform' at the end of the 1960s and early 1970s.

(4)   Jag tycker att jag alltid har haft en nära relation till mina lärare som kanske 'ni' int har haft.

(3)   Vi måste nog nia dem och vi hade stor respekt för dem och höll upp dörren för dem och...

[(1)   And as for teachers at school, that is a question of respect. Even in this day and age, I still don't think it is quite natural for the students to say *du* to their teachers, because I am of the opinion that respect suffers with the use of *du* at school. I have been a teacher myself, in the Finnish system, at Kurssikeskus, and there were students between 14 and 18 and I didn't quite like it when they would shout *sinä* [Finnish T-form] when they were addressing you. It is probably the same at Vikingaskola [a Swedish-speaking primary school in Vaasa] too, there I think the children say *du* to the teachers. There is less respect because of the *du*; that is why I quit teaching.

*(2)   I think that Maria (4) and I perhaps belong to the generation who have said *du* to their teachers all along.

*(3)   That is a generational question.

*(4)   I think that I have always had a close relationship with my teachers which perhaps you haven't.

*(3)   We had to say *ni* and we had great respect for them and held the door open for them and...]

(Vaasa, FG2, (1) male sales manager, 66; (2) female project assistant, 29; (3) female social worker, 62; (4) female university student, 24)

Teachers use T with their students and the vast majority (124/144, 86%) of our participants report having been addressed with T by their teachers. Those who report any other form of address are referring to a time that predates the '*du*-reform'. The following quotation describes the transition period when teachers stopped addressing their students by their name (i.e. third-person address) and started to use T to them:

För på 70-talet när jag gick i nian [det var när] *lärarn la bort titlarna lite grann och började säga 'du' till sina elever. <Sa de 'ni' innan?> Ja, de sa väl namnet, men de skulle aldrig säga 'du' [...] vilket de började med då, en del lärare, kanske de yngre lärarna då. Men då började det bli lite modernt att säga 'du' på 70-talet, tror jag.*

[Because in the 70s when I was in grade nine [this was when] the teacher dropped titles a little and started to say *du* to their students. *<Did they say ni before?>* Well they said the name I think, but they would never say *du* [...] which they started doing then, some teachers, perhaps the younger teachers then. But then it became a bit fashionable to say *du* in the 70s, I think.] (Gothenburg, Q7, female secretary, 50)

4.2.4   English

At school in England, first names have constituted a lowering of social distance. Some of our London male informants remembered that they were addressed by their LN by their teachers ten or more years ago:

Some teachers would, some wouldn't. I think that might have been a generational thing as well. Some of the older teachers [...] who didn't particularly build up a relationship with the students would refer to us by our last names. (London, FG, voluntary worker, 26)

Generally, there was non-reciprocal address – the teacher would use FN or LN to the student and received *Mr/Mrs* + LN from them. (Students generally did not even know teachers' first names.) Where this was not so, it indicated a special relationship. In some schools, sixth form (12th grade) students could use FN to the teachers. And sometimes there was the 'cool teacher' who permitted all the students to address them by their FN, with dubious consequences:

(1)   *When I was at school in England, like you were saying, up until sixth form we addressed all our teachers 'Mr or Mrs Such and Such', and then in sixth form some of them allowed us to call them by their Christian names.[3] However, prior to sixth form there was one teacher in the school that was like the coolest teacher in school, who allowed everyone to call him by his Christian name. And that carried a lot of weight with the kids, you know. We all thought he was like the bee's knees because we were allowed to call him by his first name.*

(2)   *I think sometimes that's a double-edged sword because sometimes the younger students, if you're 13, 14, you start trying to take liberties with that teacher then.*

(1)   *We did, yeah. We definitely over-familiarised ourselves with him and thought that we could get away with murder. Although, we sort of knew where our limitations were. But we took liberties with him that we didn't necessarily take with others.*

Moderator   *Did you respect him less?*

(1)   *I think in many ways we respected him more because he was quite a cool teacher. He wasn't just any teacher that allowed us to call him by that name. He actually was different from all the other teachers. So it wasn't just him allowing us to call him that that gave him that higher level of respect. It was other things that he did.*

(London, FG, (1) female sign language interpreter, 35; (2) male
voluntary sector worker, 26)

4.3   University

4.3.1   French

In response to the question 'How do/did you address your teachers at university? How do/did they address you?', most participants report reciprocal V (81%, 34/42), followed by non-reciprocal V to a teacher who responds

---

[3] In Britain and Ireland, 'Christian name' is used for 'first name', the term which has generally replaced it in other core English-speaking countries in response to their being recognised as secular and multi-faith societies. 'First name' does not recognise the unsuitability of the term in a multicultural society for some of whose members the first name is the equivalent of an English last name.

with T (7%, 3/42). At postgraduate level, the use of pronominal address between student and teacher can change, but often not until the student has been awarded their doctorate:

En général, un doctorant, c'est pas tout le temps qu'il tutoie son directeur. Trois quarts du temps il le vouvoie, quand même. Il peut l'appeler par son prénom mais ça dépend aussi du directeur, etc. Il le vouvoie, il passe sa thèse, [...] ils se tutoient. Si peu qu'il obtienne un poste dans la même université, il tutoiera ses anciens profs. Et c'est souvent du jour au lendemain. J'ai déjà observé ce phénomène. On passe du 'vous' au 'tu' et du 'Monsieur Machin' à Bernadette.

[In general, doctoral students don't always use *tu* with their supervisors. Three quarters of the time, they use *vous* with them. They can call them by their first name, but it depends on the supervisor, etc. They use *vous* [with their supervisor], they get awarded their thesis, [...] [then] they call each other *tu*. If they ever get a position in the same university, they will use *tu* with their former teachers. And it often happens overnight. I've noticed this phenomenon before. They go from *vous* to *tu* and from Mr What's-his-name to Bernadette.] (Paris, Q1, female student, 30)

Among students, reciprocal T is the norm, as is the case between academic colleagues. The use of *tu* between colleagues is viewed by one of our participants as stemming from May 1968:

La plupart des enseignants se tutoient. Il y a quelques collègues qui sont très arc-boutés sur le 'vous', qui sont assez vieux jeu et qui refusent de se laisser tutoyer. Dans le milieu de l'enseignement il faut quand même savoir que le tutoiement entre profs c'est vraiment issu de mai 68 hein. Donc il y a beaucoup de gens qui sont très à droite par exemple [...] qui refusent la familiarité qui va avec les relations de mai 68.

[Most academics use *tu* with one another. There are some colleagues who are very dependent on *vous*, who are quite old-fashioned and refuse to be called *tu*. In the teaching sector, one needs to know that using *tu* between teachers really came out of May 68. So there are lots of very right-wing people, for example [...] who refuse the familiarity that goes with relationships [influenced by] May 68.] (Paris, Q3, female academic, 39)

Certain French universities have retained a reputation for using T. An example is Paris VIII, created shortly after May 1968. Using T is seen as a post-68 tradition, between teachers and also between teachers and the administration, and occasionally between teachers and students:

Ça arrive à l'université qu'il y a des enseignants qui tutoient les élèves hein. Encore une fois à Paris VIII par exemple ça se fait tout le temps. C'est surtout des mecs d'ailleurs qui sont très à l'aise, qui tutoient leurs étudiants, je pense. Peut-être moins les femmes encore que, c'est peut-être un cliché. Mais je me souviens des étudiants qui avaient été un peu choqués: qui n'aimaient pas trop être tutoyés, qui se sentaient enfantilisés.

[It happens at university that there are some teachers who use *tu* with the students. Again at Paris VIII for example, it happens all the time. It's mainly blokes who are very relaxed who use *tu* with their students, I think. Perhaps women [do it] less, although that's perhaps a cliché. But I remember students who were a little shocked: who didn't like being called *tu* too much, who felt infantilised.] (Paris, Q3, female academic, 39)

Not all universities shifted ground on address forms to the same extent in 1968 and its aftermath. One of our interviewees remembers that T was used among students only at the end of the 1960s, not between teachers and students in his law faculty:

Le tutoiement c'était uniquement entre les étudiants. C'était pas entre eux et les professeurs, même en troisième cycle. <Et c'était particulier à votre fac?> *Ah peut-être, peut-être que c'était autrement dans d'autres facultés. Moi c'était droit, sciences économiques, hein. Donc c'était sans doute très marqué par le fait: bon, il se trouve qu'en France, c'est peut-être pas le cas dans toutes les autres universités européennes, mais en France les sciences économiques ont été toujours enseignées dans les facultés de Droit et les traditions des [facultés] de Droit se sont imposées, y compris dans cette question.*

[Using *tu* was only between students. It wasn't between them and the teachers, even for postgraduates. <*And was that specific to your faculty?*> Perhaps, perhaps it was different in other faculties. I was in law, economics. So it was probably very marked by the fact: it just so happens that in France, it's perhaps the case in all other European universities, but in France economics has always been taught in law faculties and law faculty traditions have imposed themselves, in this area as well.] (Paris, Q3, male secondary school teacher, 62)

Between academic and administrative staff, address practices are varied, depending on habits or personal affinities. A university administrator also observes that at her workplace administrative staff are reminded not to be too familiar with students – *c'est pas des copains* ['they're not friends']. She herself uses honorifics only, without the last name, to address students, accompanied by *vous*:

Quand je reçois des étudiants, c'est 'Bonjour mademoiselle'. Pas juste bonjour, on met 'Bonjour mademoiselle'. On donne pas le nom.

[When students come and see me, I say 'Hello, *mademoiselle*'. Not just hello, we always say 'Hello, *mademoiselle*'. We don't use their last name.] (Paris, Q3, female administrator, 48)

4.3.2   German

Students in German-speaking countries address each other as T. Prior to the student movement of the late 1960s and early 1970s, students were generally on V terms unless they were special friends and that was not revealed in public situations such as university classes. Use of T across genders among students was usually indicative of only very close relationships. Nowadays, where there are exceptions to reciprocal T among students, they are marked, intended to indicate exclusion.

In response to the question 'How do/did you address your teachers at university? How do/did they address you?', 82% of those to whom it applied (130/159) chose reciprocal V, while 13% (20/159) reported variation between T,

V and non-reciprocal V–T (teacher to student T, student to teacher V). These proportions are corroborated by the interview data with current students or people who have recently completed their studies. A male student in his mid-twenties from Mannheim sums it up as follows: *Sie* is used with professors; with other academics address is negotiated individually, based on how close their contact is. T use and compromise forms are particularly common if the student is also working as a research assistant. Variation between T, V and non-reciprocal V–T seems to occur mainly when the relationship becomes closer (e.g. between PhD student and supervisor) or when there is a double relationship (e.g. the professor is at the same time lecturer and boss, a previous lecturer becomes boss or meetings take place both at and outside university):

Mit meinem Professor, der ist auch mein Chef, und wir duzen uns [...] Wenn er mich duzt, ist das ein Signal, dass man sich duzt [...] mein Professor hat das einfach gemacht. Wir haben uns gesiezt und ab den Tag, wo ich mit ihm gearbeitet hab, hat er einfach gesagt, 'Hallo André' und da war klar, dass wir uns duzen.

[With my professor who is my boss, and we call each other *du* [...] When he calls me *du*, it's a signal for us to use *du* [...] that's simply what my professor did. We were on *Sie* terms and from the day I started working with him, he just said, 'Hi André' and it was clear that we were on *du* terms.] (Leipzig, Q3, male research assistant, 27)

As mentioned in section 3.2, a common practice is for professors and lecturers to call their students *ihr* as a group but *Sie* individually and for the students to respond with *Sie*.

According to our Vienna focus group, in small departments such as African languages and in departments teaching foreign languages with less address differentiation than German (such as Dutch) or no such differentiation (English), T is sometimes exchanged between staff and students (see also 5.2.3). The practice of using T is also initiated in fieldwork in some disciplines, but hardly ever occurs in the natural sciences.

The way professors address each other varies according to their general disposition (see 3.6) and to a lesser extent the general practices of the department or faculty. Often there are different practices coexisting between different networks in a department or faculty. Junior academics tend to address each other as T and with FN. Again, modes of address between professors and junior staff will also vary. T relations are no longer suspended in status-marked situations such as conferences, seminars and faculty meetings or even formal speeches such as at formal retirement functions and prize giving but not in PhD examinations (PO).

Sometimes an informal and a formal mode (*Lieber, sehr geehrter Herr Z*) are coupled in formal presentations. Note the number of modes of address in the opening of Professor Ruth Wodak's speech at the function at which she was awarded the Verkauf-Verlot Prize in Vienna (23 June 2003):

Sehr geehrter Herr Präsident Fischer, lieber Heinz! Lieber Wolfgang Neugebauer; sehr geehrte Frau Verkauf-Verlot, sehr geehrte Damen und Herren, liebe Freundinnen und Freunde!

Here people are addressed by FN, hon + title + LN, hon + LN, or FN + LN, and by the formal and informal equivalents of *dear*, namely *Sehr geehrte/r* or *Liebe/r*. The President is addressed both formally as *Sehr geehrter Herr Präsident Fischer* and informally as *lieber Heinz*.

Professors and administrative staff will generally exchange V + hon + LN. However, non-reciprocal address often occurs between professors and research assistants, with the professor giving V + FN and receiving V + hon + LN. Participation observation suggests that if the professor and research assistant are both female, reciprocal FN is more likely to occur than where the professor is male, regardless of the sex of the research assistant. In participant observation, we witnessed a dispute on address in a research centre between a professor in his sixties and a number of researchers in their late twenties and thirties. The professor had offered the researchers reciprocal T but they had turned this down on the grounds that this suggested equal status, which was not the case.

Titles are generally dispensed with in communication between academic colleagues regardless of rank. This varies between German-speaking locations, as we will show in Chapter 5. However, titles are usually given in formal situations, especially in writing. This means hon + full titles: *Herr/Frau Professor Dr Merkel*. Thus in the university domain too German address is more complex and difficult to capture in rules than that of French.

4.3.3   Swedish

Up until the mid-1900s, it was customary for students to address academic staff in the third person by using their title in the definite form, e.g. *Professorn* ('the professor') or by title + LN (*Professor Granqvist*), while students would be addressed by the title *Kandidaten* ('the candidate') or by title + LN (*Kandidat Svensson*),[4] also avoiding direct address. However, our data show that in contemporary use reciprocal use of T and FN is normal between academic staff and students. Of the respondents who commented, 72% (84/116) indicate that they would use T to a university teacher and 70% (81/116) say that reciprocal T and FN would be the norm. Informants who report any other modes of address than T are almost exclusively older informants, referring to a time before the '*du*-reform'. Overall, there is very little discussion in our data about contemporary address practices between students and academic staff, which is an indication that address is seen as relatively straightforward. However, the few comments that were made originate exclusively from our

---

[4] For example, in the textbook *Learn Swedish* from 1961, one of the main protagonists is a student who is addressed and referred to as *Kandidat Svensson* (Norrby 1997).

Finland-Swedish data, as illustrated by the following quotation from the second Vaasa focus group:

(1) *Däremot så jag har haft problem när jag studerade här vid universitetet, att ska jag nia professorerna? Ända sen grundskolan och i gymnasiet var det så klart, alla var bara Lars och Roger och Anette, men sen då man kom hit så visste man inte, speciellt om man skrev e-post så visste man inte, för det syns det direkt hur har jag formulerat mig. [...] för man visste att det var professorer i språk, dom lusläser ju mina mejl alltså, så då var det lite knepigt.*

(2) *Nå vad gjorde du?*

(1) *Nå jag försökte förvränga det till passiva former så att det int sku duas eller nias.*

[(1) On the other hand I had problems when I studied here at the university, should I say *ni* to the professors? Ever since primary school and in senior high school it was so obvious, everybody was just Lars and Roger and Anete, but then when you came here then you didn't know, especially if you write emails you don't know, because it is directly visible how I have expressed myself. [...] because you knew that they were professors of languages, they scrutinise my emails you know, so then it was a bit tricky.

(2) Well, what did you do?

(1) Well, I tried to distort it into passive forms so that there wouldn't be either *du* or *ni*.]
(Vaasa, FG1, (1) female project assistant, 29; (2) female social worker, 62)

4.3.4   English

At English universities students traditionally (before the late 1960s) addressed academic staff by title (*Prof* or *Dr* but not both) or Hon + LN, if they did not have a title, and staff responded with hon (*Mr* or *Miss*) + LN. Now the most common practice is for staff and students to exchange FN. However, as our London focus group agreed, this is generally initiated by academics when introducing themselves. There are exceptions: some professors do not introduce themselves and there is a general belief that they wish to keep at a distance, as this excerpt from the Newcastle focus group demonstrates:

(1)   *Do you take your lead from how they introduce themselves to you?*

(2)   *I think so, yeah. They usually introduce themselves, like 'I'm Tony' or whoever. But never 'Mr'.*

(1)   *I always referred to lecturers by their first names and normally it seemed to be OK. But when I was in Northumberland we had a professor and it was 'Professor whatever'. I didn't really ever call him by his first name. Or we just like, didn't use anything really.*

Moderator *Do you think that was because he was a professor? Of a higher status?*

(1)   *Yeah, there was a feeling – he never said what to use and he didn't invite it – he was very pleasant and nice and that but it seemed to be that we just kept it very impersonal and didn't use anything.*

Moderator   Because the personal thing wasn't invited you thought.
(1)   Yeah, he was a little bit higher.
          (Newcastle, FG, (1) male IT project manager, 45; (2) female student, 29)

The FN used by the academic to address the student may however be the full form on the student list and not the abbreviated one preferred by the student, as is shown in the following quote, again from the Newcastle focus group:

But some lecturers, when I used to study, used to call me Thomas. Even though nobody calls me Thomas. And it used to annoy me because they'd obviously learnt my name off a sheet and they'd put photos and they'd identified 'Right, this is "Thomas"' and I found that really odd because I didn't have that same kind of familiarity with them and they were sort of assuming this. <Still it's nice that they went to the trouble to learn your name.> *Well, at least ask you, 'What's your name?' rather than come out with your name, so that the students would think, as if they'd read it off your mind.* <Did you ever say to them, 'Call me Tom'?> *No, they used to insist on calling me Thomas for months and months, and I never corrected them.* (Newcastle, FG, male English teacher, 25)

Thus, in the university domain, address between staff and students in English, as in Swedish, is more symmetrical than in French and German.

4.4   Workplace

4.4.1   French

French address is characterised by a differentiation between private and public domains, in particular between the intimate spaces of the family and close friends and the public spaces of the workplace. As one of our Paris focus group members puts it: *Dans le travail on change de personalité dès qu'on met notre veste* ('At work you change your personality as soon as you put on your jacket') (Paris, FG1, waiters' captain, 28).

Table 3.7 showed the role played by status in French workplaces. While 84% of our informants address their colleagues as T and only 24% use T to their superiors, 49% address their superiors as V and 16% of communication with superiors is non-reciprocal. The use of V + FN to workplace superiors is explicitly mentioned by 15 of the French participants. One, a child care worker, describes how she uses first names with her hierarchical superior but wants to keep on using *vous* to maintain a certain distance:

Le 'vous' met une barrière quand même. C'est pas ma copine, c'est ma supérieure hiérarchique donc le 'vous', j'y tiens. [...] On a réussi à s'appeler par nos prénoms. [...] Au début j'y arrivais pas du tout parce que je trouvais ça dur parce que devant les parents il faut dire le nom de famille. Et en dehors on disait le prénom. Donc, maintenant c'est bien, mais je veux garder le 'vous'. [...] <En fait, c'est le beau compromis.> *Voilà.*

[*Vous* puts up a barrier. She's not my friend, she's my hierarchical superior, so I'm very keen on *vous*. [...] We have managed to call each other by our first names. At the beginning, I couldn't do it at all because I found it hard, because in front of the parents we had to use last names. And outside that situation we used first names. So now, it's good, but I want to keep *vous*. […] <*In fact, it's the perfect compromise.*> That's right.] (Paris, Q6, female child care worker, 34)

In those workplaces where both T and V are used, some participants make the point that using V is a way of avoiding conflict. One of the participants in the Toulouse focus group considers that *vous* serves a protective function in that the work relationship with a superior is thus free of any personal involvement or engagement:

Le vouvoiement dans une relation hiérarchique c'est aussi une façon de pas vraiment s'impliquer dans la relation. [...] On se vouvoie, il y a tellement de distance entre nous que du coup c'est plus facile de résoudre les problèmes parce qu'il n'y a aucun engagement de l'individu.

[Using *vous* in a hierarchical relationship is also a way of not really becoming involved in the relationship. […] We use *vous* with each other, there is so much distance between us that it's easier to solve problems because there is absolutely no personal commitment from the individual.] (Toulouse, FG, male bookshop assistant, 27)

There are, however, particular workplaces cited by our French participants that are considered to be sites of T use. Computing, for example, is an area where the use of T is widespread. This use of T is also said to be influenced by communication patterns in the United States (see 5.7 on language contact).

The T workplace is also common in the social services domain – *tout le monde dans le social se tutoie* ('everyone in social services uses *tu* with one another') (Paris, Q7, public legal advisor, 24) – and the fashion and music industries and the media are all work environments where the norm is to adopt egalitarian values predicated on T. One Paris focus group participant, a fashion designer, says that there are no social, age or gender barriers in the fashion and music industries as far as use of pronouns is concerned. The use of T is accompanied by a set of behaviours which serve to reinforce intimacy, including kissing on the cheek and, as she says later, having physical contact. However, she doesn't find it easy to use T with everyone because it forces too great an intimacy:

C'est vrai qu'il y a plein choses qui vont avec le tutoiement. Il y a le fait de – et ça c'est hors âge. C'est tous âges et tous sexes confondus, et toutes nationalités etc., on se tutoie tous [...] on s'embrasse – les hommes s'embrassent, ils se serrent pas la main. [...] j'ai beaucoup de mal parce que c'est pas facile en fait forcément, de tutoyer tout le monde, parce que ça fait, laisser des barrières ou ça met une proximité, qui est un peu de la promiscuité finalement. Et c'est très artificiel.

[It's true that there are lots of things that go with using *tu*. There's the fact that – and this is with all age groups and all genders and all nationalities, etc., we all use *tu* with one another […] we kiss – the men kiss, they don't shake hands. […] I have a lot of difficulty with it because it's not necessarily easy in fact to use *tu* with everyone, because it means, dropping barriers or it creates a certain closeness, which is a little too intrusive in the end. And it's very artificial.] (Paris, FG1, female fashion designer, 32)

Changes in workplace address practices are noted by some participants. A particularly illuminating example comes from a secretary who has worked in the same bank for the past 30 years and who has noted greater use of *tu* among younger employees and the disappearance of titles:

A mon travail, [...] les jeunes qui arrivent tutoient plus facilement. Un homme de vingt-cinq ans travaille avec moi et sa secrétaire a cinquante-cinq ans. Il la tutoie. Ça me choque. Effectivement le tutoiement rentre de plus en plus. Je ne pense pas que ce soit un manque de respect. Nous, on nous demandait beaucoup de soumission. [...] <Avez-vous noté une différence avec l'emploi des titres?> *Au travail, quand j'étais jeune, on s'adressait à nos supérieurs hiérarchiques avec 'monsieur' et 'madame'. Aujourd'hui l'emploi du prénom est beaucoup plus commun, même lorsqu'il y a un vouvoiement. [...]* <Et à propos des titres composés, comme 'monsieur le directeur'?> *Ils sont utilisés de moins en moins. [...] Il y eu une certaine libéralisation, on ne dira plus 'monsieur le directeur'.*

[At my workplace, [...] the young people who arrive use *tu* more easily. A 25-year-old man works with me and his secretary is 55. He uses *tu* with her. That shocks me. In fact using *tu* is coming in more and more. I don't think that it's a lack of respect. We [my generation] were asked for a great deal of submission. [...] <*Have you noted a difference in the use of titles?*> At work, when I was young, we used to address our hierarchical superiors with *monsieur* and *madame*. Nowadays the use of first names is much more common, even when it's accompanied by *vous*. [...] <*And what about titles like monsieur le directeur?*> They are used less and less. [...] There has been a certain amount of liberalisation, no one would say *monsieur le directeur* any more.] (Paris, Q5, female secretary, 49)

Certain workplace relations were influenced by the events of May 1968 and its aftermath. One participant recalls that when she was first employed as a domestic in a bourgeois family at the end of the 1960s, the family invited her to use *tu* with them:

C'était l'époque où au lycée on se disait voilà tous pareils, tous égaux, tous frères, tous bourgeois, ouvriers, et tout. Je pense qu'on a pu y croire a l'époque. Moi je sais que je me rappelle avoir travaillé comme employée de maison avec des jeunes qui étaient universitaires à l'époque, d'une famille très très aisée. Pour eux, on devait se tutoyer. Bon ils me l'ont demandé, j'ai eu beaucoup de mal. Je les ai tutoyés parce que c'était l'époque. Mais franchement, personnellement, voilà, hein, j'étais employée, je m'occupais de leurs gamins, et il y avait quelque chose qui me plaisait pas, mais l'époque voulait qu'on se tutoie. On a eu des discussions en effet, même si je crois ils ont admis aussi le fait que c'était un peu [...] utopiste quoi. On y a cru, je pense, en effet hein, tous frères, tous bourgeois et tout, oui.

[It was the time when at school we proclaimed ourselves to be all the same, all equal, all brothers, bourgeois, workers and everything. I think that we managed to believe it at the time. I know that I remember having worked as a domestic employee for some young academics from a very very well-off family. As far as they were concerned, we had to use *tu* with each other. Well, they asked me, I had a lot of difficulty with it. I used *tu* with them because of the times. But quite honestly, personally, I was an employee, I was looking after their kids, and there was something about it that I didn't like, but the times required us to use *tu* with one another. We had discussions about it in fact, even though I think they admitted that it was a little [...] utopian. We believed in it all, I think, all brothers, all bourgeois, and everything.] (Paris, Q2, female educator, 57)

She goes on to say that by the mid-1970s, everything had returned to the way it had been, at least based on her own experience, with *vous* making a return at the same time as hierarchies and ingrained habits, laid down by education, re-established themselves.

4.4.2   German

A person's status within the workplace/institution generally determines the address patterns in German, although not as much as for French. In German, colleagues are more likely to be addressed as T and superiors less likely to be addressed as V than in French, and non-reciprocal address is less prevalent. As in French, there are particular occupations characterised by universal T or rapid transition to T. These include music, especially pop music, electronic and print media, theatre, social work and sport.

For many other workers, however, the workplace has also become a domain of T + FN use in German. They may employ *du* as an aid to rapid communication – *Arbeitsstress tötet das kumpelhafte 'Du'* ('Work stress kills off the *du* of mateship') (Leipzig, FG1, male IT manager, 29). Members of the police and the clergy report the use of T to express collegiality, as do bank employees, except (in at least some cases) within earshot of customers. As a retired bank manager puts it:

In der Bank ist man nicht gewöhnt, dass sich die Schalterbeamten duzen.
[In the bank you (the customers) are not accustomed to the tellers calling each other *du*.] (Mannheim, FG1, male retired bank manager, 65)

On building sites, builders and other tradesmen exchange T + name of occupation, which denotes their status within the workplace, e.g. *Du Schlosser, komm mal her* ('Hey, carpenter, come here'); '*Du Baumeister, wo bist du?*' ('Hey, builder, where are you?') (PO). Informants from all research sites indicate that workers of all ages and status levels in the building trade exchange T. The same applies on the factory floor. One young Mannheim man reports being corrected on his first casual factory job when he addressed someone as V.

While the workplace for many is a domain of T + FN, in workplaces with strong hierarchies V is employed at least to and by superiors. Examples reported by our informants are hospitals, where the head doctor exchanges V with everyone below him/her; some companies, where departmental heads are addressed by V; the law, where judges and lawyers are addressed by V; and the German army, where V is the general pronoun of address. This is in contrast to the Austrian army, where officers are on T terms (see Chapter 5). Nurses in hospitals are addressed as *Schwester* (Sister) + FN, with either T or V, and T is now increasingly exchanged with doctors (except the doctor in charge, who exchanges V with everyone below him/her in the hierarchy). T is used especially on night duty, *weil man sehr stark auf einander angewiesen ist* ('because everyone is heavily dependent on one another') (Mannheim, Q1, female teacher and former nurse, 40).

A number of superordinates in the workplace drew attention to the need to preserve V as the pronoun of social distance between the boss and his/her subordinates to offer mutual protection in the case of conflict, as was the case for French. Several commented that terms of abuse such as *Arschloch* [arsehole] and *Trottel* [fool] are more easily collocated with *du* than with *Sie*! A female psychologist from Leipzig presented her position as follows:

Dort wo ich den Chef spiele, möchte ich mit 'Sie' angesprochen werden. [...] Da versteh ich auch meinen Chef, warum er das 'Sie' hat. Das ist ein gewisse Distanz, eine gesunde Arbeitsdistanz vielleicht...die Nähe kann schon Energie fressen.
[Where I play the boss, I want to be addressed with *Sie*. […] Then I understand why my boss has *Sie*. It is a certain distance, a healthy work distance perhaps… proximity can eat up energy.] (Leipzig, Q2, female psychologist, 30)

Some informants from Mannheim over a range of occupations felt that whether V works across hierarchical levels depends on the individuals concerned:

Entweder ich habe den Respekt oder ich habe ihn nicht, da tut das 'Sie' oder 'Du' keinen Abbruch.
[Either I have respect or I don't. *Sie* or *du* doesn't change that.] (Mannheim, Q7, male cleaner, 38)

There is also a dimension of economic management in choice of mode of address. One of our Mannheim focus group, the *Hausmeister* (janitor) of a research institute, aged in his 50s, indicated that he would use V with tradesmen to accentuate social distance and thereby ensure that he could obtain the best services from them:

Wenn ich einen Installateur oder jemanden im Haus habe, ... Handwerker, die wissen ja, dass alle Handwerker irgendwo Handwerker sind, da würde man sich duzen. Da mache ich es natürlich nicht, da halt ich Abstand auf sie, weil ich muss ja anschließend die Arbeit begutachten und muss die Studentenzettel unterschreiben und das bedeutet ja für die bares Geld und da ist es für mich einfacher wenn ich mit den Leuten per 'Sie' bleibe.
[If I have a plumber in the building, … tradesmen, they do know that all tradesmen somehow are tradesmen so you would call each other *du*. I don't do that of course, I keep some distance from them because afterwards I have to assess their work and sign their time sheets and that does mean cash for them and it is simpler for me if I remain on *Sie* terms with them.] (Mannheim, FG1, male janitor, mid-50s)

Mixed forms such as T and hon + LN can be attributed to different functions expressed by the pronoun and the nominal. A message often heard over the public address system in department stores is of the type: *Frau Müller, du wirst zur Kasse gebeten* (PO) ('Ms Müller, you (T) are asked to come to the checkout'). The *du* is the pronoun used by fellow employees at the store (expressing low social distance) and *Frau Müller* is the name by which the employee is known to the public (expressing high social distance and the status of a shop assistant). In Germany, most shop assistants wear nametags with their last names. This is believed to give them the kind of anonymity that their English-speaking counterparts enjoy with their first names. The combination of T and title in Austria is discussed in section 5.4.1.

The dominant view expressed in our focus groups and in our interviews is that staff in workplaces should decide on their modes of address by consensus and not have them imposed. Some Leipzig and Mannheim focus group participants told stories of how the imposition of *du* (including in American companies) *hat sich nicht durchgesetzt* ('has failed to get through') (Mannheim, FG1, male janitor, mid-50s).

4.4.3   Swedish

Both questionnaire and interview data clearly show that T is the norm in the Swedish-speaking workplace today, both among colleagues and in interactions with superiors. A significant indicator is the fact that the moderators had to rephrase the interview question 'How would you react if your professor or work superior suddenly addressed you by T?' to read '...by V?' to make any sense to participants.

Nowadays T is also used among colleagues and to superiors in traditionally formal and hierarchical workplaces such as hospitals, the police force and courts of law. However, the formal context of the courtroom can still be a reason for not employing T (see further discussion in section 4.8 on moving between domains). Furthermore, as pointed out in section 3.5.3, use of FN to very senior and superior staff in such contexts is not unproblematic either.

In the questionnaire data 98% (cf. Table 3.10) claimed to use reciprocal T with work colleagues over a wide range of occupations and almost as many (135/140, 96%) reported that they would exchange T + FN. In the interview data, where informants were asked to comment on address practices at workplaces where they had worked, the reported level of T is, however, somewhat lower than in the questionnaires – as outlined in Table 4.3, 76% report using T always. However, as Table 4.3 shows, the use of V in the workplace mostly concerns the transactional domain – addressing clients and customers. This will be discussed further in 4.5.3.

Table 4.3 *Swedish:* du *or* ni *in the workplace*

Address form	%
du	76
Varies with the situation	6
Ni to customers, clients	12
Ni (about the past)	5
Ni in the military	1
Ni to elderly patients	<1
3rd-pers address to elderly patients	<1
(N)	(140)

4.4.4   English

As with the other languages, workplaces using English have established address practices, whether agreed or imposed, although the variation will be in nominal, not pronominal, forms. FN is generally the norm for communication between colleagues, as discussed in the London focus group (see also 3.1.2):

I was just thinking about formality and how often or not you use it. I'm twenty-four and I don't think there's one job I've ever had where everybody's addressed each other as 'Mr' or 'Sir'. I've never called a boss anything other than their first name, ever. (London, FG, male student, 23)

In workplaces such as hospitals, where it is possible to use 'doctor' or 'nurse' to address staff, there seem to be various practices at work. A member of the Newcastle focus group comments on the changed address patterns, with nurses no longer being called 'nurse' but like doctors and others across ranks being called by FN:

Yes, quite a bit has changed. When I was first a nurse I used to get addressed as 'nurse' on the ward, when I was a student nurse. But before I retired, if ever I was in a situation where I was on the ward and addressing a patient I used to get called by my first name. So that was never done then. You were always addressed as 'nurse'. So it's gradually changed over the years and it did take a little bit of getting used to but I think it's probably better for the patients. <That was the patients as well?> Yes, that was the patients. And staff do – junior staff address senior staff by their first names. That took some getting used to. (Newcastle, FG, female retired nurse, 63)

In contrast, a nurse in her 30s from London reports that she does get addressed as 'nurse', something that she resents:

In nursing it can be very irritating because people call you 'nurse' or call out 'nurse'. They won't acknowledge you as even a person. So you have to try and make them, you know, call you your name. (London, FG, female nurse, 33)

As part of the introduction routine in English, it is possible to indicate how one prefers to be addressed and this also plays a role in determining address practices at work, as the following examples from Newcastle show:

I always just call myself Sandra Buck. (Newcastle, FG, female school administrator, 51)

I call myself Mrs Babbage. If anyone asks me who I am, I'll say 'Mrs Babbage' if it's somebody I don't know. But when I was at work, when I was getting professional documents through the post, it was always 'Ms Babbage'. (Newcastle, female retired nurse, 63)

4.5   The transactional domain

In this section we will be focusing on service encounters, but since they occur in a workplace, the boundary with section 4.4 is not always rigid. Hospitals, for instance, are a work domain and a transactional one too in that staff in hospitals also interact with patients and their families.

4.5.1   *French*

All our interview participants reported using V in service encounters and in interactions with the police. An older woman sums up the situation as follows:

En France, c'est le 'vous' qui est naturel. Que ce soit l'administration, les autorités, les responsables. Le commissariat de police à côté, je vais lui demander quelque chose, je vais lui dire 'vous'.
[In France, it's *vous* that's natural. Whether it's administration, authorities, people in charge. The police station next door, [if] I'm going to ask them something, I'm going to say *vous*.] (Paris, Q2, female retired social worker, 75)

In addition, the default nature of *vous* in shops is described as a mark of respect by one participant: *dans les magasins, c'est normal, ils disent 'vous', parce que c'est une marque de respect pour ses clients* ('in shops, it's normal, they say *vous*, because it's a mark of respect for one's clients') (Paris, Q5, male student, 22). The importance of respect was also noted by participants who volunteered in a soup kitchen, when addressing 'beneficiaries':

Avec les bénéficiaires, il y a toujours un vouvoiement, je les respecte. Pour moi c'est un respect envers: ils font déjà le premier pas de se retrouver à faire la queue pour avoir ces repas et je vois pas pourquoi j'irais les tutoyer, donc je reste toujours très poli avec eux.
[With the beneficiaries, it's always *vous*, I respect them. For me it's respect towards: they are already taking the first step in finding themselves queuing up for meals and I don't see why I would go and use *tu* with them, so I always remain very polite with them.] (Paris, Q2, male maintenance technician, 54)

While all of the French informants indicated that they expected to address and be addressed by shop assistants with V, a minority (10/72, 14%) indicated that they would use T with shop assistants in shops that they frequent regularly. Interestingly, all informants who report use of T here, except one, were male and of these males all except one were young (between 20 and 33 years of age).

The type of shop or appearance and age of the shop assistant might mean a shift towards T. In the following example, the practice of being called *tu* in record shops actually influenced the participant's own use of *tu*:

Je me souviens aussi que ça me faisait drôle lorsque dans les magasins de disques on me tutoyait plus facilement. Au début ça m'a fait drôle. Maintenant des fois c'est moi-même qui vais tutoyer ou dire 'Salut', un truc vraiment familier, alors qu'avant je ne le faisais pas. <Pourquoi ce changement alors?> *C'est la pratique je crois, le fait d'aller dans des magasins où on me tutoyait, ça m'a fait me sentir bien. C'est eux qui m'ont mis à l'aise en me tutoyant.*

[I remember too that it was odd when in record shops they used *tu* with me more easily. At first it struck me as odd. Now sometimes I'm the one who is going to use *tu* or say 'Hi', something really colloquial, whereas before I wouldn't do it. *<So why this change?>* It's the practical experience I think, the fact of going to shops where I was called *tu*, it made me feel good. They're the ones who made me feel at ease by calling me *tu*.] (Paris, Q9, accountant, 33)

The use of V-like modes, *monsieur* and *madame*, in encounters in shops is also remarked upon. One participant, who works in a women's clothing section of a prestigious department store, explains the complexities of knowing when and how to address a prospective client:

Il y a des clientes qu'on ne saluera pas, tout simplement parce qu'on voit très bien qu'elles sont là: qu'elles vont passer cinq secondes sur le stand et qu'elles vont repartir. On le sent. Il y a des personnes auxquelles on va dire 'Bonjour' tout court. 'Bonjour madame', ça va vraiment dépendre du feeling par rapport à ces personnes-là. C'est un magasin qui est un petit peu chic, il y a des personnes à hauts revenus qui passent par là. Et bon il faut toujours être souriant, toujours être poli, et parfois aller saluer une cliente peut l'importuner. Il est très très fréquent qu'on dise 'Bonjour madame' à quelqu'un qui est à cinquante centimètres de soi et que la personne ne réponde pas. [...] Il faut essayer de dire à la personne ce qu'elle a envie d'entendre et parfois 'Bonjour madame' pourra paraître un peu trop obséquieux à certaines personnes. Parfois on se trompe. [...] Mais au final, c'est du feeling, toutes les clientes sont différentes.

[There are [female] clients who you will not address, quite simply because you can see that they are going to spend five seconds in the section and they're going to leave again. You can feel it. There are people to whom you say a simple *Bonjour*. *Bonjour madame*, that's going to really depend on your feeling about these people. It's rather a chic store, there are people with high incomes who pass through. And you always have to be smiling, always polite, and sometimes going and greeting a female client can bother them. It happens very often that you say *Bonjour madame* to someone who's fifty centimetres away from you and she doesn't reply. [...] You have to try and say what the person wants to hear and sometimes *Bonjour madame* can appear a little too obsequious. [...] But in the end, it's about feeling, all clients are different.] (Paris, Q10, male sales assistant, 26)

4.5.2   German

Service encounters in German are also a strongly reciprocal V context:

In jeglicher geschäftlichen Beziehung gilt es prinzipiell, einander zu siezen, gleich welches Alter.
[In every business relationship the rule applies in principle to use *Sie* to one another, regardless of age.] (Vienna, Q10, male student, 26)

Only around 10% of the informants expect to be addressed with T, even in shops where they shop regularly. There is only a slight difference between regular and casual customers. In the former case, 17 informants (9%) report reciprocal T and there are a minimal number of instances of other modes of address.

There is variation between reciprocal T or V, avoidance (due to uncertainty) and non-reciprocal modes of address. Reciprocal T is to a large extent age dependent – of the 17 German-speaking participants who employ it, eight are aged between 21 and 30, six are in their thirties and only three are over 40. Reciprocal T is reported to be over-proportionately employed in alternative shops, internet cafés and sports stores (where the interlocutors are in the same age group). Some informants resent the lowering of social distance by the use of T on the part of salespeople, as the following quotations illustrate:

Mir fallen Situationen ein, wo's mich mehr stört, dass ich mit 'Du' angeredet werde und da würd' ich lieber gesiezt werden, [...] z.B. wenn ich in ein Geschäft gehe oder was kaufen will und ich geduzt werde, obwohl das ja quasi wie eine Art Vertrag ist, den man abschließt, [...] wo ich viel Geld ausgebe, da möcht ich eigentlich gesiezt werden.
[I can think of situations where I'd be more annoyed to be called *du*, I'd prefer to be addressed as *Sie* in such situations, […] for example when I go to a shop or I want to buy something and I'm addressed as *du*, even if that's just like a sort of contract one is entering into, […] where I'm spending a lot of money, that is where I'd actually like to be addressed as *Sie*.] (Leipzig, Q1, female PhD student, 26)

Wenn es förmlich ist, wenn es um einen Vertrag geht, kann ich es überhaupt nicht leiden, wenn man sich mit 'du' anspricht, weil man dann in so eine unformale Ebene fällt, wo es immer ganz schwer ist, seine Interessen durchzusetzen. Ein Beispiel ist, ich wollte ein Auto kaufen, da kam der Mann zu mir und sagte, was für ein tolles Auto es wär und 'du' und so, das war in diesem Moment extrem unpassend. Das war ein seriöses Geschäft, da möchte man sich nicht duzen [...] ich hab ihn zurückgesiezt, aber er hat mich geduzt. Das war ein eigenartiger Mensch. Das war unangenehm.
[In a formal situation, when it's about a contract, I just can't stand this mutual addressing with *du*, because it makes you fall on such an informal level where it is always really hard to maintain one's own interest. For example, I wanted to buy a car, and this man came to me and told me what a super car it was and [he called me] *du* and so, that was extremely inappropriate in that instance. It was a serious commercial transaction, one does not want to use *du* there […] I addressed him with *Sie*, but he continued addressing me with *du*. That was a peculiar person. It was annoying.] (Leipzig, Q3, male PhD student, 26)

This concurs with the janitor in section 4.4.2, who used V to tradesmen to avoid mateship for economic reasons.

In hospital situations, the general rule is for nurses and patients to exchange V, although nurses are traditionally addressed as *Schwester* [sister] FN, or *Pfleger* [male nurse] FN. There are changes in progress and one nurse in her thirties in a Mannheim hospital reported introducing herself as *Schwester* FN to older patients and *Frau* + LN to younger ones. There are instances of T exchange between a nurse and a patient, as is discussed by a Mannheim male nurse who contrasts communication in a general hospital with that in a psychiatric one:

Im Normalkrankenhaus gibt es oft, wenn man sich gut versteht, dass sich Pflege und Patienten duzen, es heisst ja auch Schwester Rosa oder Pfleger Peter oder sowas, das gibts bei uns nicht, die reden uns mit Nachnamen und 'Sie' an, auch um diese Konfliktgeschichte besser austragen zu können, [...] und wenn ein Patient mich verletzen will oder ärgern will, dann duzt er mich als erstes, das ist meistens das erste Mittel um auszudrücken, also du bist ja sowieso nur ein kleiner Pfleger und du hast mir gar nichts zu sagen, und dann duzen die.

[In a normal hospital it often happens that the nursing staff and patients use *du* when they get on well, it's Sister Rosa and Nurse Peter or something like that, we don't have that, they address us by our last name and *Sie*, also to better settle conflicts [...] and if a patient wants to hurt or annoy me, the first thing they do is to call me *du*, that's usually the first means to express – well, you're only a little nurse anyway and you have no right to say anything to me and then they use *du.*] (Mannheim, Q1, male nurse, 40)

4.5.3   Swedish

Our Swedish respondents to the questionnaire indicate a clear trend towards addressing staff in service encounters by T, particularly in a shop where the informant is a regular customer and thus is familiar with the staff. Some 96.5% report reciprocal T in this situation. Even in service encounters where the interlocutors are not familiar with one another, reciprocal T is by far the most frequent pattern (54.9%), but as can be gleaned from Table 4.4, there is a greater expectation of V address from staff towards customers.

In contrast to the generally strong position of T in Swedish, 20% of the informants (28/142) expect non-reciprocal address, with the shop assistant giving V, at least sometimes, while the customer uses T (or possibly plural V in a collective sense, i.e. addressing the shop as an establishment). This result supports the claim that V is making a re-entry into service encounters – the 'new *ni*' where (usually young) shop assistants address their (usually older) customers by V (Mårtensson 1986). The majority of the informants in Gothenburg who reported having been addressed by V also mentioned however that such address caused negative feelings. Use of V in service encounters is seen by them as *hysteriskt [...] löjligt* ('hysterical [...] silly') (male prosecutor, 33), which

Table 4.4 *Swedish: use of V in service encounters – unfamiliar shop assistant*

	%
T–T*	55
V–V	11
V–T	8
T–V	7
T–T/V	11
V (pl)–T	3
V–T/V	1
T/V–V	2
T–ø	1
(N)	(142)

* T–T, etc.: letter to the left indicates participant's reported use, letter to the right indicates how the shop assistant is expected to respond.

results in a *komisk effekt* ('comical effect') (female journalist and shop assistant, 29). Some participants give very colourful illustrations on how they react to the 'service-encounter V', as illustrated by the following quotation:

[Tilltalad med *ni*] *av äckliga unga manliga – och kvinnliga – expediter i tjusiga, dyra affärer. Jag blir kränkt [...] inte trevligt, känns oerhört fånigt och förlegat, det har ju varit en du-reform [...] De försöker ställa sig in, de har gått nån tretimmars försäljningsskola där de fått lära sig att det är fint.*
  [Addressed by *ni*] by disgusting young male – and female – shop assistants in fashionable, expensive shops. I feel humiliated [...] not nice, feels extremely silly and outdated, there has been a *du*-reform after all [...] They try to grease up to you, they have taken some three-hour sales school where they have learnt that it is good behaviour.] (Gothenburg, Q8, female prosecutor, 31)

The use of V in service encounters also has to do with age, in that an old person is more likely to be addressed with V than a middle-aged or younger person (see discussion in 3.4.3). However, the use of V in service encounters is not restricted to addressing very old customers. In one restaurant where one of the authors (female, mid-forties) was having dinner with a friend, she was addressed with *ni* by the waitress at a time when she was alone at the table. Curious to know whether the waitress had addressed her only or the dinner party collectively (i.e. *ni* in a plural sense), she explained the project to the waitress, who responded to her query about the use of *ni* with *Jag skulle ha sagt ni till dig med* ('I would have said V to you (T, obj.) too') which rather neatly sums up the use of service encounter *ni* in Sweden today. If it is used at all, it happens only as long as the situation is purely transactional. When the waitress was talking to the researcher about it the situation was that of two equals discussing something and *du* and *dig* were the only possible pronouns to use. The service encounter *ni* is a thin social veneer, which disappears as soon as the participant roles change ever so slightly.

Occasionally a customer in an exclusive business may be addressed as *min herre* ('Sir') – see also 3.5.3 on status – or a waitress might be called *fröken* ('miss') by a customer:

Jag jobbar som servitris så var det en svensk, relativt ung man (mellan trettio och fyrtio), och han hade en liten dotter på max. två år, som ville att jag skulle ta hans tallrik från bordet och sa 'Ursäkta mig, fröken'. Då fick man lite bekräftelse att man inte bara var en städmänniska, utan att man hade ett yrke. [Att bli kallad fröken] känns ju lite fint, för att man inte är van vid det här hemifrån. När det kommer en svensk och säger fröken till mig – det skulle inte funka om han kom och sa det när jag hade mina vanliga kläder, för då hade jag väl undrat vad han var för skum typ, men just när jag var i mitt yrke hade rätt kläder på mig och var i rätt roll, då var det väldigt bra.

[I work as a waitress so there was a Swede, relatively young man (between 30 and 40), and he had a little daughter of max two years, who wanted me to take his plate from the table and said, 'Excuse me *fröken*'. Then I felt a bit of acknowledgement that you are not just a cleaning person, but you have a profession. To be called *fröken* feels a bit exclusive, because you are not used to that kind of thing from home. When there is a Swede who says *fröken* to me – it wouldn't work if it was when I had my normal clothes, cause then I would have wondered what kind of dodgy type he was, but just when I was in my profession and had the right type of clothes and was in the right role, then it was really great.] (Gothenburg, Q3, female cleaner, 25)

The quotation above also demonstrates the importance of context in interpreting modes of address. Being addressed as *fröken* when working as a waitress, this particular participant feels that it is both positive and appropriate, while this is not the case in another context.

Overall, there is very little information in the Swedish data on the use of FN versus hon + LN, probably because hon + LN is archaic, at least in Sweden, and in the work domain FN is generally the norm (see 4.4.3). Use of FN can be an indicator of intimacy (real or perceived), as our focus group data show (see 5.7.3 for further discussion). Use of FN in the transactional domain, by salespeople and telemarketers for example, is designed to lower social distance and create a sense of commonalities between the parties. For example, we have observed how a large Swedish company, in its guidelines on customer care, instructs its staff to always address clients by FN in order to build a relationship with them. The strong trend towards T + FN could also be explained by the fact that honorifics such as *Herr* ('Mr'), *Fru* ('Mrs') and *Fröken* ('Miss') are, with few exceptions, rapidly disappearing, at least in Sweden. One exception we noted concerned online booking of plane tickets. The Swedish site of Scandinavian Airlines requires customers to choose between *Herr*, *Fru* and *Fröken* and then FN + LN.

Table 4.5 *Swedish: opinion of companies such as IKEA prescribing* du

Opinion	%
Fine	61
Fine generally, but some reservations	13
Not appropriate	4
Not good – *ni* to older	6
Not good – should be up to the salesperson	11
Advertising ploy	2
No opinion	2
(N)	(142)

While T and FN is the norm among colleagues (see 4.4.3) such as doctors and nurses, participant observation in a Swedish hospital reveals that there is some ambivalence in how to address and talk about staff with patients and visitors. For example, on a large board in a ward there was information about the medical staff working on that particular day. Nurses, nurse aids and physiotherapists were all referred to by FN whereas doctors were always referred to by FN + LN. While one explanation could be that doctors are not there as much as nurses and nurse aids and therefore are referred to by their full name, this does not explain why physiotherapists – who come only a few times a week – were referred to by FN only. We noted, however, that when staff spoke to patients or their relatives, they referred to the doctors by first name only. A nurse telling a relative of a patient *Det får du fråga Hans om* ('You'll have to ask Hans about that') was confusing, and when the nurse noticed this she clarified that Hans was the doctor.

In comparison with the widely held position among English and German speakers (cf. also Chapter 3) that people should have some say in how they are addressed by others, Swedish speakers are generally positive towards companies, such as IKEA, which prescribe use of T in interactions with their customers. As Table 4.5 shows, 61% of informants (mainly in Gothenburg) are positive and another 13% (all in Vaasa) support this with some reservations. We will discuss differences between Sweden and Finland in Chapter 5.

4.5.4   English

In the transactional domain, the mode of address in English is often a formal one, with the shop assistant addressing the customer as *Sir* or *Madam/Ma'am*. This changes to a more informal mode of address once a degree of familiarity is established. It is not a binary choice, however, because there can be a further gradual progression from *Mr, Mrs* or *Ms X* to FN. For instance, one London informant says he starts calling a client by FN 'when I've developed a relationship with that client' (London FG, male mortgage broker, 34).

Because *Sir/Madam* is a mode of address that expresses social distance, it can also be a strategy to politely distance oneself from one's interlocutor's side of the argument, as illustrated by the following excerpt from the London focus group.

(1) I was thinking, the only time since school that I've kind of ever heard the word 'Sir' used was in my last job in a call centre. The only time 'Sir' was ever really used was when people would phone up and [...] if they were kind of being rude on the phone, people would suddenly [...] call the customers 'Sir' or 'Madam', kind of almost in a quite disdainful and disparaging way. Like 'Yes Sir', 'I understand Sir', 'but Sir', that kind of thing. And that was the only time I ever heard the word 'Sir' being used formally at work. It wasn't really formal anyway.

(2) It's a kind of distancing thing.

(1) Not necessarily – yeah, distance but in a kind of quite disparaging way.

(3) That's quite interesting because I worked in a shop for a long time and it was often me, that if [...] somebody had a complaint and they were losing it, then it would often be me who would deal with it. [...] But, quite often, I would use 'Sir'. And you can use it in loads of different ways. It's a really useful word. You can use it in that way to sort of say 'I'm using this word "Sir" because you are taking the piss'. But it can also be used really as a way of dampening and calming and de-escalating a situation. [...] And it can really be used in lots of different ways to control a situation where somebody is behaving, or about to behave, really badly. And you can use the word to draw them back to a space where you're treating them respectfully and so you expect them to treat you respectfully. You're taking them and leading them to a different space just by the use of the word.

(London, FG, (1) male student, 24; (2) male solicitor, 34; (3) male student, 35)

4.6   Medium: letters

One of the interview questions explored how participants would start a letter to someone they didn't know. For *French*, the answer was nearly categorical: *Monsieur/Madame* and *vous* in the body of the letter. A very small number of respondents discussed other forms such as *Cher monsieur/chère madame* or hon + title. In the following example, one participant, a lawyer in his early thirties, makes an additional distinction between workplace and personal usage. In the former, he might use more formal expressions that include the addressee's function, such as *Monsieur le directeur*, whereas in the latter he appreciates the neutral nature of *Monsieur*:

J'aurais une tendance à donner systématiquement du Monsieur [...] en dehors du travail. Parce que j'apprécie beaucoup le côté neutre de Monsieur. Son titre finalement je m'en fous, on a tous des titres. Je ne vais pas écrire 'Monsieur le rammasseur des poubelles', alors pourquoi je dirais 'Monsieur le juge'? Ça me gêne de mettre en avant le statut social.

[I would have a tendency to systematically use *Monsieur* [...] outside work. Because I much appreciate the neutral side of *Monsieur*. In the end, I don't give a damn about titles, we all have titles. I'm not going to write *Monsieur le rammasseur des poubelles'* ['Mr Garbage Collector'], so why would I say *Monsieur le juge* ['Mr Judge']? It bothers me to put the emphasis on social status.] (Paris, Q3, male lawyer, 32, P3M2)

In *German*, nearly two thirds of interviewees (121/192, 63%) reported using the formal head, *Sehr geehrte/r*, with either *Damen* or *Herren* or *Frau X/Herr X* in letters to people they do not know well. Twenty reported they would alternate this with the less formal *Liebe/r* and two would always use the latter form. The other heads reportedly employed in letters to people you don't know well included *Hallo* (fifteen mentions), a common form in emails. In *Swedish*, address practices in this medium are clearly more informal, with *Hej* ('hello', 'hi') on its own the most frequent response (43/155, 28%). Thirteen additional participants report using *Hej* followed by either FN or FN + LN. The second most common response is *Bästa* ('dear'; literally 'best') + title + LN (17/155, 11%). Address practices are also more varied, with twenty different categories of response. There are interesting differences between the Swedish sites, which are discussed in 5.5.2.

English offers *Dear* as the common greeting in letters, but a distinction between *Sir/Madam*, hon or title + LN, and FN is made according to familiarity and formality. Several participants in the London focus group bring up non-reciprocal address patterns that sometimes emerge in letter writing and the irritation or discomfort such discrepancies might cause:

When the Labour Party got in again in '97 my father wrote a letter to Tony Blair congratulating him and saying how pleased he was and especially with the things he'd done. And I assume he wrote the letter 'Dear Mr Blair' but he would have signed it 'Mike Wells'. And he got a response, it was addressed 'Dear Mike', and I think it actually said 'Love Tony' at the bottom (much laughing), or something. Anyway, it definitely said 'Tony' and something very familiar and my dad was absolutely outraged that he'd sort of made such a kind of mis-return of this form of address. <So your dad was unimpressed by that, was he?> Yeah, yeah. He thought, you know, that Tony had written back and called my dad 'Mike' and called himself 'Tony', which was suddenly trying to make it very informal and pally and matey and it wasn't at all what he was. (London, FG, female student nurse, 29)

In the example above the focus group participant interprets the informality of Mr Blair as a conscious act of minimising social distance. However, others in the London focus group give examples of how they themselves refrain from titles and sign off with FN + LN, only to receive a reply in which they are addressed formally with hon + LN:

I've always wanted to be known as John Smythe and I sign all my documents, all my letters, I never put a title. And yet it doesn't matter how frequently I do that, I get the address back as 'Mr'. And it may be something to do with the grey hair, I don't know. I don't mind people addressing me as John Smythe at all. But in the main I find the cultural pattern still maintains that formality about 'Mr'. (London, FG, male retired secondary school teacher, 77)

The Irish focus group discussion reveals that the shift from spoken to written language can occasion a higher incidence of formal address (hon or title + LN):

(1)   *Well when I first got my PhD I wanted people to know I was a doctor but it does not matter so much. I think it's about tradition. It's the way it goes.*
(2)   *We'd never call our lecturers 'Dr' but you'd write it on essays and stuff.*
Moderator   *That's interesting – so you would write 'Mr' or 'Mrs' or 'Dr'?* [General agreement.]
(3)   *That's right. I would always put 'Mr' or 'Ms' even on an envelope.*
                     (Tralee, FG, (1) male university lecturer, 40s; (2) male student, 19; (3) female librarian, 30s)

In summary, the address systems in letters to strangers follow similar patterns to those in verbal communication first encounters. French prefers V; so does German but with the T-like *Liebe/r* ('dear') starting to encroach on the formal mode *Sehr geehrte/r*. Swedish opts for the informal *Hej* ('hi', 'hello'), sometimes followed by FN or FN + LN. English combines the single greeting *Dear*, corresponding to U, with either V-like forms (*Sir/Madam* or hon + LN) or T-like ones (FN).

4.7   Medium: computer-mediated communication

As explained in Chapter 2, we used existing chat groups (discussion forums) to ascertain how members perceived modes of address in computer-mediated communication in French, German and Swedish. In addition to observing how members of a chat group actually addressed one another, we were interested in exploring the following topics, which we asked the web master of each selected discussion forum to post for discussion on their forum:

1. Are there perceptions of a difference in modes of address online and offline, or within different areas of the web – in emails, in chat groups and in interactive blogs?
2. Have such perceptions, to your knowledge, become topics of discussion in other chat groups – regarding the use in the chat group itself, in other chat groups, or in off-line communication?
3. Is there a perception of different use of address forms (both on-line and off-line) between users of Sweden-Swedish and Finland-Swedish (for Swedish-speaking chat groups); between former West Germany vs. former East

Germany and vs. Austria (for German-speaking chat groups), and metropolitan vs. regional France, or between Paris and the south of France (for French chat groups)?

4. Are you aware of any problems in choosing an adequate address form in electronic communication in another language than [French/German/Swedish]?

In what follows, we will focus the discussion on the first two topics as they were the ones that yielded the most useful results. In many of the chat groups, members developed virtual identities, adopting nicknames; otherwise first names predominated. From this it follows that variation in address practices online is largely restricted to pronominal forms, which means that English, with its single address pronoun U, will not be discussed in this section.

4.7.1   French

Data from ten different chat groups, nine originating in France, form the basis for the following discussion (see Appendix B for listing). The general consensus among French-speaking forum members is that T is the most commonly used form for online communication and there is an acknowledgement that the same rules do not apply offline:

Personnellement, je préfère de loin vouvoyer une personne que je viens de rencontrer que de la tutoyer. Sur le net, par contre, j'avoue que j'ai plus tendance à tutoyer même si ce n'est pas d'office.

[Personally, I far prefer to use *vous* rather than *tu* with someone I have just met. On the net, however, I admit that I tend to use *tu* more, even if it's not compulsory.] (Sha-ka, Forum Marketing)

Most chat rooms and forums generally indicate that the T form is the norm and this seems to be well known by most participants. For example, one member of a language-focused forum expresses her surprise at the use of V by another member:

Le vouvoiement de Aurayfrance sur un forum m'a surprise, je ne crois pas que ce soit monnaie courante sur les forums.

[Aurayfrance's use of *vous* on a forum surprised me, I don't think it's common practice on forums.] (Valérie, Wordreference.com Forum)

Another forum member notes that the only people who have used *vous* on his forum are inexperienced internet users:

Il est extrêmement rare de voir des personnes qui vouvoient dans un forum. Pour ma part, les rares cas qui se sont présentés sur mon forum, il s'agissait de personnes assez peu à l'aise sur le net. Ce sont donc des internautes vers qui je vais plus aller car ils seront moins efficace et maladroit dans leur recherche.

[It is extremely rare to see people using *vous* in a forum. For my part, in the rare cases that have presented themselves on my forum, it was people who were uncomfortable on the net. So I'm more inclined to go towards this kind of internaut because they will be less effective and inept in their searching.] (Chooky, Forum Marketing)

The importance of online experience is underlined by another member, who talks of how participating in forums has modified her address practices online. Use of T now predominates in her forum interactions, although this still does not always feel 'natural' to her:

À mes débuts sur les forums, je vouvoyais certaines personnes et j'en tutoyais d'autres. C'était très compliqué, parce qu'au fil des diverses discussions, je ne me souvenais plus si j'avais vouvoyé ou tutoyé la personne, et étant malheureusement très perfectionniste, j'allais même jusqu'à rechercher ce détail avec le moteur de recherches.

Maintenant j'ai changé, je préfère en général le tutoiement, qui bien que n'étant pas toujours très naturel pour moi (je suis plutôt réservée et un peu distante dans la vraie vie), donne un ton plus léger aux discussions.

[When I was first on forums I would use *vous* with certain people and *tu* with others. It was very complicated because at a certain point in discussions I couldn't remember if I had used *tu* or *vous* with the person any more, and being unfortunately very much a perfectionist, I would even look up this detail with the search engine.

Now I've changed, I generally prefer using *tu*, which although not very natural for me (I'm rather reserved and a little distant in real life), gives a lighter tone to discussions.] (Pandore, Forum Santé-Psychologie de Atoute)

The notion that T gives a 'lighter tone to discussions' is echoed in different ways by other forum members. According to the following participant, to whom use of T comes easily, exchanging T on chat groups or forums reduces social distance, a view shared by at least four other participants:

Pour ma part le tutoiement m'est facile, ce n'est pas pour cela que je ne respecte pas la personne!! Il est vrai que habitué des tchat, le tutoiement est de mise, de plus je trouve qu'il peut rapprocher les personnes, les rendre plus à l'aise.

[For my part, using *tu* is easy for me, and it doesn't mean that I don't respect the [other] person. As a regular user of chat groups, it's true that *tu* is the rule, [and] I also find that it can bring people closer together, make them feel more comfortable.] (ptitloup62, Forum Marketing)

The modification of address practices online comes up in other comments which draw attention to the importance of age and particularly of topic in address choice. In the following example, the participant reflects that as he has got older and has taken to participating in more serious forums, he has modified his initial negative reaction to the use of *vous* online:

À mes débuts je fréquentais des forums dont la moyenne d'âge ne devait certainement pas dépasser vingt-cinq ans et on s'envoyait des 'tu' comme on se ramasse des oranges pendant le Carnaval de Binche. Chacun s'exprimait comme il pouvait ou plutôt comme il voulait. Depuis quelques temps je fréquente des forums d'un autre niveau, où on réfléchit

avant de laisser un 'lol' pour seule réponse ou une frimousse amusée. [...] Tout cela me
donne une vision différente des espaces de discussion et je comprends mieux le souhait
de quelques-uns à conserver le vouvoiement que je trouvais trop prétentieux et un brin
snob.

[When I was starting out I visited forums where the average age couldn't have been
more than 25 and *tu*s were being thrown around like oranges during the Binche Carnival.
Each person expressed himself as best he could, or rather as he wanted to. For a while
now I've been visiting forums of a different level, where people think before leaving a
'lol' as the only response or a smiley face. [...] All of this has given me a different vision
of discussion spaces and I understand better some people's wish to preserve *vous*, which I
used to find too pretentious and a tad snobbish.] (Katsoura, ABC de la Langue Française)

On a legal forum, one member explains how V use would be inappropriate and
negatively interpreted on other forums she takes part in. Nevertheless, after
being reprehended for using T when first joining the forum, she sees that V is
more in keeping with the spirit of a forum on legal topics:

Je participe sur d'autres forums ou le vouvoiement serait assez mal pris: du genre pour
qui se prend-il celui là ? [...] Mais bon ici c'est un forum juridique… je me suis vite fait
remettre en place à mon premier tutoiement et il est vrai qu'aprés tout nous n'avons pas
gardé les cochons ensembles.[5]

[I'm a participant in other forums where *vous* would be taken quite badly: in the sense,
'Who does he think he is, this guy?' [...] But this is a legal forum … I was quickly put in
my place after my first use of *tu* and it is true that after all we're not close friends.] (July,
Net-Iris Forum Juridique)

Finally, discussion about address is not an uncommon theme in forums. In
addition, many sites provide advice to potential members in their rules, regu-
lations and guides about the appropriateness of address forms. Two sites on the
French language have threads specifically devoted to the question of address.
On both of these sites V is the preferred if not prescribed form in use. On another
forum, the forum administrator went to the trouble of conducting a survey to
determine which address form the forum members preferred to use. The overwhelming response was use of T (96%). At the end of the forum's preamble,
explicit mention is made of the fact that T is the form used by members 'to make
life simple' – the use of T to reduce social distance between members is not put
forward as a reason and the forum explicitly recognises that some forum
members may be surprised by the prescribed use of T:

Pour se simplifier la vie, les membres du forum ont décidé d'adopter le tutoiement dans
tous les messages. Alors ne sois pas surpris…

[To make life simple, the members of the forum have decided to adopt *tu* in all
messages. So don't be surprised…] (Forum Photo Argentique)

---

[5] All quotes from the forums are rendered word by word, including deviations from French spelling
    norms.

4.7.2   German

The following discussion is based on data from eight different chat groups, seven of which originate from Germany and one from Austria (see Appendix B for listing). In German, chat groups are generally communities of T users who greet one another with *Hallo*. In this respect, they are believed to be different to real networks. The prevalence of *du* is attested by a member of a stamp collectors' chat group who self-identifies as someone who prefers *Sie* in face-to-face communication:

Im Internet ist das Duzen ein geschriebenes Gesetz.
    [On the internet the use of *du* is a written law.] (Fehldruck, Forum Showthread)

This corresponds with the position of most of the contributors to internet discussions on T and V. Another member of the same group points out that he was initially advised to stop using *Sie*:

Ich selbst habe ganz früher hier auch schon das 'Sie' verwendet. Curtis hat mich damals sehr freundlich aufgeklärt, dass hier doch das 'Du' üblich ist. Das habe ich gerne angenommen.
    [I myself did use *Sie* sometimes much earlier. Curtis very kindly instructed me that *du* was normal here. This was something that I gladly accepted.] (Herbert, Forum Showthread)

He reports that generally in chat groups, anyone employing *Sie* is regarded as an outsider:

Ich habe es auch schon in anderen Foren erlebt, dass 'Siezer' als Außenseiter betrachtet werden.
    [I already had experienced in other internet forums that people using *Sie* were regarded as outsiders.] (Herbert, Forum Showthread)

The use of V even gives an impression of rejection on the web:

Mit jemandem, den man siezt, möchte man nichts zu tun haben.
    [A person you address as *Sie* is someone you don't want to have anything to do with.] (Thilo, Forum Viewpoint)

However, there are a few chat groups (two German and one Austrian) that operate mainly with V. One contributor to the Austrian-based chat group run by the elitist daily newspaper *Der Standard* makes this observation:

Generell habe ich den Eindruck, dass der Standard.at Forum das Sie bevorzugt.
    [Generally I am under the impression that the *Standard.at* forum prefers *Sie*.] (Rafaele, Standard)

Interestingly members of all V-oriented forums think that their forum is the only one to do so:

Passt gut zum Standard, so ziemlich das Einzige Internet-Forum im deutschen Sprachraum, wo Poster per 'Sie' sind und sich teilweise sogar schwer beleidigt fühlen, wenn man duzt.

[It is just like the *Standard*, just about the only internet forum in the German language area where members are on *Sie* terms and in some cases feel very offended when they are called *du*.] (Erzbengel, der Standard)

Blogs for the high-quality German weekly *Die Zeit* are reported to be increasingly employing V, possibly because they are becoming more frequent with institutions and take on address practices from that domain:

Selbstverständlich ist auch hier das 'Du' weitaus häufiger anzutreffen als das 'Sie'; allerdings erfreuen sich Blogs auch bei offiziellen Einrichtungen immer weiter wachsender Beliebtheit. So zum Beispiel ist das 'Sie' Verwendung im Blog der Zeit-Redaktion zu finden.

[Of course *du* can be found here too far more frequently than *Sie*; however, blogs are becoming increasingly popular in official institutions. So for instance *Sie* is used in the *Zeit* editors' blog.] (LapsisInfernalis, Styleboard)

There are also some chat groups that claim that the pronoun choice is quite open and ever-changing, taking into account such aspects as respecting an individual's preference. This is the same rationale as given by many of our interviewees, who also emphasise individual variation (see 3.7):

Das hat in diesem Forum je nach aktiver Diskussionsstaffel gewechselt: Anfangs wurde noch viel gesiezt, die jetzigen Teilnehmer duzen sich öfter. Wir wollen nicht reglementieren, außer: Wenn jemand siezt, sollte das respektiert und nicht zurückgeduzt werden.

[That has changed according to the level of active discussion. At the start, a lot of *du* was still used. The current participants address each other as *du* more often. We don't want to set rules, except: if someone uses *Sie*, that has to be respected and this should not be returned with *du*.] (Webmaster, Boardunity)

Variation also occurs within one chat group according to similar patterns as in offline communication:

Es gibt aber auch innerhalb des Internets Unterschiede. In solchen Foren wie diesem wird eigentlich noch relativ oft gesiezt, weil hier wirklich sehr unterschiedliche und auch eigentlich gebildete Leute hisichtlich der unterschiedlichsten Themen miteinander kommunizieren. Dagegen wird in Foren, die sich mit einem klar abgegrenzten Spezialthema befassen, meiner Erfahrung zu neunzig prozent geduzt.

[There are also differences within the internet. In chat groups like this one *Sie* is used quite a lot because very different people with really different levels of education communicate here about the most varied topics. On the other hand, in my experience, chat groups that are concerned with a particular topic use *du* ninety per cent of the time.] (Hammerhai, Showthread)

However, given the general absence of information on age and status, social distance cannot play the same role as in offline address:

Im Internet ist es schwierig, weil ich nicht sehe, ob ein achtjähriger oder achtzigjähriger schreibt.

[On the internet it's difficult because I can't see if it's an 8 year old or an 80 year old writing.] (SaschJohn, Showthread)

One of the arguments for V on the internet is the possibility of common membership of virtual and of real networks, in which V might be used.

Es kann schon ziemlich peinlich sein, wenn man jemandem, den man im Netz dutz, persönlich kennenlernt.
[It can certainly be embarrassing if you meet someone personally whom you call *du* on the net.] (Volker, Forum Viewpoint)

This has its parallel in the issue of moving between domains (see 4.8) and between international and national networks (5.8).

4.7.3   Swedish

The questions on online address practices were distributed to six discussion forums in Finland and Sweden, but they were launched for discussion on only three forums, two in Sweden and one Swedish-speaking one in Finland (see Appendix B for further information).

Given the strong position of T generally it is hardly surprising that T is also the default form in Swedish computer-mediated communication. Respondents from the Swedish forums agree that T is used in all areas on the web – reflecting use in real life, 'offline':

Jag kan bara svara för mig själv, men jag försöker bemöta folk på ungefär samma sätt online som i verkliga livet. Jag har läst franska, och förstår en del tyska, och jag tycker att överförandet av 'ni' (vous, sie, whatever) till svenskan som ett försök till artighet är rent åt skogen. Innan du-reformen i Sverige, tilltalade man överordnade med titel ('Godmorgon, ingenjör Andersson'), och niade nedåt ('Är ni helt från vettet Andersson, sådär kan man inte göra'). Att ungdomar nuförtiden (oj, nu lät jag betydligt äldre än vad jag är) niar pensionärer och förväntar sig en positiv respons bara för att de läst tyska är som sagt åt skogen enligt mig. Jag skulle tro att i nittionio procent av allt elektroniskt jag läser på nätet används 'du', och i all epost jag får också. ... eller kort och gott 'jag duar överallt'.
[I can only speak for myself, but I try to treat people approximately the same online as in real life. I have studied French, and understand some German, and I think the transfer of *ni* (*vous*, *sie*, whatever[6]) to Swedish as an attempt at politeness is completely off the wall. Before the *du*-reform in Sweden, you addressed a superior with a title ('Good morning, engineer Andersson') and used *ni* downwards ('Are you (*ni*) out of your mind Andersson, you can't do it like that'). The fact that youths nowadays (oops, now I sound a lot older than I am) use *ni* to retirees and expect a positive response just because they have studied German is, as I said, off the wall, from my point of view. I would think that in 99% of everything electronic I read on the net *du* is used, and in all email I get as well. ... Or short and sweet 'I use *du* everywhere'.] (Tuborg, Forum Flashback)

It was, however, also pointed out that in blogs it is often the case that there is no use of direct address and it may be more common to use the personal

---

[6] *Whatever* is said in English.

pronoun *den* ('it') and the indefinite pronoun *man* ('one'), referring to an unspecified collective, in the same way as *they* is sometimes used impersonally in English.

Bloggaren skriver för en obestämd mottagare som sällan tilltalas. Man ser inte 'Du som läser detta kanske tror att…' eller motsvarande. Det är nog isåfall vanligare att använda 'Den' eller 'Man'.
[The blogger writes for an unspecified addressee who seldom is addressed. You don't see 'You who read this perhaps think that…' or similar. In such a case it is more common to use *Den* (lit. 'it') or *Man* ('one', 'they').] (JesperT, Forum Privata affärer)

The fact that the blogger is writing for a collective explains why *du* is not used, but not why *ni* (as the second-person plural) is not employed. A possible explanation is that *ni* is avoided precisely because it could be mistaken for formal, singular address (V). This aspect will be further explored in Chapter 5 in the discussion on letters (5.5.2).

While all contributors to the Finland-Swedish forum claimed to use *du* in chat groups and discussion forums, half of them said that they would use *ni* to address strangers in written and oral business communication. This difference in written communication (including emails) between the Swedish and Finland-Swedish research sites will be addressed in more detail in Chapter 5.

To what extent were forum members aware of discussions about address use *within* chat groups/news forums, or in any other net-based communication as well as 'offline'? Most (six of eight who commented) say that there is no discussion about address practices in the forums they participate in:

Jag har inte upplevt några diskussioner om tilltalsbruk i andra forum. Annat än av skojkommentarer som att 'jag säger alltid du till alla utom till dig och bror din'. Som är en gammal skröna om hur masar tilltalar kungar.
[I haven't experienced any discussions about address use in other forums. Other than comments said jokingly such as 'I always say *du* to everybody except to *du* and *din* (T, 'your') brother'. Which is an old tale about how people from Darlecarlia address kings.] (God Tro, Forum Privata affärer)

4.8   Moving between domains

Moving between domains can affect choice of address form in various ways. First, in French, two individuals can know each other in two different domains and use different forms in each. An example from one of our French interviews involves meeting someone for the first time informally at a party and using *tu* with them. Later in the evening it becomes apparent that *le statut social de la personne fait que dans d'autres circonstances je l'aurais vouvoyé* ('The social status of the person means that in other circumstances I would have used *vous* with them') (Paris, female academic, 39). One of our Finland-Swedish participants comments on the difficulty of moving to informal modes of address when there is a domain shift:

Ni när man presenterat någon inför klassen, sen svårt att sätta bort titlarna när man titulerat [inför studenterna] som professor Karlsson.

[(You use) 'ni' when you introduce somebody to the class, then it's difficult to do away with titles when you have used the title Professor Karlsson in front of the students.] (Vaasa, FG1, female university lecturer, 48)

An example from a court of law in Gothenburg also demonstrates that the formal context of the courtroom can lead to a switch to formal modes of address while the same colleagues would employ T outside the courtroom:

Ja, i rättegångssituationen finns domare – en äldre dam – som använder min titel, åklagare [...] <Hur vill domaren att du ska kalla henne?> Vet inte, jag säger ordföranden för nån slags respekt. Står vi och pratar säger jag 'du', inte 'ni'.

[Yes, in the situation of a court case there are judges – an older lady – who uses my title, prosecutor [...] <How does the judge want you to address her?> Don't know, I say your honour (lit. chairperson) out of some sort of respect. If we stand around talking I say *du*, not *ni*.] (Gothenburg, Q8, female prosecutor, 31)

An example from German concerns a case of double relationships, such as a colleague in the work domain and a family friend in the social domain. A foreign visiting academic in Germany was addressed as T by the spouses of two German colleagues (one male, one female) but this does not occur automatically, for they did not exchange T with the spouse of their local colleague.

Second, the use of T in one domain can influence the speaker to start using T in other domains. One French participant who works at IKEA notes that his use of *tu* in the workplace has spread to other domains in his life. One of the matters of concern in the German chat group data (4.7.2) was that chat group members using T online would meet offline and be constrained in their address choices. A retired nuclear physicist reported to us that when he was employed in the Ministry of Environment, the entry of the Greens into the government heralded the arrival of new colleagues who knew each other from Greens politics. They were on T terms and appeared to the existing staff to be excluding them with the use of V, the pronoun normally used in the department.

Third, within a particular domain, a change of topic, reflecting a change of role relationship, can motivate a shift in address form. One French participant observes that although she and her boss use *vous* with each other at work, when they talk about personal experiences they occasionally use *tu*: *des fois on raconte ses expériences personnelles et c'est vrai que dans ces moments-là elle va plus peut-être sortir le 'tu' que le 'vous'* ('sometimes we talk about our personal experiences and it's true that in those moments she is more likely to use *tu* than *vous*') (Paris, female child care worker, 24). This has not been attested in any of our German data.

4.9   Concluding remarks

This chapter has dealt with modes of address signalling inclusion in (or, by implication, exclusion from) a group. The institutions and domains discussed in this chapter are generally characterised by well-established address practices not requiring choices (family, students) or practices established periodically by imposition or contract (particularly workplaces).

In the family domain, modes of address mark both inclusivity (T in French and German) and status (non-reciprocity in address between parents and children – kinship term vs. FN – something that is common to all four languages). In French and German, the fuzzy edges of the family (uncles/aunts, children's partners and partners' parents) present a challenge to otherwise clear-cut address practices as inclusion and exclusion is more arbitrary there. In French, German and English, social distance between teachers and students in the school domain is marked by non-reciprocity of address developed through the education system. The exception, reciprocity of V at the upper secondary level, is the general practice in France. This is being relaxed in Germany. In the university domain, address between students – T and FN – is based on common ground and the recognition of an absence of social distance. It is the most T-oriented situation outside the family. Modes of address employed by academics to one another are open to negotiation, with both status and common ground playing a role in determining degree of social distance. In communication between staff and students, English and Swedish have gone furthest to remove any indicators of social distance in address, and in the other two languages, individual, institutional and departmental differences lead to considerable variation.

Modes of address in the workplace are generally part of an identity formation in which the interaction of inclusivity and status plays a prominent part. Where common practices develop, they are promoted by the need for efficiency, a common work culture and the avoidance of face threats in potential conflict situations.

English, not having pronominal choice of address, makes more use of nominal modes of address such as *Sir/Madam* in the transactional domain, which can serve as a face saver in a dispute in a negatively polite service encounter context, and hon + LN versus FN. The use of *Sir/Madam* in English and the re-emergence of *ni* as a form of address to the older customers by younger sales assistants in Swedish service encounters are in keeping with a new transactional politeness (although in both languages the V or V-like use was seen as not entirely positive, in English from the point of view of the giver (at times) and in Swedish from the point of view of the receiver). *Sir/Madam* makes English transactional address, being tripartite (*Sir/Madam*, hon + LN, FN), as complex as that of French (*monsieur/madame*, hon + LN, FN) and more complex than the other two languages.

In Swedish, the predominance of T puts more pressure on the FN/LN choice to express social distance, as is the case in English with its single pronoun of address. In the past, Swedish was characterised by avoidance strategies where, for example, older relatives, teachers and very senior colleagues were addressed indirectly by kinship term or title and using third-person address. German modes of address with partners' parents indicate both the difficulty of pinpointing the appropriate time for a transition to T and the greater use of T in German than in French. The distinction between French and German workplace address patterns is not very clear-cut. It does seem that generally hierarchy plays a much greater role in French workplace address than in Swedish, with English and German in intermediate positions. Also, there are a small number of professions (media, journalism, fashion, high technology, social services) in which T is employed between workplace colleagues more generally in French than in German.

In letters, the choice of opener generally involves tension between formality and informality in English, German and Swedish, whereas in French there is nearly complete agreement over the (formal) forms to be used. Almost all chat groups use T, although the desirability of that is not always universally accepted and a few interest-specific forums in French and German opt for V.

These issues will be developed further in Chapter 6. In the following chapter, we will focus on national variation in address and also on the impact of language contact on modes of address.

5   National variation

So far we have explored address in our four languages as a whole without focusing on differences between national varieties. This chapter is largely devoted to variation in perceptions and use of address forms in some national varieties of German, Swedish and English. As national variation in these three languages takes different forms, the content of the sections on the three languages will not be readily comparable. We begin with the customary reminder that the English data are limited and serve as a point of reference.

The chapter opens with an overview of the national varieties that form part of our investigation, followed by a comparative analysis of modes of address in the countries under study. We then turn to address in letters and the national variation discernible, as well as general awareness of national variation. The chapter concludes with an examination of the impact of language contact on address and the influence of address choices in business and multinational companies on national address practices.

5.1   National varieties

5.1.1   German in Germany and Austria, and the former East–West division

Variation between the Austrian and German national varieties of Standard German results from separate cultural and sociopolitical development, especially from the late eighteenth century and including the formation of separate states (1871, 1918, 1945). After a conflict between the pan-German and pro-independence elements in Austria, the post-World War II years were characterised by increasing national consciousness and the acceptance of the notion of an independent Austrian nation. The codification of Austrian Standard German as a national variety has been controversial, particularly in relation to the definition of standard and the degree of distance from German Standard German. However, it has been demonstrated that variation between the Austrian and German national varieties extends beyond the lexical, phonological and morphosyntactic levels to the pragmatic (Muhr 1987, 1994, Clyne, Fernandez and Muhr 2003).

The term 'national variety' is somewhat problematic for our data in German. While the distinction between German and Austrian communication patterns has developed over centuries, the variation between East and West German ones originated from the postwar division of Germany – effectively from 1945 to 1990 – into a communist eastern state and a capitalist western state. This created different socio-economic and political systems which led to separate cultural developments and different systems of communication. It was a very deep division because of the lack of contact between the two Germanies (cf. 5.2.1). Far more so than in the case of Austria, the term 'nation' for the German Democratic Republic (GDR) was a political one rather than a cultural one. In the GDR, people tended to have both a public and private register. The public register was employed by the party functionaries, bureaucrats and the media, and usually by all people interacting with them (Hellmann 1978, Schlosser 1991, Lerchner 1992, Gärtner 1992). Features of GDR German are now used largely to share past experiences (Hellmann 1990, Clyne 1995: 78–87; see also Stevenson 2002). So for the eastern Germans today, address differences are not only regional, they are also historical, marking the difference between what it was like in the GDR and what it is like in post-unification Germany.

5.1.2   Swedish in Sweden and Finland

With the rise of Sweden as a nation state (which included Finland) in the sixteenth century, Swedish became a symbol of the new nationhood and corpus planning was undertaken to ensure that the use of Swedish would extend to public domains previously dominated by Latin and, to a lesser extent, German and French. There was also a political interest in safeguarding Swedish against Danish influence, as Denmark was the other main player in Scandinavia at that time (Teleman 2002). Finland remained part of Sweden until 1809, when it was lost to Russia, but Swedish remained the language of the bureaucracy. By the time Finland became an independent state in 1917, Finnish was the dominant language, not only in government and the civil service but also in society in general. As a result of industrialisation, and hence urbanisation, many formerly Swedish-speaking areas became rapidly fennicised (Tandefelt 1994). Today the Swedish-speaking minority makes up slightly over 5% of the population and is found predominantly in the coastal areas in the south and the west (Osthrobothnia, of which Vaasa is a centre) and on the Åland Islands. While Finland-Swedish is considered a variety of standard Swedish, it also has the status of an official language in Finland (Tandefelt 2006). However, Swedish in Finland is under heavy influence from Finnish, particularly in vocabulary, but also in pragmatics (Reuter 1992, Saari 1995), and Finland-Swedish has been described as more formal and using more negative politeness strategies compared with Sweden-Swedish (Fremer 1998, Saari 1995). Finland-Swedish language planning aims at maintaining similarity between the two Swedish national varieties and therefore advises against the use of unnecessary loan words and loan translations from Finnish (Hällström and Reuter 2000). It has probably also led to a desire to keep Swedish 'intact' and relatively free of Finnish influence. For Swedes in Sweden this means that the Finland-Swedish vocabulary seems slightly archaic.

5.1.3   English in Ireland

Irish English is the result of the asymmetrical relations between the national language, Irish, and the colonial language, English, over the past 600 years. While Irish and English are the two official languages of Ireland, about 95% of the population speak English as a first language (Ó Laoire 2005: 253), with more than 5% using Irish 'to a greater or lesser extent' (Ó Laoire 2005: 254). The decline of Irish can be attributed to colonialisation, cultural domination and power relations. Irish survived Anglo-Norman colonisation in the eleventh and twelfth centuries and the Statute of Kilkenny (1366) banning the use of Irish by English speakers among themselves in the small English-speaking area. The hostilities of the seventeenth century and English subjugation of Ireland outlawed Irish and made it an instrument of defiance. The greatest shift to English occurred in the years after the famine (1840s), which affected the Irish speakers most (Crowley 2000, Ó Laoire 2005: 286).

Irish became an important symbol of independence. The Irish revival movement was originally liberal and secular, unlike the independence movement, which was linked to Catholicism (Ó Laoire 2005: 291). In the Irish Republic (1937), Irish became a compulsory subject in public examinations and a prerequisite for admission to the public service and the legal profession but never the home language of a significant population. The Irish Foreign Affairs Department was willing for English to be regarded as its working language when it joined the European Community, though this has been reviewed at Ireland's request on the acceptance of Estonian, Latvian, Lithuanian and Maltese as official languages following EU enlargement. Irish became an EU official language as from 2007 (Ó Laoire 2005: 305–6).

Over the centuries, English affected by an Irish substratum (phonology, morphosyntax and discourse patterns) rather than Irish itself was for many the practical linguistic marker of national identity (Crystal 1993: 336–9, Macarthur 1992: 530).

5.2   Pronoun use according to national variety: German

5.2.1   The special case of eastern Germany

Before we explore address in certain domains, a discussion of the specific situation in eastern Germany would be useful. A polarisation of social and cultural values there has characterised the aftermath of the fall of the Berlin wall in 1989. Unlike western Europe, the GDR was not affected by the student movement but there was a mode of address of solidarity imposed by the Communist Party, namely use of *Genosse* ('comrade') and T. Consequently there is considerable reluctance in the middle and older generations in Leipzig – those who have lived through the GDR – to accept T use in a more public register. A retired physiotherapist believes that she is less inclined than a westerner to accept the imposition of *du* address at a workplace:

Ich finde, das kann man nicht machen. Das ist zu diktatorisch. Da kommt mein DDR-Bürger raus. Das ist nämlich die Diskrepanz auch zu vielen Westdeutschen.

[I don't think I can do that [referring to the imposition of *du*]. It's too dictatorial. There's my GDR background coming out. That is just the difference from many West Germans.] (Leipzig, Q3, female retired physiotherapist, 65)

Yet there are those who miss the solidarity of GDR days, when incomes were fairly level and people socialised across social groups.

Früher haben die Leute [...] zusammen im Garten gegrillt, der Oberarzt und der Fliesenleger.

[People used to have barbecues together in the backyard, the head doctor and the tiler.] (Leipzig, FG2, male taxi driver, 38)

Of the Leipzig interviewees, 46 of 66 believe that people have become more anti-social. Some members of the Leipzig focus group and 12 Leipzig interviewees mentioned nostalgically that T was used more in those days, as opposed to four who thought less *du* was used and 11 who believed the situation had not changed. Those who noted a decreased use of T since 1989 included 9 out of 30 aged over 35. A retired teacher reports:

Die Menschen waren sich näher als jetzt, d.h. der soziale Kontakt war enger[...] ja, es gab menschliche Wärme, Solidarität in weit größerem Maße als jetzt, [...] jetzt ist sich mehr oder weniger jeder selbst der Nächste.

[People were closer than now, that is, social contact was closer [...] yes, there was human warmth, solidarity to a much greater extent than now [...] now everyone themselves is their neighbour.] (Leipzig, Q7, female retired teacher, 75)

Generally people are also reported to now be more reserved and formal, hence less use of *du*.

Die Menschen sind verschlossener geworden. Zu DDR-Zeiten hat man sich [...] eher geduzt.

[People have become more reserved. In GDR times you were [...] more inclined to use *du*.] (Leipzig, Q1, male IT manager, 30)

Es ist eindeutig zum 'Sie' übergegangen. Ich bin auch der Meinung, dass die Menschen nicht mehr so locker mit einander umgehen, wie es früher mal war.

[There has been a clear change to *Sie*. I too am of the opinion that people don't interact as informally as they used to.] (Leipzig, Q5, female economist/engineer, 47)

Table 5.1 *German: How do you address your superiors at work? How do they address you?*

	T–T (%)	T or V–T or V* (%)	V–V (%)	n/a (%)	(N)
Mannheim	25	6	69	3	(66)
Leipzig	27	8	71	5	(66)
Vienna	59	3	38	12	(66)
Total	34	6	60	7	(198)

* Non-reciprocal use: one participant each in Leipzig and Mannheim uses V with superiors but receives T.

Table 5.2 *German: How do you address your co-workers? How do they address you?*

	T–T (%)	T/V–T/V (%)	V–V (%)	n/a (%)	(N)
Mannheim	64	17	19	3	(66)
Leipzig	55	32	12	2	(66)
Vienna	81	13	6	5	(66)
Total	67	21	13	9	(198)

The changed political situation itself is considered a factor by an administrative officer and translator, who expressed the view that some people are suddenly using *Sie* to hide something about their past:

Ich stelle heute fest, dass Leute, die sich früher gekannt haben und dann sich wiederse- hen, dass sie sich nicht unbedingt mehr duzen. Um seriöser zu sein, das weiss ich nicht, um was zu vertuschen vielleicht, weil manche um ihre Vergangenheit nicht umgehen können, was weiss ich, in der Partei oder FDJ-Leute oder sonst wo gearbeitet haben, die siezen sich auf einmal.

[I notice these days that people who used to know each other and then meet again, that they don't necessarily call each other *du*. To be serious, I don't know if it is to hide something because some people can't deal with their past, whatever, in the party or Freie Deutsche Jugend (Communist youth organisation) people or wherever else they worked, they suddenly use *Sie*.] (Leipzig, Q3, female administrative officer and translator, 52)

5.2.2   Workplace

Tables 5.1 and 5.2 indicate the greater use of *du* in Vienna in the workplace. While in work situations Leipzig people use V more than Mannheimers, the reverse holds for non-work situations. Also, with grandparents' friends Leipzigers use more T than anyone else, whereas use of T with parents' friends

Table 5.3 *German: address between teachers and students at university*

	T–T (%)	T/V–T/V* (%)	V–V (%)	other (%)	n/a (%)	(N)
Mannheim	2	12	81	5	35	(66)
Leipzig	–	9	90	2	14	(66)
Vienna	–	17	75	9	11	(66)
Total	<1	13	82	5	20	(198)

*Reciprocal T in some interactions, reciprocal V in others and some non-reciprocal address, receiving V from the teacher.

is equally distributed in Leipzig and Mannheim. These results reflect the eastern Germans' practice of differentiating between the public and private language discussed in the previous section.

Of the three research sites, the one where, according to the network interviews, T is used most in the workplace is Vienna. As indicated in Table 5.1, nearly 60% of the Vienna sample exchanged T with superiors at work, as opposed to one in four in Mannheim and just over one in five in Leipzig. The variation in T use between the three locations is significant at $p < 0.01$. Table 5.2 shows that over 80% in Vienna exchange T with colleagues in contrast to less than 65% of the Mannheim sample and about 55% of those in Leipzig. The variation between the three locations in T use with colleagues is significant at $p < 0.05$.

5.2.3   University

As will be gleaned from Table 5.3, university staff and students predominantly use V to each other (the variation between the three locations in V use between university teachers and students is significant at $p < 0.005$). The main alternative is non-reciprocal T from staff to students and V from students to staff. This is slightly more common in Vienna than in Mannheim and especially in Leipzig.

However, some of our informants report a gradual introduction of more informal communication in universities since 1989, including some lecturers (but not professors) starting *du* relationships with students. Such comments originate from people of different age groups and therefore with varying amounts of experience of the GDR.

5.3   Pronoun use according to national variety: Swedish

Given the default position of T (not V as in French and German) in Swedish, it is interesting to observe where V would be typically used across the research sites.

Table 5.4 *Swedish: situations for V address in both Swedish sites*

Addressee	Q.	Gothenburg		Vaasa	
		N	%	N	%
A considerably older person of the opposite sex	1d	72	46	72	70.8
Friends of grandparents	23	65	49	62	45.2
Email to stranger	38	70	43	66	69.7

Table 5.5 *Swedish: additional situations for V address in Vaasa*

Addressee	Q.	Gothenburg		Vaasa	
		%	N	%	N
A considerably older person of the same sex	1c	36	72	69	72
A considerably older police officer of the same sex	5c	15	72	58	72
A considerably older police officer of the opposite sex	5d	17	72	60	72
Friends of parents whom you do not know	23	25	71	45	65
Email to a client	32	30	53	61	64

There are only three situations that would make about half, or more, of the informants abandon *du* address in both research locations, but, as outlined in Table 5.4, in two of those situations the use of V is substantially higher in Vaasa. Statistically, overall, national variation is significant at $p < 0.01$; questions 1d and 38 are significant at $p < 0.05$; question 23 is not significant.

While there are only three situations that would lead to substantial use of V (around 50% or more) in Gothenburg, five additional situations are reported to occasion substantial V address in Vaasa (see Table 5.5). The results for Gothenburg are included for comparison. The differences between the sites in these additional situations are quite striking. Only about 15% of the Gothenburg informants would consider addressing a considerably older police officer with V, while close to 60% of the Vaasa informants report V use here. About twice as many Vaasa informants would address a considerably older person of the same sex or a client with V compared with those in Gothenburg.

A consistent finding is that, for Swedish speakers, the addressee should be unfamiliar in order to occasion use of any form of address other than *du*. The variables that promote use of V in both sites are *age* and *medium*. In Vaasa, the additional variable of *status* – real or perceived status differences between the informant and the interlocutor – appears to be of some importance, whereas this is not the case in the Sweden-Swedish data: compared with Vaasa, very few of the Gothenburg informants report that they would address an older police officer or a client by V. Although some of the factors that tend to lead to the shift from *du* are the same for both sites, there is also some systematic variation between the national varieties in how the informants report using address pronouns or avoid address altogether.

5.3.1   Social variables: age

One of the interview questions asked informants to nominate a threshold age for V and the results demonstrate great variation both within and across sites. Firstly, many participants say that there is no such V-age and that they would use universal *du*. This is particularly the case in Gothenburg, where it is the most frequent response (35/72, 49%). It is the second most common in Vaasa (13/72, 18%), which underscores the greater use of *du* in Sweden compared with Finland. Secondly, many informants are of the opinion that other factors are more important than age as such. This is the most frequent reply in Vaasa (24/72, 33%), which is an indication that address usage is dynamic and negotiated in the situation at hand, and not simply correlated to a certain age. Thirdly, while there is substantial variation in both sites for those informants who do give an age for V address, the Swedish informants generally select a higher age than their Vaasa counterparts.

For those informants who give a threshold age for V, the average is 70.2 and the median 75 in Gothenburg (based on 23 responses), while in Vaasa the average is 59 and the median 60 (based on 34 responses). (Where an informant gives a range, e.g. 70–80, an average has been calculated.) Not only is the V-age considerably lower in Vaasa, there are also more informants who state an age, although many of them also say that it is difficult and that other factors play a role as well. Furthermore, it is interesting to compare the age range at the two sites: in Vaasa it spans from 14 to 100; in Gothenburg the lowest age mentioned is 55 and the highest 100.

There is a trend in the Gothenburg data for those informants who give a V-age to conjure up images of the very old and frail, who would – perhaps – be addressed with *ni*. The following quotation from one of the interviews illustrates this:

Jag kan själv känna att väldigt gamla skröpliga människor tilltalar jag gärna med ‚ni', *för att man känner att man inte vill komma nära dem, för att de verkar så skröpliga. Det* *är ett sätt att hålla distans på ett trevligt sätt och kanske ett sätt för att få dem att känna* *sig trygga och bekväma, och att saker kan få vara så som de vill ha det tills de dör.*

[I myself can feel that I quite like to address very old, frail people with *ni*, because you feel that you don't want to get close to them because they seem so frail. It is a way of keeping the distance in a nice way, and perhaps a way of making them feel secure and comfortable, and that things are allowed to be in a way they like until they die.] (Gothenburg, Q10, female journalist, 29)

There is no direct equivalent in the Finland-Swedish data to these Swedish images of the very old who would possibly be addressed by *ni*. This can be linked to the fact that for those who give a V-age in Vaasa, this age is considerably lower:

Jag har själv blivit uppfostrad att äldre personer ska man ge plats i bussen och öppna dörren och tilltala med ni-form, så äldre människor, men vem är äldre, så det är ju också lite svårt. Det beror också på vilken typ av människa det är, om det är en äldre människa som ser ut som om han skulle vilja bli tilltalad med 'ni', så då tilltalar man som 'ni', men en annan skulle kanske känna det väldigt obekvämt om man skulle säga 'ni'. Åldern är nog det viktigaste. Om man grovt tippar så 60 år och uppåt.

[I myself was brought up to give older people a seat on the bus, open the door and address with *ni*, so older people [should be addressed by *ni*], but who is older, so that's a bit difficult too. It also depends on what type of person it is, if it is an older person who looks like he would like to be addressed by *ni*, well, then you address with *ni*, but another one would perhaps feel very uncomfortable if you were to say *ni*. Age is probably the most important. If you give a rough estimate then 60 years and older.] (Vaasa, Q6, female project leader, 41)

However, the most conspicuous trend in Vaasa is for age alone not to determine address behaviour. The following quotation is representative of ways in which many Vaasa informants reply to this question:

Som sagt jag tycker det beror mera på sammanhangen än på åldern i många fall, det beror på vem det är som tilltalar och vem som blir tilltalad. Om det är en riktigt ung person som tilltalar, kan man nia en femtioåring men den personen kan ju bli sårad, det vet man aldrig och int ens alla femtioåringar ska man nia. Det är beroende på sammanhanget, är man i nåt serviceyrke i en sån typ av affär där det hör till att nia så niar man kanske alla kunder från 40 år. Med äldre människor, sjutti, åtti år.

[Like I said I think it depends on the situations more than age in many cases, it depends on who it is who is addressing and who gets addressed. If it is a really young person who addresses, you can use *ni* to a 50 year old, but that person might get hurt, that you never know, and not all 50 year olds should be addressed with *ni*. It depends on the situation, if you are in a service profession in a type of shop where it is expected to use *ni*, then you perhaps will address customers with *ni* from 40. With older people, from 70, 80.] (Vaasa, Q4, female translator and interpreter, 39)

This points to two important issues not addressed in the Swedish interviews. On the one hand the Finland-Swedes are more likely to give a lower age threshold for V address (and hence there are no images of the extremely old as the only candidates for such address). On the other hand the Finland-Swedes tend to describe address behaviour as more complex and contingent on several factors, compared with their Swedish counterparts. As outlined above, the most frequent reply in Sweden is that there is no age threshold for V, and *du* address is universal:

Jag tycker inte om 'ni', tycker inte man ska göra skillnad på folk och folk, och ålder ska inte ha med det att göra.

[I don't like *ni*, don't think you should differentiate between people and age shouldn't have anything to do with it.] (Gothenburg, Q1, female journalist, 30)

Accordingly the fact that *ni* is used more in Finland-Swedish means that address behaviour is something which requires thought and negotiation, compared with the more straightforward address patterns in Sweden, where *du* dominates.

5.3.2   Social variables: status

As mentioned above, in the questionnaire results from Vaasa *status* was an additional factor (in addition to unfamiliarity, age and medium) in V address. About 60% of the informants reported that they would address a considerably older police officer as V. This should be compared with the Sweden-Swedish questionnaires where only about 15% of the informants reported that they would use V (see Table 5.5 above) in this way. It is, however, also apparent from the data that status alone cannot be the explanation for the address choice of the Vaasa informants: a same-age or younger police officer would be addressed by T to a much greater extent also in Vaasa (about 80%). Thus the interpretation is that *status* interacts with age.

Table 5.6 summarises attitudes to the indiscriminate use of *du* in TV and radio interviews. While there is quite strong support for general T in the Swedish data (over 75% indicate that this is generally suitable), only about half of the Finland-Swedes find such a practice generally acceptable and as few as ten Finland-Swedish informants have no reservations at all. The informants certainly perceive a difference in address usage between the Swedish and Finnish media:

Vi ser mycket på SVT och faktiskt har det hänt nån situation där jag har gapat och stirrat att, 'oho, det var ledigt!' Men det är nu svensk stil. Int har jag nånting emot, men man blir lite så där när det kommer en situation när reportern drar till med 'du' på direkten att man blir lite oho!

[We watch SVT [Sweden's state television] a lot and there have actually been occasions when I've been gob-smacked and stared, 'Gee, that was casual!' But, then again, that's just the Swedish style. Not that I've got anything against it – it's just that there are occasions when the reporter goes straight into using *du* and it makes you go a bit oh!] (Vaasa, Q7, male specialist consultant, 63)

The Swedish informants are generally more favourably disposed to universal *du*, demonstrating the strong sense of egalitarianism in Swedish society:

Lämpligt, jag tycker inte artigheten behöver sitta i om det är 'du' eller 'ni'.

[[It is] suitable, I don't think politeness has to be a question of *du* or *ni*.] (Gothenburg, Q8, female lawyer, 30)

For those informants who do have reservations, differences in status between interviewer and interviewee is the most important factor for questioning the use of universal *du* (see Table 5.6).

In the Sweden-Swedish data, most comments concern the unsuitability of addressing the king or another member of the royal family as *du* (12).

Table 5.6 *Swedish: attitudes to the use of universal* du *in TV and radio interviews*

T not suitable for addressing:	Gothenburg	Vaasa
the king and royal family	12	6[1]
people in high positions, e.g. prime minister, president, experts	8	28
elderly people	5	11
(N)	(16)*	(35)

* The number of informants does not match the number of responses as several informants list more than one type of addressee who should not be addressed by T.

The following response gives a description of the exceptional status of the royal family:

Det är väldigt lämpligt att dom är konsekventa i TV därför att annars så kan nån tänka att varför kallar han honom för 'ni' och mig för 'du' [...] – att man gör lika. Jag tror inte nån reagerar om man säger 'ni' till kungen och drottningen och 'du' till andra, men där går gränsen.

[It is very appropriate for them to be consistent on TV because otherwise somebody might think why did they call him *ni* and me *du* [...] – that you do the same. I don't think anybody reacts if you say *ni* to the king and queen but *du* to others, but that's where I draw the line.] (Gothenburg, Q6, female speech pathologist, 51)

In Vaasa most informants mention the president of Finland as worthy of more formal address, which could be seen as the republic's counterpart to the Swedish royals, but they also mention other senior politicians, experts and celebrities much more often than the Gothenburg informants, thus underscoring the higher sensitivity within the Finland-Swedish community towards status differences:

I regel är det lämpligt, men jag blir nog störd om republikens president eller kungen i Sverige duas av reportern. Ställningen är av sådan art att här är det artigt att nia. Men i Finland, nog säger vi ju Herr Statsminister också, säkert de här riksdagsmänniskorna också, det är positionen som avgör, det en viss artighet då och då är det lämpligt att de niar och de förmedlar ju då via tv till människorna att har man nått en sån position är man värd att visas aktning.

[As a rule it [*du*] is suitable, but I get irritated if the president of the republic or the king of Sweden are addressed by *du* by the reporter. Their position is of such a kind that here it is polite to say *ni*. But in Finland I think we say Mr Prime Minister too, surely also these parliamentarians too, it is the position that decides, a certain level of politeness then and then it is suitable that they say *ni* and they are conveying via TV to people that if somebody has reached a certain position you are worthy of being shown some respect.] (Vaasa, Q10, female retired lecturer, 63)

[1] Referring to the Swedish king and royal family.

5.3.3   Workplace

As discussed in section 4.4.3, status hierarchies in the workplace generally do not lead to any differentiation in address behaviour; the normal mode of address is *du* in both national varieties, both to colleagues and superiors. However, there is some use of V in Vaasa in certain marked situations, such as addressing the managing director, professors or other very senior representatives of the company or institution. The quotations below display the important relation between status and social distance, or lack of familiarity. When our Vaasa informants talk about work-related status differences, they tend to focus on somebody at the very top of the hierarchy such as the director of the entire corporation, whose status is indisputable:

Ingen niar på ABB men om Finlands högsta chef skulle komma på besök så niar man honom.
[Nobody uses *ni* at ABB but if the managing director of ABB in Finland visited us, we would say *ni* to him.] (Vaasa, FG1, female sales manager, 29)

This is also intrinsically linked to a perceived lack of common ground, enforced by the physical distance (the representatives of the head office are from Helsinki or from overseas) and thus also a lack of familiarity. As reported in Chapter 3, unfamiliarity is a condition for the use of V in both Swedish national varieties, but its interaction with other variables – age, status and how formal the situation is – reveals sharp differences between the two varieties.

In universities, a status hierarchy still seems to be alive in Vaasa, at least compared with the situation in Sweden, as the following quotation from the Vaasa focus group illustrates:

Nu har jag inte hunnit jobba så mycket utan jag har forskat innan jag fick det här arbetet jag har nu och på universitetet så där såg man nog tydligare vilka som var professorer som man inte gick och talade med för de var så pass högtidliga och sen hade man sina närmaste, assistenter och professorer som man jobba närmast med som man dua. Men chefen på institutionen kände jag att jag skulle behöva nia. Det var en ganska tydlig hierarki. Det känns som ett vassare klimat.
[Now I haven't had time to work so much, but I was a researcher before I got this job, and at university I think you noticed more clearly who were professors who you didn't walk up to and started talking to because they were quite formal and then you had your closest [colleagues], assistants and professors who you were working closely with who you addressed with *du*. But the head of department I felt I needed to say *ni* to. It was a fairly clear-cut hierarchy. It felt like a more piercing climate.] (Vaasa, Q5, female municipal secretary, 28)

This is clearly different from the Swedish workplaces, where there is no evidence of (contemporary) use of *ni*, not even to the very senior superiors (see 3.5.3).

Another work-related difference between the sites concerns addressing clients. As was pointed out in the introduction to the Swedish data in this chapter, the questionnaire results demonstrate a much higher incidence of *ni* in Vaasa (61%)

than in Gothenburg (31%) when addressing a customer or client. The tendency to
address clients with *ni* in Vaasa is also borne out in the interviews (see Chapter 4).

5.4   Nominal modes of address

5.4.1   German

In all German-speaking sites, FN tends to correspond with T use and hon + LN
with V use, with the exceptions discussed in Chapter 3. However, the use of titles
correlates with V in Germany but not necessarily in Vienna, where, for instance,
Grüß Dich Herr Botschafter (using T with the title *Ambassador*) does occur.

One aspect of national variation mentioned by all of the focus groups and
many interviewees was the greater use of titles in Austria. In Germany, a
declining use of titles and a relaxation of their use was reported, though they
were still employed by the older generation. In Mannheim, as illustrated in the
following exchange, positions varied between acceptance, when the person
with a title attached importance to them (3 and 4), and complete rejection of
what was considered arrogance (1 and 2):

(1)   *Also ich gebrauch keine Titel. Also mein Mann ist Professor, niemals stellt
       er sich mit Titel vor, [...] kenne aber Leute, die penetrant auf ihre Titel
       abheben und das berührt mich in einer Weise merkwürdig. Eine Dame hat
       sich vorgesellt mit den Worten: mein Name ist Doktor Soundso, so viel Zeit
       muss sein (Gelächter)*
(2)   *Also da kann man natürlich auf den Charakter einer Dame schließen.*
(3)   *Ja aber sie hat ja auch dafür was geleistet, wenn sie das gerne haben möchte, finde
       ich jetzt nicht so.*
(1)   *Mich berührt das unangenehm, also ich empfinde es als peinlich. [...]*
(4)   *Wenn jemand seine Titel hören will, dann kriegt er den von mir zu hören aber nur
       damit es keinen Stress gibt.*
[(1)   So I don't use titles. Well, my husband is a professor; he never introduces himself
       with his title [but I] know people who insist on their title and that affects me in a
       strange kind of way. One lady introduced herself with the words 'My name is Doctor
       So-and-so, and there has to be time for me to say that'. (*Laughter*)
(2)   So this way you can deduce the character of a lady.
(3)   Yes but she has achieved something for it, if she wants it, I don't see it that way.
(1)   It affects me in an unpleasant way, well, I feel embarrassed about it. [...]
(4)   If someone wants to hear their title, then they will hear it from me but only so that
       there is no stress.]
                   (Mannheim, FG2, (1) female secondary school teacher, late 40s; (2) male,
                             unemployed/home duties, 40s; (3) female publisher's editor, 26;
                                                                  (4) male student, 27)

In Austria, titles are considered part of people's names and their omission can cause
offence. They are employed especially in hierarchical situations, such as those that

Table 5.7 *German: number of interviewees reporting use of titles in the workplace*

Use of titles with:	Mannheim	Leipzig	Vienna	Total
superiors at work	–	7	9	16
work colleagues at same level	–	1	3	4
teachers	2	–	53	55
university teachers	4	13	56	73
(N)				(148)

exist in institutions typical of the church, hospitals, law courts and universities. Titles are seen as useful in communication with bureaucracy and to locate people socially. They do not necessarily increase the social distance, which is expressed by V.

Table 5.7 shows that no use of titles in the workplace is reported by Mannheim interviewees in the network interviews, whereas a small number of interviewees in Vienna and Leipzig report using titles with superiors and colleagues at work. The variation between the three locations is statistically significant at the following levels: superiors $p < 0.01$; colleagues $p < 0.05$; teachers $p < 0.005$; university teachers $p < 0.005$. Of a total of 73 participants who reported use of titles with university teachers, more than two thirds (56) were from Vienna. The greater use of titles to academics in Leipzig than in Mannheim can be attributed to the address mode at the time of the GDR, where there had not been a student revolution – *Professor* X, not *Herr* X, which emerged during the student revolution as the democratic mode of address in West German universities. In the GDR, academic titles were used as a mark of respect. *Herr*, on the other hand, was officially considered a bourgeois mode of address.

One of the reasons for schoolteachers being addressed by their titles in Vienna is that upper secondary school teachers in Austria carry the title of *Professor*, not to be confused with *Universitätsprofessoren* ('university professor').

The substantial use of both T and titles in Vienna may seem paradoxical but it is in fact a carryover from the Austro-Hungarian Empire, which was characterised by the high frequency of T use in both the military officers' corps and state bureaucracy (Sproß 2001: 121–3) as well as the use of titles within the imperial public service and beyond. The usage seems to have spread from there into the wider community, particularly the workplace. With regard to titles, the post-imperial continuity is corroborated by similarities between contemporary Austrian and Czech usage that differ from both western and eastern German usage (Ehlers 2004).

5.4.2   Swedish

With T being the default form of address, in particular in Sweden-Swedish, this could be expected to always co-occur with first names. However, there are indications to the contrary in our data. In 3.5.3, we noted how a relatively junior lawyer in Gothenburg feels comfortable addressing senior superiors with T but hesitates to use their first names. We also showed how informants in both Gothenburg and Vaasa express their reservations about being addressed by their first name by perfect strangers in transactional encounters (see 4.5.3). In other words, T use is generally expected and serves as a neutral form of address (except for some very formal or marked situations; see 5.3.2 and 5.3.3), while use of first names suggests a certain level of familiarity between interlocutors. There are also differences between the locations, with more use of first names to characterise people in Gothenburg (see 5.8).

The use of hon or title + LN is very restricted in Swedish, although, as outlined in the sections above on status-related address, there is a tendency among Vaasa informants not only to use V more but also to match this with use of hon/title + LN. The differences between the sites are also borne out in our data on written communication, which we address below in section 5.5.

5.4.3   English

Here the focus is on modes of address where there are *differences* reported in the focus groups. One such difference is in the use of *mate* as a T-like nominal mode of address (see also Chapter 3). It is very common in England among males to express informality and low social distance. One male English focus group member reported: '"Mate" is ubiquitous. I think everyone uses "mate"' (Newcastle, NM2, male English teacher, 25). It does not entail a particularly special relationship, according to another participant in the same focus group, 'because I don't think saying "mate" implies a big connection' (Newcastle, FG, unidentified male). *Mate* is very little used in Ireland and our Irish focus group identified it as English-English. The same applies to other informal modes of address, including *love*, *pet* and *dear*, used outside the family or an intimate setting:

(1) *I think it's different here in Ireland. I mean we don't use 'love' or 'darling' or 'pet' a lot, do we? In England it's all 'love' and 'mate' and things like that.*
(2) *Yeah, that's definitely true. When we lived in London it was all 'mate' and 'love.' It's true we don't use these terms of endearment so much.*
                              (Tralee, FG, (1) male student, 40s, bilingual; (2) female nurse, 30s)

One characteristically Irish mode of address attributed to the elderly address-ing younger people is *boy* or *girl*:

You'd sometimes hear people saying 'girl' in Ireland. Especially older people, 'Sit down there girl for yourself' and it might sound rude but I think it comes from Irish – we'd say that as respect when talking to a girl – 'Suigh ansan a chailín' ['sit down there girl'].
(Tralee, FG, male student, bilingual, 40s)

Boy as a mode of address is based on Irish *abhuachaill*. Such traditional Irish modes of address are on the decline, according to our focus group. Plural *yous*, which is often identified with Irish English, did not rate a mention in the Tralee focus group. It is still in use in Dublin and Northern Ireland (Muiris Ó Laoire, personal communication).

V-like *Sir/Madam* as formal nominal modes of address in the transactional domain are also very common in England, even though some of our English informants believe they are not employed as much as a generation ago (see Chapter 4). Again, our Irish informants characterise these as English-English modes of address that Irish people do not normally employ:

(1)   *When I lived in England I think the English use 'Sir' and 'Madam' a lot more [...] you know, in a nice way I suppose [...] than we do in Ireland you know – on the streets in the shops with the police there, it is all 'Madam'. I found it very polite but very formal too you know [...] I don't think I suppose we are like that in Ireland.*

(2)   *No, we are not like that at all. I mean, when did someone call anyone 'Sir' here outside the classroom maybe?*
                              (Tralee, FG, (1) female postgraduate student, bilingual who has also
                              acquired Spanish, 21; (2) male college lecturer, bilingual who
                              has also acquired French, 40s)

The non-use of *mate* and the evaluation of *Sir/Madam* as unnatural in Irish-English was confirmed by nine additional academic informants from all over Ireland but now resident in Dublin. But some could find instances where *Sir* could be heard in Ireland – from staff in posh restaurants and hotels and in pupil–teacher interaction at school. Irish-English would simply use the neutral pronoun *you* (*Are you coming?*) if they were unfamiliar with the interlocutor, or FN or hon + LN (*Are you coming, Paddy? Or Mr Donovan?*) if they were familiar with them. The non-use of *Sir/Madam* is understandable considering the tradition of non-compliance to authority in the face of centuries of colonial subjugation. One of our informants, a male bilingual student in his 40s, attributes it to the absence of an equivalent of *Monsieur* in Irish. The Irish appear to see themselves as less formal than the English. On the other hand, the modes of address *love, dear* and *pet*, and even *mate*, identified with England, are informal.

5.5   Modes of address in letters

5.5.1   German

In letters to people they do not know, Leipzig and Vienna informants distinguished themselves from their Mannheim counterparts in adhering to the traditional formula, in this case *Sehr geehrte/r* (see Table 5.8). Nine of our 66 Viennese informants alternated this with *Liebe/r Herr/Frau X* and a considerable minority

Table 5.8 *German: how to start a letter to somebody you do not know*

Category	Opener	Leipzig (N=66)	Mannheim (N=50)	Vienna (N=66)
1	Always *Sehr geehrte Damen und Herren/ Sehr geehrte Frau X, Sehr geehrter Herr Y*	50	27	45 *
2	*Sehr geehrte ...* or variant depending on context	10	16	13
3a	Always *Liebe/r ...*	–	–	3
3b	Always *Hello*	1	–	–
4	Only choice between *du/Sie* mentioned	5	7	3

* Two elderly women in Vienna (aged 76 und 80) reported using *Sehr geehrter Herr X* to men and *Verehrte (gnädige) Frau* to women.

of Mannheimers (14/66) alternated it with *Hello* (especially in emails) depending on the context, degree of formality and age of addressee (if known). A single Leipziger, a 75-year-old woman, preferred the old GDR form '*Werte/r...*' which she considered less formal than *Sehr geehrte/r*.

5.5.2   Swedish

In general, moving from spoken discourse to the written medium also involves a higher likelihood of more formality, including the greater use of V and of honorifics and/or titles. But there are also clear-cut differences between the Swedish-speaking sites in this respect. Again, Finland-Swedish comes across as more formal than Sweden-Swedish.

One of the questions explored how informants would start a letter to a person whom they do not know. Table 5.9 summarises the responses given to this question.

While the standard greeting in both Swedish varieties tends to be *Hej* ('Hi', 'Hello') – sometimes followed by FN or FN + LN – the results also demonstrate that the Finland-Swedes opt for rather formal greetings to a much larger extent than the Swedes. In Vaasa as many as thirty-two suggestions include the formal phrase *Bästa* (lit. 'Best', but equivalent to 'Dear' in formal greetings such as 'Dear Sir' or 'Dear Mr Smith') whereas only fourteen responses in Gothenburg do so. It is also noteworthy that the use of *Bästa* is most often combined with honorifics or title and full name of the addressee in Vaasa, whereas this is rarely the case in Gothenburg. Overall, the results indicate higher reported use of honorifics and titles in Finland-Swedish, whereas the Sweden-Swedes report much more frequent use of FN only. It is also noteworthy that the Gothenburg

Table 5.9 *Swedish: how to start a letter to somebody you do not know*

Variant	Gothen.	Vaasa
Till den det berör/ Beträffande/ Angående/ jag skriver med anledning av... (To whom it may concern/ Regarding/Regarding/ I am writing regarding...)	8	1
Hon./title + LN	1	3
Bästa[2] (lit. 'Best') + kontaktperson/mottagare (contact person/recipient)	–	4
Bästa + hon./title + LN	3	14
Bästa + FN + LN	5	10
Bästa+ FN	6	3
Kära[3] ('Dear') + FN	1	2
FN + LN	8	3
Hej ('Hello', 'Hi')	23	20
Hej + FN + LN	4	2
Hej + FN	7	–
FN	3	–
Depends on situation	3	10
Neutral phrase/avoid address	3	–
Don't know/no reply	3	4
Other	5	4
Total responses*	83	79

* The numbers do not correspond exactly with the number of respondents as a few give more than one alternative.

participants are more inclined to nominate a set of terms such as *Till den det berör* ('To whom it may concern') which could be interpreted as strategies to avoid direct address. This is a further indication that the use of *ni* is problematic in Sweden-Swedish.

In the questionnaire we also asked about addressing an unknown person in an email with *du* or *ni*. Here slightly more than 60% of the Vaasa informants say they would use *ni* whereas only about 30% of the Gothenburg participants would. These results are substantiated by the interview responses.

5.5.3   English

Dear..., *Hello* and *Hi* are used similarly in England and Ireland, with any differentiation based on medium (*Dear...* for written correspondence and *Hello* and *Hi* common in email), degree of formality, degree of familiarity and

---

[2] *Bästa* sometimes also occurs in the masculine form *Bäste*.
[3] *Kära* (lit. 'dear') has connotations of intimacy and is not directly equivalent to 'Dear' as part of a formal greeting in English.

age of interlocutor(s) rather than on national variety of English. In formal letters the use of hon + LN is the standard way of addressing the recipient according to the focus group participants and there are no differences recorded between the research sites in this respect.

5.6 Awareness of national variation in German and Swedish

The interview data reflect the characteristic of asymmetrical pluricentricity that people from the dominant nation(s) using the language will be poorly informed about the other national varieties, sometimes equating them with regional varieties (Clyne 1992: 460).

Twenty-three German informants, eight from Leipzig and fifteen from Mannheim, think that there is more T use in Austria than in Germany. They often mention that it is 'wie Bayern' (like Bavaria), or that their experience is limited to holidays where T is more likely anyway.

However, almost twice as many German informants (forty-four), twenty-two from Leipzig and twelve from Mannheim, think that V is used more frequently in Austria and often associate it with the well-known use of titles there. The confusion between the function of titles and of pronouns is reflected in the following quotations. This corresponds to the well-attested finding in dialectological research (see e.g. Mattheier 1980) that people will recognise dialects from closer proximity better than those from further afield.

In Österreich, glaub ich, ist es konservativer, aber es wirkt lockerer.
[In Austria I think it's more conservative but it gives a more informal impression.] (Leipzig, Q5, male solicitor, 39)

Man lächelt sehr oft über die vielen, vielen Titel, die in Österreich benutzt werden [Hofrat, Geheimrat, Doktor, Magister], nie würde ein Deutscher den Magister-Titel ... auch in den Mund nehmen, in Österreich sehr, sehr häufig [...] und das ist die Welt, wie sie sich darstellt auf den ersten Blick. Aber sobald man Menschen besser kennt, und das ist in Österreich schon ab dem 5. oder 6. Glas Wein, kommt da sehr schnell das 'Du', sehr viel früher als in Deutschland. Während Menschen jahrelang nebeneinander wohnen können und sich noch siezen, ist in Österreich oft schon nach wenigen Wochen das 'Du' da [...] auf den ersten Blick ist die Distanz grösser, aber später viel näher.
[People are very often amused about the many, many titles that are used in Austria (*Hofrat* [nearest equivalent: privy councillor], *Geheimrat* [nearest equivalent: privy councillor], *doctor*, *master*), a German would never say these titles, in Austria very, very often [...] and that is the world that is presented on the surface. But as soon as you know people better, and in Austria, that is the case starting with the fifth or sixth glass of wine, *du* is used. Much faster than in Germany. While people live next to each other for years and still call each other *Sie*, *du* is often used in Austria after a few weeks [...] at first sight the distance is greater but afterwards it is much closer.] (Mannheim, Q10, male junior academic, 29)

Twenty-three Viennese informants believe that address use in Germany is generally more informal (i.e. more T). Many of them associate this with more informal greetings in Germany such as *Hallo* and *Tschüß*.

Of the Swedish informants, 40% have no opinion at all about Finland-Swedish usage, whereas this is the case for only 3% of the Vaasa informants. These figures confirm earlier findings that the dominant nation in pluricentric situations tends not to engage with the other variety and displays ignorance of its features (Clyne 1992: 460). Furthermore, the overwhelming majority (75%) of the Vaasa informants are of the opinion that Sweden-Swedish is more informal, with more use of *du* than Finland-Swedish. Some Vaasa informants refer to the ubiquitous T (*du*) as typically Swedish, even a practice that forms part of the national character of the Swedes:

I Sverige säger alla 'du', utom till kungen.
[In Sweden everybody says *du* except to the king.] (Vaasa, FG1, male retired police officer, 67)

Det svenska duandet är ju så väldigt, väldigt svenskt.
[The Swedish use of *du* is so terribly, terribly Swedish.] (Vaasa, Q3, female chief librarian, 49)

In contrast, most of the Gothenburg informants who express an opinion claim that Finland-Swedish is more formal, old-fashioned and/or has a higher frequency of *ni*. However, it is worth noting that many who present a view are uncertain, as is evidenced by the high level of hedging in many responses:

Jag har absolut ingen aning men jag har en känsla av att den finlandssvenska delen är mer formell.
[I have absolutely no idea but I have a feeling that the Finland-Swedish part is more formal.] (Gothenburg, Q7, female assistant gardener, 52)

5.7   Language contact

Globalisation, migration and new technologies have brought address systems into contact with those of other languages. As we have seen in previous chapters, the changes in the pronominal system of Swedish occurred due to internal socio-political changes in Sweden and to a lesser extent in Finland. However, the nominal system is more volatile and subject to influence from other languages. Because in German T and FN tend to go hand in hand, as do V and hon + LN, the increased FN use due to language and culture contact can flow on to increased T use. The single most important contact influence on address in all three languages is from English and this is referred to in both our interviews and focus groups.

In the case of English-English and Irish-English, it is American-English that is the main influence. *Babe*, used between marriage partners, was given as an example by one of our Newcastle informants:

Certainly a few years ago I couldn't see me and my missus referring to each other as 'babe' like a couple of New York hip hop artists. It just seems that these things drift in. There's no way when I was a kid would two grown people refer to themselves as that. And that seems to have crept in. (Newcastle, FG, IT project manager, 45)

5.7.1   English first names and German T – the global and the local context

We have observed people meeting in first-name contexts socially or institutionally, for instance at international conferences and associated social gatherings where English is frequently employed as a *lingua franca*. They will sometimes face a dilemma when they next meet on a similar or different occasion in a German-speaking country (especially Germany). There they continue FN use and may extend it to T, even if they had previously been on V terms in the local context. Usually this happens quite painlessly. However, there is potential for embarrassment if there are closer colleagues with whom they are on V terms. One of our Viennese informants comments on this in a business context:

In einem englischsprachigen Land, auch geschäftlich, wenn man mit einem englisch-sprachigen Kollegen den Vornamen verwendet, dann wird man auch mit dem deutsch-sprechend zu Vornamen übergehen. Wenn man zurückkommt ist es anders, nicht mit der bestimmten Person, da würde man so bleiben, aber nicht mit den anderen.

[In an English-speaking country, even on business, when you use first names with an English-speaking colleague, you will immediately go over to first names in German. On your return it's different, not with the particular person, you would continue the mode of address with them, but not with the others.] (Vienna, Q5, male technician, 31)

In addition, two Mannheim focus group members – a policeman of about forty and a female arts teacher, aged about thirty – report on people temporarily increasing their use of *du* after their return from extended stays in America. Some of our informants, especially in Leipzig, attributed the increased use of *du* in German to American influence:

Heute wird mehr 'Du' gesagt, [...] es ist langsam, schrittweise gekommen mit den Medien, eine Entwicklung von Amerika her.

[Today more *du* is used, [...] it has come slowly, step by step with the media, a development from America.] (Leipzig, Q6, male engineer, 36)

The use of *du* and first names among staff and between staff and students in university English departments is also commented on. For example, one twenty-eight-year-old male student in Mannheim (Q3) states that there is *bewusstes Duzen bei den Anglisten* ('a conscious use of *du* in English departments') (cf. 4.3.2).

The more formal rules in German than in English can pose a cultural problem for German speakers. One Mannheim student indicated he could not really speak German with one of his English lecturers because he did not know which pronoun to use:

Das ist auch ein Grund, warum ich mit dem Kerl gar nicht Deutsch rede.
[That is another reason why I don't speak German with the fellow.] (Mannheim, Q3, male student, 26)

A typical problem for German-speaking teachers of German in English-speaking countries is choice of address pronoun:

Da hatte ich größte Probleme damit, die jetzt zu duzen auf deutsch, aber siezen wäre dann auch komisch gewesen.
[I had the biggest problems addressing her with *du* [referring to a fellow teacher and mentor] but using *Sie* would have been funny too.] (Mannheim, Q3, male student, 28)

5.7.2   Dilemmas of the transfer of English first-name use into Swedish

Although Swedish is similar to English in that it is, according to many participants, a 'one-pronoun' society, the English address system is not without its challenges for speakers of Sweden-Swedish. Some of our participants claim that English address conventions are difficult to learn because they allow for both more formality (use of honorifics and titles) and more informality (use of first name).

According to our initial focus group data, an increased use of first names in addressing people is often attributed to the Anglo-American influence on Swedish. In recent years, it has become increasingly common for people to be addressed by their first name by perfect strangers, e.g. sales people or civil servants. Such use of first names is associated with false intimacy and a trend in society that the participants find both irritating and calculating, as the following quotation from the Gothenburg group reveals:

Det är fruktansvärt obehagligt med förnamnstilltal… förnamnet är privat. Vem är du? Vad har du för rätt att känna till eller använda mitt förnamn? Så reagerar jag när vilt främmande människor använder mitt förnamn.
[It is terribly unpleasant this address with first names…your first name is private. Who are you? What right have you to know or use my first name? That is the way I react when complete strangers use my first name.] (Gothenburg, FG1, female cashier at McDonald's, 20)

Irrespective of their age, all focus group participants in both Gothenburg and Vaasa agree that perceived intimacy is signalled by use of FN. Introducing oneself and addressing people by FN only is seen as a habit imported from English, but in the Finland-Swedish data Sweden is also mentioned as a source of this change, as illustrated in the following quotation from the initial focus group:

Jag har blivit uppfostrad med att presentera mig med hela namnet, bara förnamnet beror på intryck från Sverige, den demokratiska processen. Duandet.
[I have been brought up to introduce myself by my full name; the use of first name only is due to influence from Sweden, the democratic process. The use of *du*.] (Vaasa, FG1, female social worker, 59)

Variation between the two national varieties of Swedish is also emphasised by the second focus group in Vaasa. In the quote below the participants are discussing the trend of using first names, mostly agreeing that it is likely to be more prevalent in Sweden than Finland and a trend which could be attributed to globalisation and American influence:

(1)   Men används förnamnen i tal på det här sättet mer i sverigesvenskan än finlandssvenskan?
(2)   De gör nog det.
(1)   Ja, det gör det för jag sku som väldigt sällan använda förnamn.
(2)   Det tyder ju den här undersökningen på också.
(3)   Men har man nåt ärende så: 'hörrdu Carola'.
(1)   Jo, men du upprepar det ju int tre gånger efter att ha fått uppmärksamheten.
       [...]
(4)   Globalisering.
(1)   Jag sku nog tippa på någo Amerikainfluenser, ja kanske i och med tv och sånt.

[(1)   But are first names used in spoken language in this way more in Sweden-Swedish than in Finland-Swedish?
(2)   It is, surely.
(1)   Yes, it is, because I would very rarely use first names.
(2)   This investigation indicates that too.
(3)   But if you have some business, then: 'listen Carola'.
(1)   Yes, but you don't repeat the name three times after you got her attention.
       [...]
(4)   Globalisation.
(1)   I would guess at some sort of American influences, well perhaps because of TV and such.]

(Vaasa, FG2, (1) female project assistant, 26; (2) male retired police officer, 67; (3) female social worker, 59; (4) male sales manager, 63)

5.7.3   Honorifics and titles – Swedish perception of English formality

While the increased use of first names is regarded as an import from English, there is no evidence of the more formal aspects of English address having made it into Swedish. On the contrary, comments made by the interviewees often illustrate how completely impossible and outdated use of honorifics such as *Herr, Fru* or *Fröken* would seem in contemporary Swedish:

Samtidigt är det bra att man kan visa respekten, att man säger 'ni'. Men det kommer mera fram i engelskan att de säger 'Mr' och 'Mrs' hela tiden. Om någon skulle säga fröken Korpimäki här så skulle jag nog anse att personen i fråga är helt bakom.

[At the same time it is good to be able to show respect, to say *ni*. But that comes through more in English by them saying *Mr* and *Mrs* all the time. If somebody would say *Miss Korpimäki* here I think I would consider the person in question completely stupid.]
(Vaasa, Q6, female student, 27)

As the quotation above illustrates, when asked about advantages and disadvantages of the English address system, the informants often comment on the fact that English uses means other than address pronouns to convey a certain level of respect or politeness, which would not be readily transferred into Swedish.

5.8   Business/multinational companies

Two large Swedish multinational companies, the furniture retailer IKEA and the clothing/fashion company H&M, have imposed the use of the informal address pronoun within the company and when addressing customers, even where traditionally V address would be the natural choice in such encounters. When IKEA started using *du* in Germany and Austria on signs in stores, in catalogues and on websites, some customers reacted negatively. These included young internet-literate customers, as can be seen from a number of German blogs (see e.g. Sdun 2004). An Austrian newspaper conducted a survey, from which it was able to conclude (Schacherreitner 2004) that *Herr und Frau Österreicher sehen offensichtlich keinen zwingenden Grund, mit jemandem per Du zu sein, bloß weil man ihm das Regal Billy oder den Sessel Vilma abgekauft hat* ('Mr and Ms Austria evidently see no compelling reason to be on *du* terms with someone just because they have bought a Billy bookshelf or a Vilma chair from them'). H&M's requirement of T use within the company even led to some legal action on the part of an employee (Sakowski not dated).

In response to a question on attitude towards companies that prescribe a mode of address, some of our German-speaking informants express an awareness that Swedish norms have influenced usage in Swedish companies in German-speaking countries and have some sympathy for it:

Das nehme ich als Eigenart des Landes.
[I take that to be a feature of the country.] (Vienna, Q4, female retiree, 83)

Ja, mein Gott, wenn das zu deren Firmenphilosophie gehört und sie aus einem Land stammen, in dem das Du ganz normal ist; ja why not?
[Yes, for goodness sake, if it is part of their company philosophy and they are from a country where it is quite normal; yes *why not?*[4]] (Mannheim, Q2, female laboratory assistant, 35)

Generally, the responses of our participants to IKEA's *du* use vis-à-vis customers and in advertising were less negative than those surveyed by the newspaper and varied from *freundlich* ('friendly') via *eine gute Verkaufsstrategie* ('a good sales strategy') to '*störend*' ('disturbing').

Business contacts and other professional engagements in other countries and across language boundaries can also result in different address behaviour

---

[4] In English.

depending on the cultural and linguistic background of one's interlocutor. For the Vaasa informants, all of whom are bilingual and use both Swedish and Finnish in their daily life, the different pragmatic norms of the languages can pose problems, as one of the interviewees put it:

Det är jättesvårt i och med att man är tvåspråkig, använder finska och svenska och man vet att man beter sig annorlunda, det kommer mycket naturligare att du niar på finska än vad det gör på svenska så det är svårt att tänka sig in i olika situationer och tänka att du enbart har svenska att ta till eftersom du dagligen liksom ändå använder både finskan och svenskan.

[It is really difficult because you are bilingual, use Finnish and Swedish, and you know that you behave differently, it comes much more natural to use *ni* in Finnish than it does in Swedish so it is difficult to imagine different situations and imagine that you only would have access to Swedish since you use both Finnish and Swedish daily anyway, you know.] (Vaasa, Q2, female project manager, 30)

While many of the Vaasa informants are in daily contact with Finnish speakers through their work, close work-related contacts with Sweden are also very common and several informants also come in regular contact with people from other nations. These varied contacts make them perceptible to differences in address usage, as illustrated in the following exchange from the Vaasa focus group between two women:

(1)	*På vårt jobb märks det ganska bra. Leverantörer: stor skillnad mellan Sverige – 'du' genast fast det är första kontakten. Inom Finland: 'ni', mera hövligt. Tyskland 'ni'. Hövligt 'ni'. Telefonsamtal: lite hövligare när man ringer så blir det mer hövligt med 'ni'.*
Moderator	*Tyskarna niar så då niar du.*
(2)	*man ska veta när man ska säga 'ni' eller 'Sir' i europeiska projekt.*
[(1)	At our workplace it is quite noticeable. Contractors: big difference between Sweden: *du* immediately even if it is the first contact. Within Finland: *ni*, more polite. Germany: *ni*. Polite *ni*. Phone conversations: a bit more polite when you phone, so it is more polite with *ni*.
Moderator	So the Germans say *ni* so then you also use *ni*.
(2)	One should know when to say *ni* or *Sir* in European projects.]

(Vaasa, FG1, (1) female purchaser, 29; (2) female teacher, 48)

It is perhaps not surprising to find that the majority of the Gothenburg informants (80%) have no objection to a *du* policy as practised by IKEA. However, it is interesting to note that support for such a policy is much less pronounced in the Finland-Swedish data (40%).

The reservations put forward by the Finland Swedes deal with addressing older people, but also reveal the language contact situation, as informants point out that Finnish speakers are less likely to approve of it:

Nej, jag tycker inte det är lämpligt p.g.a. att de har så mycket finska kunder och jag tror inte att finnarna tycker om det, men för svenska kunder tror jag nog det går för fullt. Men som sagt de har både finska och svenska kunder och inte vet de om det är en svensk eller finsk kund som kommer. Jag tror inte finska kunder tycker om det, i synnerhet de från Helsingforstrakten.

[No, I don't think it is suitable for the reason that they have so many Finnish customers and I don't think the Finns like it, but for Swedish [i.e. Finland-Swedes] customers I think it works fully. But like I said, they have both Finnish and Swedish customers and they don't know if it is a Swedish or Finnish customer who is approaching. I don't think Finnish customers like it, in particular if they are from the Helsinki region.] (Vaasa, Q5, male retired engineer, 78)

5.9   Concluding remarks

This chapter has compared the role of modes of address in human relations in different societies or nations using the same language rather than examining the entire language area. We discussed how English, German and Swedish all show different national variation patterns in modes of address based on sociocultural history and cultural values. The indications from the English focus group data are that Irish-English has gone furthest in the avoidance of even nominal modes of address such as the V-like *Sir/Madam* or the T-like ones *mate* and/or *dear* used beyond the family or intimate context. This would suggest that social distance is of greater importance in England but also that the tendency towards negative politeness is more developed in Ireland than in England.

Finland-Swedish and Sweden-Swedish differ in terms of address, with *ni* still playing some role in marking formality and different degrees of social distance in Finland. In Sweden, there are few functions for *ni*. In Vaasa, unlike Gothenburg, status is still an important factor in some decisions on address. Thus, the use of V to elderly people by the young as a marker of social distance does not give the impression of social exclusion the way it does in Gothenburg. In Vaasa, too, degree of social distance is negotiated in the choice of both address pronouns and nominal modes of address, though to a lesser extent than in England, Austria, Germany (or indeed France), and nominals in England. In Sweden-Swedish, social distance plays a role in the choice of FN or FN + LN rather than in address pronoun choice.

In German, there are quantitative rather than absolute differences based on social, cultural and political history, ongoing traditions and reactions to previous imposition. A greater use of *du* is reported and accepted in Vienna than in Germany. *Du* is reported to be used less in Leipzig now than in GDR times, at least in the middle and older generations. This is variously attributed to the effect of distaste for obligatory *du*, part of an imposed identity within the GDR Communist Party, and a loss of the previously more open, more collective identity since the fall of the Berlin wall. The younger generation is largely freed of that dilemma. There is variation between those who feel their individual right to determining sameness and difference was disrupted in the GDR and those who prefer to make a decision on common ground – they do not see social distance as important. The Leipzig data thus show that the legacy of the GDR affects people differentially. There is still evidence of split identity – imposed publicly (more V) and negotiated privately (often choice of T). The higher incidence of both *du* and titles in Vienna can be traced to practices that have their origin in the days of the Austro-Hungarian Empire. It demonstrates that status can be expressed by title, without being in opposition with a low degree of social distance on the basis of affect, solidarity and familiarity, leading to the choice of T.

As is the case with other aspects of national varieties, people using dominant varieties of a pluricentric language do not know much about the address patterns in non-dominant varieties. In the case of address, there is confusion about whether other national varieties are more or less formal.

Globalisation, travel, conferences and international networks have all facilitated contact-induced changes in modes of address. For instance, English influence has led to the increased use of FN and, by extension, of T and V + FN in the first language as well as dilemmas on how to address some people in first-language contexts. Swedish influence, which has led to default T being imposed in some Swedish companies in German-speaking countries, has generated different attitudes on the part of the local populations. Language contact has also led to some challenges to the expression of human relations through modes of address to the point where some people will avoid employing their first language in order to avoid a face-threatening act by the use of a particular pronoun. This is an issue that is not usually raised in the discussion of English hegemony in the contemporary world.

Our next and final chapter will attempt to develop some of these questions and those arising from previous chapters into a theoretical model.

6   Conclusions

6.1   Introduction

This chapter summarises the findings of the study and proposes a model for choice of address mode. This is based on grammatical and pragmatic comparisons between the languages, the address preferences of individuals or networks, contextual factors and a set of six principles of address mode choice focusing on degree of social distance.

In this study, we have focused on three languages, French, German and Swedish. They share quite similar pronominal resources for address, namely a binary system in at least the singular (in the case of German, in the plural too). The fourth language, English, which we have considered in a more peripheral way as a point of reference, does not offer a binary pronominal system of address. However, it has shown how nominal features (notably FN vs. hon [with or without title] + LN, but also V-like modes of address *Sir, Madam* and T-like ones such as *mate, dear*) can fulfil similar functions as the pronominal modes in the other languages. How linguistic resources such as pronouns are utilised pragmatically to manage human relations is informed by cultural and/or sub-cultural values and social structures as well as by contextual factors, all subject to sociopolitical change. This means that the same grammatical devices can be used quite differently across and within languages. In French, and to a large extent in German, the pronouns T and V drive the entire address system; T is linked with FN (or kinship term) and V with hon (and/or title) and LN.

In French and especially in German, variation and change in address have made the rules and their social significance more difficult and challenging to interpret. In Swedish, however, the widespread use of T has given FN vs. FN + LN some of the differentiating roles played by T and V in French and German. Following a period of cumbersome address patterns based on negative politeness (1.5, 2.3.4), Swedish has adjusted its grammatical resources so that T (*du*) is the default pronoun and the V form (*ni*) is still available but utilised only in very specific contexts. English can often avoid explicit address for three reasons. One is the single pronoun of address (U in our terminology). The second is the occurrence of address nominals only as vocatives. Third, second-person verb morphology is not dictated by pronouns the way it is in French and German.

Furthermore, German has the additional pronominal form *ihr*, which is used as a resource in two ways: to enable the speaker to include on T terms a group of people who are (a) partially (or wholly) in a T network or (b) members of an institution within which a T-type relationship exists. This ambiguity gives German speakers an intermediate form in the plural which has similarities with English U. As for Swedish *ni*, it is ambiguous in two ways. First, it is the plural of both T and V. Second, particularly in Sweden-Swedish, the context-specific use of *ni* mentioned above has resulted in a degree of generational miscommunication arising from an intention of politeness among younger people and an interpretation of exclusion and condescension on the part of the elderly, to whom it is addressed.

While in French and German it is usually the pronoun that drives the nominal modes, this is not always so. T + title, T + LN and V + FN are all possible combinations. The use of T with titles in Austrian German, in the education sector to address teachers (5.4.1) but also in the public service, indicates that two modes of address used together can have different functions – T for lowering social distance and title to designate status. The same applies in German to the use of T with hon + LN, used by employees to one another in public situations in department stores (4.4.2). T expresses a lowering of social distance and hon + FN confirms workplace employee status within earshot of the customers. Another compromise combination is V + FN, attested in both French and German. For instance, instead of T being used in the workplace for lowering social distance, it is FN that takes on this role and it is the pronoun V which designates status in a hierarchical work relationship (see 4.4). V + FN is also used in the family, particularly with a partner's parents, and this combination marks respect and low social distance.

6.2   Towards a model

Our data, from interviews, focus groups, participant observation and chat groups, have given insights into how users of the project languages decide which mode of address to use to whom and when (cf. Fishman 1965). In Chapter 4, our examination of address in various institutions and domains highlighted well-established address practices not requiring choices, for example within the close family and among students, as well as practices established by imposition or hierarchy, particularly in the workplace. Chapter 3 investigated how speakers can use the pronominal and nominal modes of address available in each language to express common ground, a degree of social distance and group boundaries.

The choice of address mode is an act of identity (cf. Le Page and Tabouret-Keller 1985). It is a spontaneous or a reasoned response to how much of themselves speakers discover in their interlocutor, or, to put it another way, the extent to which speakers share common ground with their interlocutor. There are many ways in which common ground can be perceived – through membership of particular groups, common interests, or common sociopolitical views, for example, and through non-linguistic indices such as dress and outward appearance. The choice of address mode determines, or reflects the perception of, a higher or lower degree of social distance. Familiarity can promote the inclination to lower social distance by triggering the T form. Substantial age differences play a particular role in expressing a high degree of social distance in Swedish, especially in Sweden, and are the basis for non-reciprocal V address (Chapter 3). It is in the two languages that offer the greatest choice, French and German, that T is associated with positive politeness (Brown and Levinson 1987) and V or avoidance with negative politeness, often to prevent face threats to oneself and others (2.3.1).

Whether the choice of address mode is rational or emotional, it is a decision on inclusion or exclusion, on whether or where to draw a group boundary between that person and oneself or between them and us. In English, French and German, mode of address choice (T and/or nominal) is made on the basis of sameness, i.e. low degree of social distance. In Swedish, where communication presupposes general membership of an almost universal mainstream, it is difference that is expressed by mode of address (V), which separates small groups (royal family or very much older people) warranting special status and esteem. It is also expressed in the reintroduction of V into Sweden-Swedish service encounters in which some young shop assistants address (usually older) customers by V (4.5.3). However, V is more prevalent in Finland-Swedish, which adopts similar patterns of address to French and German but in a far more limited way, with T still being used frequently in contexts served by V in French and German (5.2.2, 5.3.2, 5.4.2).

In Chapter 2, we noted the usefulness of a multidimensional, dynamic model in the conceptualisation of social distance (cf. Svennevig 1999). Our own model of address practices presented below underlines the importance of multidimensionality, comprising three scales, a set of principles and a number of contextual factors. It compares grammar and pragmatics of the languages, general principles across languages and contextual factors that may or may not apply. The tripartite model is dynamic in the sense that grammatical resources in a language interact with the principles of use – which in turn are contextually sensitive (the factors). There is overlap between the scale of sameness and difference and the principle of social identification, but these entities have different functions in the model.

(a)   Scale of grammatical resources

German – French – Swedish – English

French, German and Swedish all offer pronouns of address. In the first two languages, they drive nominal modes of address such as FN and hon + title and/or LN. German differentiates between T and V in both the singular and plural, and only French and German verb morphology is marked by personal pronoun. Swedish has potentially the same pronoun resources as French but has effectively abandoned one of them. English has done this completely. There are other grammatical devices such as *on* in French and to a lesser extent *man* in German, which together with the passive (especially in Swedish) are grammatical devices of address pronoun avoidance.

(b)   Scale of V-ness

French – German – Swedish – English

We have also seen in our data chapters that French employs V and V-like modes most, quantitatively more than German, the language with the most similar results. Swedish has almost abandoned V and V-like modes. English, with its pronoun U, does without T and V altogether, but employs T-like nominals, such as FN, *mate* and *dear*, and V-like ones such as hon + LN, title, *Sir* or *Madam*, which express lower and higher social distance respectively.

If we differentiate national varieties, Finland-Swedish should come between German and Sweden-Swedish and German (Standard) German should precede Austrian (Standard) German. Irish-English could come at the end of the scale as it utilises even nominal resources sparsely to express social distance. The national variety scale can be represented as follows:

French – German (Standard) German – Austrian (Standard) German – Finland-Swedish – Sweden-Swedish – English-English – Irish-English

(c)   Scale of sameness

French – German – English – Swedish

French, German and English in descending order all employ sameness (common ground) as a major criterion for T (or T-like) address. It is in French that the distinction between T and V is the strongest and thus the shift to T based on sameness has the most salience. In German, where there is more ambivalence about T and V, the sameness criterion is less central. In English, with its one pronoun U, there is no imperative to mark sameness (or difference). Swedish, in contrast, automatically employs T address, whereas difference (lack of common ground) can be a reason for V address.

As has already been intimated, human relations are primarily issues of identity, of inclusion and exclusion and of face. These are at the fore of the decision-making process when a choice of address mode is made, or a transition to another address mode is initiated, on the basis of a set of principles. These principles are formulated through a series of questions; however, this is not to say that people consciously raise these questions in their interactions. They are simply a device for illustrating each principle.

1. *Familiarity Principle:*
   Do I know this person?
2. *Maturity Principle:*
   Do I perceive this person to be an adult?
3. *Relative Age Principle:*
   Do I perceive this person to be considerably older than me? Or younger?
4. *Network Membership Principle:*
   Is this person a regular and accepted member within a group I belong to?
5. *Social Identification Principle:*
   Do I perceive this person to be similar to or different from me?
6. *Address Mode Accommodation Principle:*
   If this person uses T (or V), or a T-like (or V-like) address with me, will I do the same?

Principles 1, 2 and 4 concern absolute assessments of the interlocutor, whereas principles 3 and 5 consider the other in relation to oneself and 5 relates to address mode per se. Principle 2 can promote a mode of address based on negative politeness, avoiding T or T-like modes which might encroach on the interlocutor's autonomy. Principle 3 provides a basis for inclusion or exclusion, motivating T (T-like) or V (V-like) modes. This is one of the factors enabling a speaker to decide choice of address mode.

As we have seen (Chapter 3), principles 2 and 3 are not quite as clear-cut or as readily discernible as might be expected and can lead to face threats when the mode of address implies membership of a different age group to the one which people imagine themselves to belong to. Principles 1, 4 and 5 also relate to inclusion or exclusion, and the chosen mode of address denotes degree of social distance. Principle 6 concerns speakers' orientation towards their interlocutor and the extent to which they converge to, or diverge from, their interlocutor's address choices.

As we have seen in Chapters 3, 4 and 5, all these principles depend on factors such as:

(a) the address rules of the language and/or the national variety according to the scales above;
(b) the address preferences of the network and/or the individual; together with
(c) the contextual factors (domain, institution, medium).

The interface between scales, principles and factors will enable people to decide where on the continuum of social distance they would like to place the interlocutor and consequently on the scale of mode of address (T/T-like, V/V-like). If we consider the four project languages, it is clear that the languages differ in terms of which scales and/or principles apply. In French and German, all principles come into play, which is not the case for Swedish: because of the position of Swedish on the Scale of Grammatical Resources and the Scale of Sameness, the Maturity Principle will have no effect on address mode, though the Relative Age Principle might.

In addition, our data from chat groups show a medium in which T is very widely used as a default pronoun in French, German and Swedish, albeit not quite as universally as anticipated by the participants. The members of chat groups know very little about one another, though many of the forums are based on common ground. The information required for the Relative Age Principle (or even the Social Identification Principle) to be put into operation is generally not available to the interlocutors. Here it is the Network Membership Principle that predominates.

6.3   Non-reciprocity and transition

Although non-reciprocity is generally associated with oppressive power structures, there appears to be a survival or even a resurgence of it. This is an expression of a high degree of social distance by a person whose status does not allow them to include the other in their group and exchange reciprocal T or first name. This may be because of the social distance felt or because of the face relations with others which might be adversely affected. Thus in German, choosing a mode of address has become most difficult. The degree of variation in address patterns is greatest and the social significance of the interlocutor's choice of address mode may not be easily discernible. So address becomes a sort of communication game that people play or have to play. It can entail avoidance of address mode or waiting for the other to use a pronominal or nominal mode of address. To at least some extent this applies to all our languages and is part of the dynamics associated with the negotiation of multiple identities, some shared and some not. However, because in English the mode of address is only nominal and therefore not embedded in the grammatical system and the use of V is so limited in Swedish, the issue is relevant especially to German and French.

While the practice of address is similar in French and German, there are also important differences. Not only does quantitative analysis demonstrate a greater use of T employed in German than in French in similar situations, there is also a considerable minority of our informants, especially young adults, who deny the social significance of T and V in German. In German and also in French, there is substantial grey territory between the clear-cut T and V areas, and speakers characterise themselves as more T or more V users. Such characterisations are among the stylistic features of a younger, more urban and bourgeois or egalitarian image (cf. Morford 1997). In addition, the fuzzy boundaries of certain domains such as the family permit much leeway for individual choice and negotiation in both languages (see 4.1.1 and 4.1.2).

The T pronoun, and, in English, FN, are on the increase in the workplace, whether to promote company identity or as a marker of low social distance among colleagues; yet the irreversible nature of T relationships in French and German, workplace mobility and the requirements of the transactional domain keep the reins on this development, for V can avoid the semblance of favouritism. In English too the V-like nominal modes of address *Sir* and *Madam* can ensure that social distance is preserved in a conflict situation within the domain of service encounters.

As far as transition is concerned, the mode of address in first encounters in French and German tends to be V, except within institutions or networks that are characterised by T address. However, there may be early or later opportunities for a transition from V to T. Traditionally this was a rite of passage ceremoniously celebrated or performed according to particular rules, such as the older person offering a T relationship to the younger one. This can be an event, such as leaving school or completing a doctorate, leading the teacher or supervisor to offer a T relationship, but the transition can also occur spontaneously. Such transitional practices previously occurred in Swedish, the language which has undergone the most radical changes in modes of address.

6.4   Address and cultural values in the face of sociopolitical change

Through globalisation, migration, travel and new technologies, languages and by extension their address systems are increasingly in contact. We have seen the way in which modes of address express human relations and how important the role of cultural values is in this. This connection is challenged by dyads and larger groupings interacting across languages and cultures, as is evident from the perceptions of others' address systems and dilemmas associated with them. These include a fear of using your first language with some people with whom you have developed a T-like relationship in English, one which would not be possible in your first language. Transfer of Swedish address rules into German in Swedish multinational workplaces in German-speaking countries has led to difficulties in industrial relations and service encounters.

Both cyclical developments and large-scale variation detract from the predictive power of Brown and Gilman's (1960) projected tendencies. Their prediction that V will yield to T can be supported only in a differentiated way. This has largely become the case in Sweden-Swedish, but even there *ni* has undergone something of a resurgence in service encounters between young and old and occasionally in some status-marked situations. Swedish had earlier moved quite swiftly from a society in which the dropping of titles was accompanied by very strict social conventions to one in which no transition of modes of address needed to be negotiated. This rapid development had no parallel in any of the other languages considered here.

In French, and particularly in German, the widespread effects of the T ideology of the student movement have waned. In German, they are limited to like-minded networks of 'baby boomers' and especially to the university domain, where T address among students remains general. An ongoing effect of the student revolution in German is the large-scale dropping of titles in informal communication. In France, the events of May 1968 and their aftermath were initiated by both students and workers, and the French data show the extent to which the (mainly transitory) effects of the time on both pronominal and nominal address practices continue to be discussed, nearly forty years later. The T ideology has remained in some tertiary institutions, where T is the norm among students, staff and administrators. It is also the source of the current widespread T use among university academics and among students, particularly among those with certain leftist political leanings, as well as those known as *soixante-huitards* ('sixty-eighters').

Yet this study has drawn attention to some new developments. A new pervasive individualism, explicitly remarked upon by the majority of our participants, has led to a reluctance to have address practices imposed. Across the languages, there is a desire to reserve the right to decide which pronominal or nominal mode of address they are to be addressed by whom.

The issue of imposition featured most particularly in the eastern part of Germany, where some members of the older and middle generations rejected the general use of T because the SED (Communist Party) had imposed it on its members in the days of the German Democratic Republic. The majority of French interview participants were not in favour of the imposition of the T form in the workplace and members of the English focus groups also expressed resentment of imposition of address modes. A new transactional politeness has brought *Sir/Madam* and *ni* back in England and Sweden respectively. Globalisation has brought languages with different address systems into contact. People are thus more aware of other ways of 'doing address'.

6.5   The special contributions of this study

Each of our data-collection methods – focus groups, closed and open question-naires, participant observation, chat groups – has made a unique contribution to the totality of the project. The focus groups have enabled us to ascertain the salient issues around address in the community. The lively discussions and debates between people of different backgrounds in terms of age/generation, education/ occupation and gender are conducive to exploring the extent of variation and change, especially since address proved to be an issue of interest and concern in the various communities under investigation. The issues discussed in the focus groups could be explored further in participant observation. Moreover, they could be addressed explicitly in both the quantitative and qualitative sections of the interviews, which yielded comparative results both within and between research sites and languages. The chat groups have provided a different forum for discussion on address within a medium that is itself a factor in changes in choice of mode of address. The large amount of qualitative data has provided the quotations throughout the book in which the voices of many of our participants may be heard. The reflective nature of these quotations demonstrates how much thought people give to choice of address mode.

Adopting a pluricentric model of languages has enabled us to ascertain the effects of cultural values on address in particular national varieties. Contact with Finnish, which has a more conservative address system than Swedish, has contributed to a greater use of V in Finland-Swedish than in Sweden-Swedish; issues of status and formality still play an important role in a residual T/V dichotomy, though not nearly as much as in French or German. Also, the age threshold for the use of V is considerably lower in Finland-Swedish than in Sweden-Swedish. The differences between the Austrian and German national varieties of German are relative rather than absolute. The greater use of T and of titles in Austria reflects sociopolitical and cultural history. Meanwhile, eastern German address modes reflect both a hankering for a more collective society and distaste for the communist past. The continuing variation between attitudes to and practice in address in western and eastern Germany nearly two decades after the fall of the Berlin wall, though they were separated for only four, demonstrates the impact of sociocultural history on address. Our Irish focus group comments on the lack of V-like nominal modes of address (*Sir*, *Madam*) in Irish English may be largely in reaction to English colonialism. All this underlines the 'depth' of pragmatic aspects of a language.

Our findings are not without surprises. Everywhere address is more complex than we might have anticipated. Even in Sweden-Swedish, with its dominance of universal T, the distinction between T and V use still engages people and makes them agonise over what is an appropriate mode of address. In some domains such as the law, titles and third-person address still occur as a relic of earlier address practices. In Finland-Swedish, status-marked V is far more prevalent than in Sweden-Swedish. There are paradoxes, such as German speakers, noted for their uncertainty avoidance (Hofstede 1991: 57, but cf. Behrens 2007) and the importance they attach to commitment as a cultural value, extolling the pleasures of fathoming out what meaning their interlocutor attributes to a T or V use, while yet others deny the social significance of T and V.

What we believe previous studies have neglected and ours has been able to capture is *variation* in address within each language. Differences in modes of address between and within each of the languages reflect cultural and sub-cultural values, largely conditioned by social and political history. So T or T-like exchange is especially strong in young adults in English, German and French and in professional and common-interest networks. It is also prevalent in chat groups, but not as universally as is often assumed (we are not including Swedish in this consideration as T predominates in almost all contexts in that language).

6.6   Some general issues

This project confirms some general issues. One is that national varieties of a pluricentric language, even with relatively small differences in morphosyntax, show deep pragmatic variation related to cultural values developed out of long or short periods of nationhood or statehood with different national priorities of communication. Address is one of the outstanding examples of this, as can be seen in relation to Swedish in Sweden and Finland and German in Austria and the western and eastern parts of Germany. Our study confirms research on pluricentric languages focused on lexicon, morphosyntax and phonology, which demonstrates that speakers of dominant national varieties of a language are largely unaware of the features of other national varieties (cf. articles in Clyne 1992).

A second issue is that the popular term 'polite' for the V form is not appropriate as there are many ways of being polite, which can equally involve the T-form. In Swedish, some older informants consider V to be impolite and condescending, demonstrating the conflicting social values attached to address in contemporary Sweden.

Third, address in language contact situations accentuates one of the major problems of English domination of international communication. English address modes can deal simply and efficiently with what may seem difficult or problematic but do not give people from 'other' cultural backgrounds scope to express human relationships based on their cultural values.

The study underlines the complementary roles played by grammatical typology and pragmatics in the investigation of address, which exemplifies significantly the contribution of language to human relations.

Appendix A: written questionnaire (filled in by participant)

Informants were asked to circle the pronoun of address used (T or V) AND, where applicable, whether they used the first name or Mr/Ms + surname to address a particular person. They were also asked to indicate which forms they expected to be addressed with in return by the person in question.

1. Imagine that you are in an unknown town in .... and that you need to ask someone for directions to the train station. How would you address a person of:

   the same age and of the same sex?
   the same age but of a different sex?
   considerably older and of the same sex?
   considerably older but of a different sex?
   younger and of the same sex?
   younger but of a different sex?
   How would you expect to be addressed by each of these people?

2. Let's say that you enter a shop to ask for an article.

How would you address the sales person?	T	V
How would they address you?	T	V
Is there anything in this situation that would make you change the pronoun of address?	age of sales person	□
Please rank by importance (1 = most important)	sex of sales person	□
	dress of sales person	□
	type of shop	□
	other:	□

3. Let's say that you enter a shop where you regularly make purchases.

How would you address the sales person?	T	V
How would they address you?	T	V

4. If you called a public   T   V   first name   Mr/Ms+
    authority, for example the   surname
    local council, to ask about
    rubbish collection, how would
    you start the conversation?
5. If you needed to go to the police, how would you address an officer of:
      the same age and of the same sex?
      the same age but of the opposite sex?
      considerably older and of the same sex?
      considerably older but of the opposite sex?
      younger and of the same sex?
      younger but of a different sex?

Informants were then asked to indicate whether they used T or V AND whether they used the first name, a kinship term or another term of address (e.g. Mr/Ms + surname, surname only, etc.) to address a particular person, and also what forms each person used with them.

Father
Mother
Stepfather (if applicable)
Stepmother (if applicable)
Maternal grandmother
Maternal grandfather
Paternal grandmother
Paternal grandfather
A friend of your grandparents
A friend of your parents whom you have not met before
Your closest friend's parents
Your partner's parents
Your superiors at work
Other co-workers
Clients (if applicable)
Your teachers when you went to school
Your lecturers, professors, etc. at university
To an unknown person when writing an email
At school, how old were you when you started to be addressed as V by your teachers? If applicable, when did you attend university?

Interview questions

1. How often do you go abroad? What are the purposes of those trips? Which countries have you been to?

2. Are you politically active, for example in a political party, an organisation like Amnesty International or Greenpeace? Are you a member of any such organisation?

3. Are you a member of any other organisation or club, e.g. a sports club, a trade union, a religious organisation, or an internet chat group?

4. Do you think that the .... society has changed in the last 10–15 years?
   a). in the way people behave towards each other?
   b). in the way the welfare state works?
   If so, how do you feel about these changes?

5. How do you think welfare should be financed and distributed in society?

6. Is there any legislation that has been passed in recent years that you feel uneasy about?

7. How do you feel about people from other countries settling in ....?

8. How would you describe your immediate neighbours? Do you have a good relationship with them? Do you see them often?

9. How do you address your neighbours?

10. How do they address you?

11. How do you start a letter to a person you do not know?

12. Have you ever received any positive or negative reactions to your address usage? If so, please describe the situation(s).

13. Have you ever been addressed with a form you didn't expect? When? By whom? How did you react to that? How did you perceive it?

14. How would you react to your professor or work superior suddenly addressing you as T (if applicable)?

15. From what age should a person be addressed with V?

16. Would you like to be addressed more formally/less formally more often? Why?/Why not?

17. Does it matter to you when people use a different term of address to you than you do to them?

18. In radio and on television, for example in news programmes, T is often used by the interviewers regardless of who they are interviewing. Do you think that such an address usage is impolite or is it appropriate and polite? Why/why not?
    [modified version for French and German] In radio and on television, especially in talk shows, T is sometimes used by the interviewers regardless of who they are interviewing. Do you think that such an address usage is impolite or is it appropriate and polite? Why/why not?

19. How do you feel about companies which prescribe the T form (for example, IKEA)?

20. What has been the practice of address forms in workplaces where you have worked previously?
21. Have you noticed any changes in the way people address each other over the last 10–15 years? If so, can you describe the changes?
22. (If the interviewee has lived in different places in ....) Have you noticed whether people address each other differently in different regions? If so, how?
23. Do you think address terms are used in a different way in other .... -speaking countries?
24. In English there is only one form of address – *you*. Would you describe the system of choice in your language as cumbersome/less friendly/more polite, or would you say that you appreciate the choice? Why?
25. Could any of the forms of address be used in a derogatory sense? How?
26. Would you address other .... speakers with T and/or by their first name if you met them abroad, particularly in an English-speaking country? Why/why not? Under what circumstances?
27. How do you feel about the T and V forms in general?
28. Had you thought about these issues before the interview?
29. Do you have any other comments or questions on address usage?

Appendix B: chat groups

French

1. ABC de la Langue Française (Languefrancaise.net) forum
2. Defensedufrancais forum
3. Forum-marketing.com
4. France5.fr forum
5. Langue-fr.net forum
6. Nafsep.org forum
7. Net-iris.fr forum
8. PCinpact forum
9. Photo Argentique (35mm-compact.com) forum
10. Wordreference.com forum

German

1. Boardunity (German)
2. Der Standard (Austrian)
3. Showarticles (German)
4. Showthread (German)
5. Simpson's Paradise (German)
6. Styleboard (German)
7. Viewpoints (German)
8. Webstyle Times (German)

Swedish

1. Flashback
2. Privata affärer (Swedish business magazine)
3. Vasabladet forum (Finland-Swedish newspaper)

References

Adams, George Brendan. 1985. Linguistic cross-links in phonology and grammar. In S. O'Baoill (ed.). *Papers on Irish English*, 27–35. Dublin: IRAAL.

Agha, Asif. 2007. *Language and Social Relations*. Studies in the Social and Cultural Foundations of Language 24. Cambridge: Cambridge University Press.

Ahlgren, Perry. 1978. *Tilltalsordet ni. Dess semantik och användning i historiskt perspektiv*. Uppsala: Almqvist and Wiksell.

Allensbach. 2003. Weniger schnell per 'du'. *Allensbacher Berichte* 9/2003. www.ifd-allensbach.de/pdf/prd_0309.pdf (last accessed 15 December 2007).

Amendt, Gerhard. 1995. *Du oder Sie: 1945 – 1968 – 1995*. Bremen: Ikaru-Verlag.

Ammon, Ulrich *et al.* 2004. *Variantenwörterbuch des Deutschen*. Berlin: De Gruyter.

Bakhtin, Michael. 1986. The problems of speech genres. In Emerson, Caryl and Holquist, Michael (eds.). *Speech Genres and Other Late Essays*. Austin, TX: University of Texas Press.

Bargiela, Francesca, Corinne Boz, Lily Gokzadze, Abdurrahman Hamza, Sara Mills and Nino Rukhadze. 2002. Ethnocentrism, politeness and naming strategies. *Working Papers on the Web 3: Linguistic politeness and context*. www.shu.ac.uk/wpw/politeness/bargiela.htm (last accessed 15 December 2007).

Barthes, Roland. 1971. Ecrivains, intellectuels, professeurs. *Tel quel*, 47: 1–15.

Bayer, Klaus. 1979. Die Anredepromina Du und Sie. *Deutsche Sprache*, 3: 212–19.

Behrens, Leila. 2007. *Konservierung von Stereotypen mit Hilfe der Statistik: Geert Hofstede und sein kulturvergleichendes Modell*. Arbeitspapier 51, Neue Folge. Cologne: Institut für Linguistik, Universität.

Besch, Werner. 1998. *Il Duzen, Siezen, Titulierem*. Göttingen: Vandenhoeck and Ruprecht.

Birch, Barbara M. 1995. Quaker Plain Speech: A policy of linguistic divergence. *International Journal of the Sociology of Language*, 116: 39–59.

Braun, Friederike. 1988. *Terms of Address: Problems of patterns and usage in various languages and cultures*. Berlin: Mouton de Gruyter.

Brown, Penelope and Stephen Levinson. 1987. *Politeness: Some universals in language usage*. Cambridge: Cambridge University Press.

Brown, Roger and Albert Gilman. 1960. The pronouns of power and solidarity. In T. A. Sebeok (ed.). *Style in Language*. Cambridge, MA: MIT Press. 253–76.

Calvet, Louis-Jean. 1976. A tu et à vous. *Le Français dans le Monde*, 118: 14–18.

Clark, Herbert. 1996. *Using Language*. Cambridge: Cambridge University Press.

Clyne, Michael (ed.). 1992. *Pluricentric Languages*. Berlin: Mouton de Gruyter.

Clyne, Michael. 1995. *The German Language in a Changing Europe*. Cambridge: Cambridge University Press.

Clyne, Michael. 2006. Some thoughts on pragmatics, sociolinguistic variation and intercultural communication. *Intercultural Pragmatics*, 3: 95–105.

Clyne, Michael and Sandra Kipp. 1999. *Pluricentric Languages in an Immigrant Context*. Berlin: Mouton de Gruyter.

Clyne, Michael and Sandra Kipp. 2006. *Tiles in a Multilingual Mosaic: Macedonian, Somali and Filipino in Melbourne*. Canberra: Pacific Linguistics.

Clyne, Michael, Sue Fernandez and Rudolf Muhr. 2003. Communicative styles in a contact situation. *Journal of German Linguistics*, 15: 95–154.

Clyne, Michael, Heinz L. Kretzenbacher, Catrin Norrby and Doris Schüpbach. 2006. Perceptions of variation and change in German and Swedish address. *Journal of Sociolinguistics*, 10 (3): 287–319.

Coffen, Béatrice. 2002. *Histoire culturelle des pronoms d'adresse. Vers une typologie des systèmes allocutoires dans les langues romanes*. Paris: Honoré Champion.

Coffen, Béatrice. 2003. Rôle attribué aux pronoms d'adresse dans la construction identitaire individuelle. Paper presented at the *Colloquium Pronoms du 2e personne et formes d'adresse dans les langues d'Europe*, 6–8 March 2003, Institut Cervantes, Paris.

Coupland, Nikolas. 2001. Language, situation and the relational self: Theorizing dialect-style in sociolinguistics. In Penelope Eckert and John R. Rickford (eds.). *Style and Sociolinguistic Variation*. Cambridge: Cambridge University Press. 185–210.

Crowley, Terry. 2000. *The Politics of Language in Ireland, 1366–1922*. London: Routledge.

Crumley, Bruce. 2006. Pardon your French. Hit or miss? A formal debate forms over the correct form of address. *Time Europe*, 30 April.

Crystal, David. 1993. *Cambridge Encyclopedia of the English Language*, second edition. Cambridge: Cambridge University Press.

Davies, Bronwyn and Rom Harré. 1990. Positioning: The discursive production of selves. *Journal for the Theory of Social Behaviour*, 20 (1): 43–63.

Eckert, Penelope and John R. Rickford (eds.). 2001. *Style and Sociolinguistic Variation*. Cambridge: Cambridge University Press.

Ehlers, Klaas-Hinrich. 2004. Zur Anrede mit Titeln in Deutschland, Österreich und Tschechien. Ergebnisse einer Fragebogenerhebung. Brücken. *Germanistisches Jahrbuch Tschechien-Slowakei* NF.12: 85–115.

Ervin-Tripp, Susan. 1986. On sociolinguistic rules: Alternation and co-occurrence. In John J. Gumperz and Dell Hymes (eds.). *Directions in Sociolinguistics: The ethnography of communication*. Reissued with corrections and additions, Oxford: Blackwell. 213–50.

Filppula, Markku. 1999. *The Grammar of Irish English: Language in Hibernian style*. London, New York: Routledge.

Fishman, Joshua A. 1965. Who speaks what language to whom and when? *Linguistique*, 2: 67–88.

Formentelli, Maicol. 2007. The vocative mate in contemporary English: A corpus based study. In A. Sansò (ed.). *Language Resources and Linguistic Theory*. Milan: Franco Angeli. 180–99.

Fraser, Bruce. 1990. Perspectives on politeness. *Journal of Pragmatics*, 14: 219–36.

Fraser, Bruce and William Nolen. 1981. The association of deference with linguistic form. *International Journal of the Sociology of Language*, 27: 93–110.

Fremer, Maria. 1998. Tilltal och omtal i samtal. *Språkbruk*, 2: 5–10.

Folktinget. 2003. Språkfördelningen i Svenskfinland. www.kaapeli.fi/~fti/pdf/publikationer/ Sprakfordelningen2003.pdf (last accessed 28 April 2007).

Gardner-Chloros, Penelope. 1991. Ni tu ni vous: principes et paradoxes dans l'emploi des pronoms d'allocution en français contemporain. *Journal of French Language Studies*, 1 (1): 139–55.

Gardner-Chloros, Penelope. 2004. Le développement historique de T/V en français et en anglais: parallélisme et divergence. *Franco-British Studies 33–34* (Autumn 2003–Spring 2004). Special Issue: Second person pronouns and forms of address in the languages of contemporary Europe. 90–99.

Gardner-Chloros, Penelope. 2007. Tu/vous choices: An 'Act of Identity'? In Mari Jones and Wendy Ayres-Bennett (eds.). *The French Language and Questions of Identity*. Oxford: Legenda. 106–16.

Gärtner, Detlev. 1992. Vom Sekretärsdeutsch zur Kommerzsprache. In Gotthard Lerchner (ed.). *Sprachkultur im Wandel. Anmerkungen zur Kommunikationskultur*. Frankfurt: Lang. 203–62.

Giles, Howard (ed.). 1984. The dynamics of speech accommodation. Special Issue. *International Journal of the Sociology of Language*, 46.

Giles, Howard, Nikolas Coupland and Justine Coupland. 1991. Accommodation theory: Communication, context and consequence. In Howard Giles, Nikolas Coupland and Justine Coupland (eds.). *Contexts of Accommodation*. Cambridge: Cambridge University Press. 1–67.

Goffman, Erving. 1959. *The Presentation of Self in Everyday Life*. Harmondsworth: Penguin.

Goffman, Erving. 1967. On face-work. An analysis of ritual elements in social inter-action. In Erving Goffman (ed.). *Interactional Ritual: Essays on face-to-face behaviour*. New York: Anchor Books. 5–45.

Graddol, David and Joan Swan. 1989. *Gender Voices*. Oxford: Blackwell and Open University.

Greater London Authority. 2006a. *Greater London Demographic Review 2005*. London: Date Management and Analysis Group, Greater London Authority. www.london. gov.uk/gla/publications/factsandfigures/factsfigures/population.jsp (last accessed 23 March 2007).

Greater London Authority. 2006b. *A Summary of Countries of Birth in London. DMAG Update*. www.london.gov.uk/gla/publications/factsandfigures/dmag-update-2006-09. pdf (last accessed 9 April 2007).

Greenbaum, Thomas L. 1998. *The Handbook for Focus Group Research*, second edition. Thousand Oaks, CA: Sage.

Gumperz, John. 1982. *Discourse Strategies*. Cambridge: Cambridge University Press.

Hällström, Charlotta and Michael Reuter. 2000. *Finlandssvensk ordbok*. Helsinki: Schildts.

Halmøy, Odile. 1999. Le vouvoiement en français: forme non-marquée de la seconde personne du singulier. In Jane Nystedt (ed.). *XIV Skandinaviska Romanistkongressen*. Stockholm: Acta Universitatis Stockhomiensis.

Harré, Rom and Luk van Langenhove. 1999. *Positioning Theory: Moral contexts of interactional action*. Oxford: Blackwell.

Havu, Eva. 2005. Quand les Français tutoient-ils? Paper presented at the *XVIe Congrès des romanistes scandinaves*, 25–27 August 2005, Copenhagen. www.ruc.dk/cuid/publikationer/publikationer/XVI-SRK-Pub/KFL/KFL06-Havu (last accessed 15 December 2007).

Havu, Eva. 2006. L'emploi des pronoms d'adresse en français: étude sociolinguistique et comparaison avec le finnois. In Irma Taavitsainen, Juhani Härmä and Jarmo Korhonen (eds.). *Dialogic language use. Dimensions du dialogisme. Dialogischer Sprachgebrauch.* Helsinki: Socieété Néophilologique. 225–40.

Hellmann, Manfred. 1978. Sprache zwischen Ost und West – Überlegungen zur Wortschatzdifferenzierung zwischen BRD und DDR und ihren Folgen. In Wolfgang Kühlwein und Günter Radden (eds.). *Sprache und Kultur – Studien zu Diglossie, Gastarbeiterproblematik und kulturelle Integration.* Tübingen: Narr. 15–54.

Hellmann, Manfred. 1990. Sprachgebrauch nach der Wende: eine erste Bestandaufnahme. *Muttersprache*, 100: 266–86.

Hickey, Leo and Miranda Stewart (eds.). 2005. *Politeness in Europe.* Clevedon: Multilingual Matters.

Hickey, Raymond. 2003. The German address system: Binary and scalar system at once. In Irma Raavitsainen and Andreas Jucker (eds.). *Diachronic Perspectives on Address Form Systems.* Amsterdam: Benjamins. 401–25.

Hill, Ben, Sachiko Ide, Shoko Ikuta, Akiko Kawasaki and Tsunao Ogino. 1986. Universals of linguistic politeness: Quantitative evidence from Japanese and American English. *Journal of Pragmatics*, 10: 347–71.

Hofstede, Geert. 1991. *Cultures and Organizations.* London: McGraw-Hill.

Holmes, Janet. 2001. *An Introduction to Sociolinguistics.* London: Longman.

Holtgraves, Thomas. 2001. Politeness. In W. Peter Robinson and Howard Giles (eds.). *The New Handbook of Language and Social Psychology.* Chichester: John Wiley & Sons. 341–55.

Hughson, Jo-anne. 2001. *Le tu et le vous: Étude sociolinguistique dans la banlieue parisienne.* Unpublished Diplôme d'études approfondies. Université Paris-X, Nanterre.

Hughson, Jo-anne. 2005. Spanish address pronoun usage in an inter-cultural immigrant context: Language, social and cultural values among Spanish–English bilinguals in Australia. Unpublished Ph.D. Thesis. University of Melbourne.

Ide, Sachiko. 1989. Formal forms and discernment. *Multilingua*, 8: 223–48.

Joseph, John. 1989. Review of terms of address: Problems of patterns and usage in various languages and cultures by Friederike Braun. *Language*, 65 (4): 852–7.

Joseph, John. 2004. *Language and Identity: National, ethnic, religious.* Basingstoke, New York: Palgrave Macmillan.

Kachru, Braj. 1982. *The Other Tongue.* Champaign, IL: University of Illinois Press.

Kallen, Jeffrey. 2005. Politeness in Ireland: '…in Ireland, it's done without being said'. In Leo Hickey and Miranda Stewart (eds.). *Politeness in Europe.* Clevedon: Multilingual Matters. 130–44.

Kallmeyer, Werner. 2003. Sagen Sie bitte du zu mir. Werner Kallmeyer, Soziolinguist am Institut für Deutsche Sprache in Mannheim, über die Kunst der richtigen Anrede. Das Gespräch führte Cosima Schmitt (Werner Kallmeyer, Sociolinguist at the Institute for German Language in Mannheim, on the art of correct address. Conversation with Cosima Schmitt). *Die Zeit*, 58.27, 26 Juni 2003.

Kasper, Gabriele. 1994. Politeness. In R. E. Asher (ed.). *The Encyclopedia of Language and Linguistics 6.* Oxford: Pergamon Press. 3206–11.

Kerbrat-Orecchioni, Catherine. 1992. *Les interactions verbales,* vol. II. Paris: Armand Colin.

Kipp, Sandra, Michael Clyne and Anne Pauwels. 1995. *Immigration and Australia's Language Resources.* Canberra: AGPS.

Kretzenbacher, Heinz L. 1991. Vom Sie zum Du – und retour? In Heinz L. Kretzenbacher and Uwe Segebrecht. *Vom Sie zum Du – mehr als eine neue Konvention? Antworten auf die Preisfrage der Deutschen Akademie für Sprache und Dichtung vom Jahr 1989.* Hamburg, Zurich: Luchterhand Literaturverlag. 9–77.

Labov, William. 1972. *Sociolinguistic Patterns.* Philadephia, PA: University of Pennsylvania Press.

Lakoff, Robin. 1973. The logic of politeness; or, minding your p's and q's. Papers from the *Ninth Regional Meeting, Chicago Linguistics Society,* 292–305.

Lakoff, Robin and Sachiko Ide (eds.). 2005. *Broadening the Horizon of Linguistic Politeness.* Amsterdam, Philadelphia: John Benjamins.

Lambert, Wallace E. and G. Richard Tucker. 1976. *Tu, Vous, Usted.* Rowley, MA: Newbury House.

Leech, Geoffrey N. 1983. *Principles of Pragmatics.* London: Longman.

Leech, Geoffrey N. 1999. The distribution and function of vocatives in American and British English conversation. In Hilde Hasselgård and Signe Oksefiell (eds.). *Out of Corpora: Studies in honour of Stig Johansson.* Amsterdam, Philadelphia: Rodopi. 107–118.

Le Page, Robert B. and Andrée Tabouret-Keller. 1985. *Acts of Identity: Creole-based approaches to language and ethnicity.* Cambridge: Cambridge University Press.

Lerchner, Gotthard. 1992. Broiler, Plast(e) und Datsche machen noch nicht den Unterschied. Fremdheit und Toleranz in einer polyzentrischen deutschen Kommunikationskultur. In Gotthard Lerchner (ed.). *Sprachkultur im Wandel: Anmerkungen zur Kommunikationskultur.* Frankfurt: Lang. 297–332.

L'Express. 2006. D'où viennent les Parisiens. Dossier spécial. *L'Express,* 30 November.

Linell, Per. 1998. *Approaching Dialogue: Talk, interaction and contexts in dialogical perspectives.* Amsterdam, Philadelphia: John Benjamins.

Lüdi, Georges. 1992. French as a pluricentric language. In Michael Clyne (ed.). *Pluricentric Languages.* Berlin: Mouton de Gruyter. 149–78.

Macarthur, Tom (ed.). 1992. *The Oxford Companion to the English Language.* Oxford: Oxford University Press.

Maley, Catherine. 1974. *The Pronouns of Address in Modern Standard French.* University, MS: University of Mississippi Romance Monographs.

Mara, Johanna and Lena Huldén. 2000. *Hälsningsvanor, tilltal och omtal i Svenskfinland under 1900-talet. Källan 2.* Helsinki: Svenska litteratursällskapet i Finland.

Mårtensson, Eva. 1986. Det nya niandet. *Nordlund 10.* Lund: Dept. of Nordic Languages. 35–79.

Matsumoto, Yoshiko. 1989. Politeness and conversational universal observations from Japanese. *Multilingua,* 8: 200–21.

Mattheier, Klaus J. 1980. *Pragmatik und Semantik der Dialekte.* Heidelberg: Winter.

McCarthy, Michael and Anne O'Keeffe. 2003. 'What's in a name?' Vocatives in casual conversations and radio phone-in calls. In Pepi Leistyna and Charles F. Meyer (eds.). *Corpus Analysis: Language structure and language use.* Amsterdam, New York: Rodopi. 153–85.

Morford, Janet. 1997. Social indexicality in French pronominal address. *Journal of Linguistic Anthropology,* 7 (1): 3–37.

Mühlhäusler, Peter and Rom Harré. 1990. You: The grammatical expression of social relations. In Peter Mühlhäusler and Rom Harré (eds.). *Pronouns and People: The linguistic construction of social and personal identity.* Oxford: Blackwell. 131–67.

Muhr, Rudolf. 1987. Regionale Unterschiede im Gebrauch von Beziehungsindikatoren zwischen der Bundesrepublik Deutschland und Österreich und ihre Auswirkungen auf den Unterricht in Deutsch als Fremdsprachen, dargestellt an Modalpartikeln. In Lutz Göetze (ed.). *Deutsch als Fremdsprache: Situation eines Faches.* Bonn: Dürrsche Buchhandlung. 144–56.

Muhr, Rudolf. 1994. Entschuldigen Sie, Frau Kollegin… Sprechaktrealisierungsunterschiede an Universitäten in Österreich und Deutschland. In Susanne Bachleitner-Held (ed.). *Verbale Interaktion.* Salzburg: Kovac. 126–44.

Muhr, Rudolf and Peter Sellner. 2006. *Zehn Jahre Forschung zum Österreichischen Deutsch 1995–2005: Eine Bilanz.* Frankfurt: Lang.

Niedzielski, Nancy A. and Dennis Richard Preston. 2000. *Folk Linguistics.* Berlin: Mouton de Gruyter.

Norrby, Catrin. 1997. Kandidat Svensson, du eller ni – om utvecklingen av tilltalsskicket i svenskan. In Anders-Börje Andersson *et al.* (eds.). *Svenska som andraspråk och andra språk: Festskrift till Gunnar Tingbjörn.* Gothenburg: Department of Swedish Language, Gothenburg University. 319–28.

Norrby, Catrin and Gisela Håkansson. 2004. 'Kan jag hjälpa dig med något?' Om tilltal i en servicesituation. *Språk & Stil,* 13: 6–34.

Nyblom, Heidi. 2006. The use of address pronouns among Finnish and Finland-Swedish students. *Australian Review of Applied Linguistics,* 29 (2): 19.1–19.12

Ò Laoire, Muiris. 2005. The Language Planning Situation in Ireland. *Current Issues in Language Planning,* 6: 251–314.

Paulston, Christina Bratt. 1976. Pronouns of address in Swedish: Social class semantics and changing system. *Language in Society,* 5: 359–86.

Pauwels, Anne. 1998. *Women Changing Language.* London: Longman.

Pavlenko, Aneta and Adrian Blackledge. 2004. Introduction. Theoretical approaches to the study of negotiation of identities in multilingual contexts. In Aneta Pavlenko and Adrian Blackledge (eds.). *Negotiation of Identities in Multilingual Contexts.* Clevedon: Multilingual Matters. 1–33.

Peeters, Bert. 2004. Tu ou vous? *Zeitschrift für französische Sprache und Literatur,* 114: 1–17.

Peyret, Emmanuèle. 2006. C'est "mademoiselle" ou "madame"? *Libération,* 12 April.

Plevoets, Koen, Dirk Speelman and Dirk Geeraerts. 2008. The distribution of T/V pronouns in Netherlandic and Belgian Dutch. In Schneider and Barron, 181–210.

Ransmayr, Jutta. 2006. *Der Status des Österreichischen Deutsch an nicht-deutschsprachigen Universitäten.* Frankfurt: Lang.

Reuter, Mikael. 1992. Swedish as a pluricentric language. In Michael Clyne (ed.). *Pluricentric Languages.* Berlin: Mouton de Gruyter. 101–16.

Romaine, Suzanne. 2001. A corpus-based view of gender in British and American English. In Marlis Hellinger and Hudumod Bussmann (eds.). *Gender Across*

Languages: The linguistic representation of women and men. Vol 1. Amsterdam, Philadelphia, PA: John Benjamins. 153–75.

Saari, Mirjaa. 1995. 'Jo, nu kunde vi festa nog'. Synpunkter på svenskt språkbruk i Sverige och Finland. *Folkmålsstudier*, 36: 75–108.

Sacks, Harvey. 1992. Lecture 6. In Gail Jefferson (ed.). *Lectures on Conversation*. Vols. 1–2. Oxford: Blackwell. 40–8.

Sakowski, Klaus. Not dated. Geduzt werden im Betrieb – LAG Hamm. *Juristische Beiträge Arbeitsrecht*. www.sakowski.de/arb-r/arb-r13.html (accessed 24 September 2004).

Schacherreitner, Christian. 2004. Sie Trottel, du! *ÖNachrichten* 06/03/04. www.nachrichten. at/magazin/wochenende/252744?PHPSESSID= (accessed 24 September 2004).

Schlosser, Horst-Dieter. 1991. Deutsche Teilung, deutsche Einheit und die Sprache der Deutschen. *Politik und Zeitgeschichte, Beilage zur Wochenzeitung Das Parlament*, B17/91: 13–21.

Schneider, Klaus and Anne Barron (eds.). 2008. *Variational Pragmatics*. Amsterdam: Benjamins.

Sdun, Nora. 2004. Individuelle Kommodität. Textem 24/08/04. www.textem.de/index. php?id=25&backPID=1&tt_news=183 (accessed 24 September 2004).

Seidman, Michael. 2004. *The Imaginary Revolution: Parisian students and workers in 1968*. New York, Oxford: Berghahn Books.

Sifianou, Maria. 1992. *Politeness Phenomena in England and Greece: A cross-cultural perspective*. Oxford: Oxford University Press.

Spencer-Oatey, Helen. 1996. Reconsidering power and distance. *Journal of Pragmatics*, 26 (1): 1–24.

Sproß, Elfriede Monika. 2001. Das Du-Wort. Zur Anrede im Umgang mit anderen. Unpublished PhD thesis. Karl-Franzens-Universitat, Graz.

Stevenson, Patrick. 2002. *Language and German Disunity*. Oxford: Oxford University Press.

Stewart, Miranda. 2005. Politeness in Britain: 'It's only a suggestion…'. In Leo Hickey and Miranda Stewart (eds.). *Politeness in Europe*. Clevedon: Multilingual Matters. 116–29.

Svennevig, Jan. 1999. *Getting Acquainted in Conversation. A study of initial interactions*. Amsterdam, Philadelphia: Benjamins.

Tajfel, Henri. 1974. Social identity and intergroup behaviour. *Social Science Information*, 13: 65–93.

Tandefelt, Marika. 1994. Urbanization and Bilingualism. In Bengt Nordberg and Norbert Dittmar (eds.). *Urbanization and Language Change in Fenno-Scandinavia*. Berlin: Walter de Gruyter. 246–73.

Tandefelt, Marika. 2006. Tänk om…Handlingsprogram för svenskan i Finland. [Imagine if…Action plan for Swedish in Finland.] *Språk i Norden 2006*. 57–66.

Teleman, Ulf. 2002. *Ära, rikedom & reda: Svensk språkvård och språkpolitik under äldre nyare tid*. Stockholm: Norstedts Ordbok.

Teleman, Ulf. 2003. *Tradis och funkis: Svensk språkvård och språkpolitik efter 1800*. Stockholm: Norstedts Ordbok.

Thompson, Robert W. 1992. Spanish as a pluricentric language. In Michael Clyne (1992), 45–70.

Trudgill, Peter. 1974. *The Social Differentiation of English in Norwich*. Cambridge: Cambridge University Press.

Trudgill, Peter. 1986. *Dialects in Contact*. Oxford: Blackwell.

Trudgill, Peter and Jean Hannah. 1985. *International English*. London: Arnold.

Tykesson-Bergman, Ingela. 2006. *Samtal i butik: Språklig interaktion mellan biträden och kunder*. Stockholm Studies in Scandinavian Philology. New Series 41. Stockholm University.

Upton, Clive and John D. A. Widdowson. 2006. *An Atlas of English Dialects*, second edition. London, New York: Routledge.

Vanderkerckhove, Reinhild. 2005. Belgian Dutch versus Netherlandic Dutch: New patterns of divergence? On pronouns of address and dimunitives. *Multilingua*, 24: 379–98.

Vermaas, J. A. M. 2002. *Veranderingen in de Nederlandse aanspraakvormen van de dertiende t/m de twintigste eeuw*. Utrecht: LOT.

Wahrig, Gerhard. 1977 [1968]. *Deutsches Wörterbuch*. Gütersloh: Bertelsmann.

Wales, Katie. 1996. *Personal Pronouns in Present-Day English*. Cambridge: Cambridge University Press.

Wales, Katie. 2003. Second person pronouns in contemporary English: The end of a story or just the beginning? *Franco-British Studies*, 33–34: 172–85.

Wales, Katie. 2006. *Northern English: A cultural and social history*. Cambridge: Cambridge University Press.

Watts, Richard J. 1989. Relevance and relational work: Linguistic politeness as politic behaviour. *Multilingua*, 8: 131–66.

Watts, Richard J. 1991. *Power in Family Discourse*. Berlin: Mouton de Gruyter.

Watts, Richard J. 2003. *Politeness*. Cambridge: Cambridge University Press.

Watts, Richard J., Sachiko Ide and Konrad Ehlich (eds.). 1992. *Politeness in Language: Studies in its history, theory and practice*. Berlin: Mouton de Gruyter.

Wellander, Erik. 1935. *Tilltalsordet Ni*. Stockholm: C.E. Fritzes Bokförlags Aktiebolag.

Winter, Joanne and Anne Pauwels. 2007. *Miss*ing me and *Ms*ing the other: Courtesy titles for women in Englishes. *Australian Review of Applied Linguistics*, 30 (1): DOI:10.2104/aral0708.

Yli-Vakkuri, Valma. 2005. Politeness in Finland: Evasion at all costs. In Leo Hickey and Miranda Stewart (eds.). *Politeness in Europe*. Clevedon: Multilingual Matters. 189–202.

Zimmerman, Don. 1998. Identity, context and interaction. In Charles Antaki and Sue Widdicombe (eds.). *Identities in Talk*. London: Sage. 89–106.

Index